Discretionary Justice

CRITICAL ISSUES IN CRIME AND SOCIETY
Raymond J. Michalowski, Series Editor

Critical Issues in Crime and Society is oriented toward critical analysis of contemporary problems in crime and justice. The series is open to a broad range of topics, including specific types of crime, wrongful behavior by economically or politically powerful actors, controversies over justice system practices, and issues related to the intersection of identity, crime, and justice. It is committed to offering thoughtful works that are accessible to scholars and professional criminologists, general readers, and students.

For a list of titles in the series, see the last page of the book.

Discretionary Justice

LOOKING INSIDE A JUVENILE DRUG COURT

LESLIE PAIK

RUTGERS UNIVERSITY PRESS
New Brunswick, New Jersey, and London

LIBRARY OF CONGRESS CATALOGING-IN-PUBLICATION DATA

Paik, Leslie.
  Discretionary justice : looking inside a juvenile drug court / Leslie Paik.
    p. cm. — (Critical issues in crime and society)
  Includes bibliographical references and index.
  ISBN 978-0-8135-5006-0 (hardcover : alk. paper) — ISBN 978-0-8135-5007-7
(pbk. : alk. paper)
  1. Juvenile courts—California. 2. Drug courts—California. 3. Youth—Drug
use—California. 4. Drug abuse—Treatment—Law and legislation—California.
5. Juvenile delinquents—Rehabilitation—California. I. Title.
  KFC1196.P35 2011
  345.794'02770269—dc22

                                 2010048420

A British Cataloging-in-Publication record for this book is available
from the British Library.

Visit our Web site: http://rutgerspress.rutgers.edu

Manufactured in the United States of America

CONTENTS

Preface and Acknowledgments

THE IDEA FOR THIS BOOK began before I started graduate school. In the mid-1990s I worked at a nonprofit legal organization that designed, implemented, and evaluated drug courts and other problem-solving courts. I saw the value of these courts—helping offenders kick their drug addiction, keeping them out of prison—but I also worried about the courts' potential Big Brother impact on the offenders with their expectations of behavioral change. As I was discussing these thoughts with a senior staff member who had been involved in criminal justice policy for twenty years, she responded that while it sounded like we were imposing white middle-class values onto poor minorities, nothing else had worked. I still think about that conversation often—namely, if these courts do help to keep people out of jail or prison, are their moralistic expectations of behavior worth it, especially considering the experience of policy practitioners who have seen countless other attempts at reform fail?

I went to graduate school to explore that question but then was confronted with another equally confounding one. I was trying to defend my coworker's view of drug courts to a faculty member, who asked the following question, which I'm paraphrasing here: "While the courts' goals are honorable, wouldn't it be better to spend the money on improving our decaying schools, building affordable housing, and increasing the number of jobs?" In other words, we should be addressing the social problems that policy makers acknowledged were often the root causes for the crimes committed by the offenders entering these specialized courts, instead of focusing on those individuals to change their behaviors.

Those two questions explain the impetus for this book—how can we understand drug courts from both the practical policy view and the broader sociological perspective? How can I straddle the lines between the two audiences without forsaking the analysis? It means that I need to question the ideological premises of drug courts of accountability and therapeutic jurisprudence without accepting them at face value. Yet, at the same time, I do not want to reduce drug courts to being Orwellian expansions of social control over docile bodies of drug offenders without also raising the possible practical value in such courts. In short, I have attempted to validate the efforts of the drug court staff members, who are tirelessly dedicated to "doing good," while also questioning the iatrogenic effect that their efforts can produce.

My hope is that policy makers will come away from this book with a newfound perspective about the unintended consequences of these courts and the courage not to jump on board any reform train that appears to work. I equally hope that academics will see how debunking policy reforms is not a helpful approach to rectifying the social inequalities created by the contemporary justice system.

Over the years, many people have helped me develop and think through the ideas presented in this book. First and foremost, my mentor since graduate school, Robert Emerson, has been unswerving in his support and willingness to read draft after draft. Working with him has been a privilege, as it has taught me how to be a better ethnographer and scholar. He pushed me to push myself, to constantly question the validity of my claims and the ever important connection to the data. The late Melvin Pollner also provided invaluable guidance during the dissertation phase of this project. I fondly remember our long conversations about the theoretical implications of my work, bolstered with a healthy dose of humor and laughter. I also want to thank my fellow graduate students, specifically Sal Zerilli and Julie Peggar, in the social control working group that helped move the dissertation writing along. Finally, my dear friends and colleagues, Alexes Harris, Nikki Jones, Carla Shedd, and L'Heureux Lewis, read later versions of the manuscript as it evolved from the dissertation stage.

I could not have finished this manuscript without the wonderful support of the Ohio State University Crime and Justice Summer Research Institute. My time there gave me an extra push at the final stage when all I wanted to do was throw the manuscript in a drawer. Special thanks to Laurie Krivo, Ruth Peterson, Steve Lopez, Aaron Kupchik, and the other participants in the 2009 SRI cohort.

I'm forever grateful to Marlie Wasserman and Peter Mickulas at Rutgers University Press for their immediate enthusiasm and support for the book, as well as the anonymous reviewers who provided wonderfully detailed feedback on the manuscript. Lastly, Tori-Ann Haywood provided much-needed research assistance in the last phases of the writing.

Chapter 5 is reprinted with permission from *Law and Society Review* 40, no. 4 (2006): 931–962. Excerpts from chapter 7 appeared in an article in *Law and Social Inquiry* 34, no. 3 (2009): 569–602. Chapter 6 was prepared with the assistance of a grant from the PSC-CUNY program. The American Sociological Association Minority Fellowship Program and the National Science Foundation also supported this work.

Finally, this book could not have been written without the kindness and generosity of the juvenile drug court staff and the youth participants and their families who let me into their lives at the court, in their homes, and in their communities. I am eternally indebted to them for allowing me the opportunity to be part of their world, at least for a little while.

Discretionary Justice

CHAPTER 1

Inside the Black Box of
Drug Court Justice

During its weekly review meeting before court, the staff talks about Molly, a white sixteen-year-old who has been in the drug court for two months. While the staff applauds the fact that she went to school every day, her electronic house-arrest monitoring device shows that she left the house one night from 11 P.M. until 5 A.M. This is a major concern for staff since Molly can only leave the house if accompanied by a parent. A probation officer speculates that she was out all night with her boyfriend. The drug counselor does not know what happened since she has not heard Molly's side of the story. They debate the validity of the house arrest report until another probation officer asks, "What are we doing with Molly?" The judge speculates that if Molly was using drugs, she will not bother to show up today for court. The public defender suggests sending Molly to juvenile hall for the weekend for staying out all night. When Molly and her mom appear before the court, the public defender starts the proceedings by saying she has a home supervision violation for leaving the house that night. Molly explains that she was at a friend's house, but when pressed further by the judge about whether it was a girlfriend or a boyfriend, she denies having a boyfriend. The judge then tells her that she will spend a weekend in juvenile hall and reminds her to drug test before leaving court that day.[1]

Drug courts like this one are intended to be new types of alternatives to incarceration for drug offenders. No time seems more perfect for such alternatives than now. The devastating effects of mass incarceration largely fueled by the War on Drugs cannot be ignored: communities are destabilized; children grow up without parents; ex-offenders cannot find jobs, housing, or educational opportunities; and the democratic process is compromised by the many ex-offenders who lose their right to vote.[2] The need for drug reform is not simply a moral or political issue: in dire economic times, states can no longer afford to keep locking up people. The National Conference of State Legislatures (2009) reports that state estimates for correctional spending in fiscal year 2008 are $39.8 billion, and the Department of Justice (2004) indicates the increases in state prison budgets are outpacing the increases in state spending on schools or hospitals. While the need to change our drug policy is clear, the solution is not as easy to find. It seems too radical to most people to let drug offenders out of prison on their own or to legalize some drugs to reduce the number of people going to jail. So the question remains: what is the next step in current drug policy that has been characterized by the 1992 study of two prominent legal scholars, Malcolm Feeley and Jonathan Simon, as the new penology in which we classify and manage "dangerous" groups of people? How can we transition to a more humane, practical, and reasonable policy about drug offenders?

Drug courts appear to offer one such step. Started in 1989 in Miami, drug courts divert drug offenders into drug treatment instead of prison, with court staff supervising the offenders' progress in treatment. These courts have a little of everything to appease multiple and divergent interest groups such as liberals, conservatives, drug treatment professionals, and legal practitioners. Drug offenders can stay out of jail or prison and get the treatment they need. Unlike previous diversions to treatment programs, drug courts closely supervise and manage potentially "dangerous" offenders while they are in the community. As a result, the offenders know that if they mess up they go back to jail. If they do well, they not only stay out of jail but become sober and responsible citizens. This comprehensive approach has fueled public support for drug courts. In July 2009 there were 2,264 such courts in all fifty states (U.S. Department of Justice 2009); over 400,000 adults and youths were processed through these courts between 1998 and 2005 (Center for Families, Children, and the Courts 2006). According to the National Drug Court Institute, "there are over 99,100 drug court clients currently being served" as of December 31, 2008.[3] And in a 2007 article in USA Today, C. West Huddleston, the executive director of the National Drug Court Institute, estimated that drug courts could help an additional four million people (Unze 2007).

Given their popularity, drug courts have become perhaps the most prominent model of a broader legal movement called therapeutic jurisprudence. Initially conceptualized by two law professors, David B. Wexler and Bruce Winick,[4] for mental health law, this movement encourages legal practitioners to help offenders address issues such as drug use, unemployment, and homelessness instead of processing them simply in terms of the legal offense. To accomplish this therapeutic goal, drug courts establish their own set of expectations (e.g., attendance in drug treatment and court, abstinence from drug use) and tools (e.g., drug tests) to hold offenders accountable to their treatment plan. If the offenders do not meet these expectations, the staff can use a series of graduated sanctions (e.g., short-term jail stays, community service) and rewards (e.g., movie tickets, gift certificates) to encourage them to comply with the drug court.

This study looks at the drug court staff's evaluative process of offenders' compliance and noncompliance to better understand the nature of the court's therapeutic intervention. While the link between compliance and drug treatment may seem illogical, drug courts incorporate a key component of self-help drug treatment programs that involves learning to take responsibility for one's drug use and actions. Framed as accountability in the therapeutic jurisprudence literature, this kind of individual responsibility involves two main components. One part of the accountability message calls for youths to account for their actions, in the dual sense of taking ownership to fix their problems—such as controlling their drug use—and confessing when they fail in their attempt—that is, admitting "guilt" in committing "noncompliant" actions. The second component involves youths being held accountable by staff. If the youths do something wrong, they agree to be exposed to the court's sanctions, or its punishments. In other words, accountability in the juvenile drug court refers to the dual idea of being accountable and being held accountable for one's actions.

To convey this multifaceted message of accountability, the drug courts assess individual acts of noncompliance and compliance. The subsequent court decisions are geared not toward the offenders' rehabilitation as people but with the correction to their noncompliant actions. In this way, accountability has an inherent tension of therapy and punishment. This form of tough love therapy involves accepting some kind of punishment to learn not to do it again.[5]

This study also shows how accountability is crafted through the staff's negotiated and socially constructed views of the youths' noncompliance and compliance. It conducts an intensive case study of staff decision-making practices in a juvenile drug court in southern California and asks the following questions: what do accountability and noncompliance mean on a day-to-day basis for the staff, youths, and their parents? How are accountability and noncompliance assessed, interpreted, and implemented by staff in actual organizational circumstances? To answer these questions, I focus specifically on how the staff constructs and negotiates youth noncompliance in its decision-making process. As the opening vignette hints, this process is not necessarily seamless. Staff members debate with one another about the nature, validity, and severity of a youth's noncompliance.

BUILDING BLOCKS OF ACCOUNTABILITY: NONCOMPLIANCE AS A SOCIAL CONSTRUCTION

Because a central feature of drug courts is individual accountability, many would assume that the offenders' ultimate case outcome would be shaped mainly by their lack of motivation to take responsibility for their actions and stop using drugs. This book argues that view is too limited because the outcomes are based on staff assessments of offender noncompliance. Those assessments are, upon closer inspection, social constructions by staff. What drug court staff considers noncompliant is a variety of trivial actions that could be seen elsewhere as normal behavior. As the introductory vignette noted, the juvenile drug court staff could assess youths as noncompliant for their relationships, adherence to curfew, school attendance, and drug use. Some of these behaviors are not criminal outside of the drug court; however, youths in the drug court could face criminal-like sanctions like short-term stays in juvenile hall for those behaviors.[6] The focus of the juvenile drug court, then, is about not only regulating drug use but also reshaping these youths into more responsible citizens who engage in positive activities. In addition, drug court staff often holds youths responsible for things that are not always within their control. For example, staff once sent a youth to juvenile hall for a cur-few violation; the real reason was to appease his disgruntled and frustrated mom before she kicked him out of the home completely.

To prove this view of noncompliance as a social construction, this study demonstrates how noncompliance is a product of staff interpretations about youths' behavior and situations amid a limited amount of organizational responses at the staff's disposal.[7] Seen in this light, the youths' final case outcomes are actually an accumulation of several staff decisions classifying trivial youth actions as noncompliant or compliant. This book explores a variety of factors that influence these decisions, such as the staff's notion of the youth's character, the youth's demographics, and the youth's family and organizational factors related to drug testing and court resources.

Youth-Related Factors

One factor would be the staff's assessments of the youth's character. This notion of character is not as permanent as the kinds of moral character found by sociologist Robert Emerson in his study of a juvenile court. In his 1969 book, *Judging Delinquents*, Emerson outlined the influence of moral character on the legal decision-making process, as the judge made his final decision based on his sense of the youths as "good," "bad," or "sick." Because the drug court makes many frequent decisions about youths' mundane behaviors over a long period of time, there is a temporality to staff assessments of character that could change from one court decision to another. The staff's sense of the youths' character, then, is tied more to establishing their contin-ued viability in the court, as the staff is constantly refining its approach to working with them.

The staff's decisions also appeared to vary by the youths' race, gender, and socioeconomic class. While the staff did not explicitly mention race or socioeconomic class in their discussions, those differences did emerge in its seemingly neutral descriptions of youths as "mentally ill" and "wannabe gang members" (e.g., white middle-class youths) versus the "manipulators" and "gangsters" (e.g., Latino working-class youths).[8] Gender issues came up more explicitly in how the staff interpreted and responded to the youths' behaviors. As found in traditional juvenile courts, home troubles for girls differed greatly from those for boys: parents of female participants were more likely to tell staff when their youths were violating curfew or had "inappropriate" boyfriends. Another key gender difference occurred when the youth client was expecting a baby. The staff immediately transferred pregnant youths to another probation program for expecting mothers because it was assumed they would be unable to meet the drug court requirements while keeping their prenatal appointments. Soon-to-be fathers, on the other hand, were described as having an added motivation to stay clean.

Non–Youth-Related Factors

Other factors shaping staff's assessments of youth noncompliance pertain to broader issues beyond the staff's view of individual youths. Drug test results were perhaps the most influential of all information used in the staff's decision-making process. While drug test results might be seen as scientific fact, staff might still interpret the same results for two tests differently, depending on a variety of issues, such as the type of drug or the person who administered the test. The youth's family also affected the staff's decision-making process, particularly when the parent chose to either share or hide information about potential youth noncompliance with the staff. Finally, as with any other court, the juvenile drug court staff had to work within a specific organizational context of limited resources, external agencies, and caseload pressures. For example, if the court staff did not have treatment programs or schools to send the youths to, it had to reassess decisions concerning the youths' noncompliance and expectations of the youths' ability to change.

Discretionary Justice considers how each of these factors inform, but do not determine, staff's judgments about youth noncompliance. The staff decision-making process is a fluid process in which the staff selects and interprets certain youth actions as relevant. Noncompliance, therefore, is a status created during staff interactions that could change from week to week. Moreover, the driving question for those staff discussions is "What do we do with this youth now?"

Workability

To explore the fluid and practical nature of youth noncompliance, this study uses the concept of the youths' workability. By "workability" I mean the staff's sense of how it can best influence the youths to adhere to the court's requirements and to learn to be accountable. This sense is continuously revised over time, as staff determines which court response will work best for the youths in specific situations. As such, the concept of workability conveys both an idea of informed guesswork and staff persistence to coach the youths to remedy their noncompliant behavior. In addition, workability conveys the multifaceted and multi-actor character of individual accountability. Workability is based on not only youths' actions or desires to comply with the court but also the staff's ability to work with the youths based on the court's fluctuating organizational resources. In this sense, a staff member might decide a youth is no longer workable because of the court's failure to respond to that youth's issues, regardless of the youth's motivation in the court. This dual notion of workability—involving both staff and youth actions—eventually crafts the youth's pathway in the court as the staff figures out in what ways and for how long it can influence youth behavior.

DRUG COURTS: A NEW FORM OF SOCIAL CONTROL AND PUNISHMENT?

This fine-grained analysis of the juvenile drug court staff's decision-making practices is not merely a descriptive exercise; it illuminates how the court's assessments of noncompliance and the underlying goal of cultivating individual accountability are an expanded form of social control and punishment. This study sees the social control found in drug court as an unlikely combination and reinterpretation of three contemporary sociolegal concepts: the culture of control, the new penology, and the therapeutic state. Similar to the contemporary forms of rehabilitation described by sociologist David Garland in his book *The Culture of Control*, drug courts' therapeutic intervention focuses on "offence behavior and the habits most closely associated with it" (2001, 176). Drug courts also rely on actuarial assessment and management techniques discussed in the new penology by Malcolm Feeley and Jonathan Simon (1992). However, they do so not to manage the risk of groups of offenders but to motivate them to engage in drug treatment and improve offenders' self-esteem. In his book *The Therapeutic State*, sociologist James Nolan claims this therapeutic turn is now the central concern of the state, as various institutional settings like courts, schools, and public assistance agencies are increasingly focusing on helping individuals improve themselves. This therapeutic orientation allows for and legitimates a broader involvement of governmental presence in peoples' everyday lives in civil society. *Discretionary Justice* offers an additional layer to that compiled view of social control: the therapeutic jurisprudence offered in drug court, operationalized as noncompliance or compliance, subjects drug court participants to greater amounts of surveillance and, as a result, leads them to face the possibility of punishment for behaviors that otherwise might be seen as normal or mundane.[9]

In viewing drug courts as a surveillance mechanism disguised as treatment, *Discretionary Justice* also argues that the drug courts represent a revised contemporary form of the total institution. While this statement seems odd, since the drug court clients are not locked up in one physical space to be constantly monitored, the actual work of the drug court mirrors much of what sociologist Erving Goffman documents in *Asylums* (1961). In the mental hospital, Goffman shows how staff scrutinized, interpreted, and recast client behaviors in a therapeutic light, using a variety of techniques such as case records, mortification, looping, and the ward system. So, while the drug court is not a total institution, since the clients are not inmates in a locked controlled facility, it is replicating that environment of surveillance in the community, a panopticon without walls, so to speak.[10] To do so, the drug court staff uses other types of surveillance, such as drug testing and electronic house arrest to monitor clients.

I advance this understanding of drug courts as new total institutions by conducting an ethnography of a juvenile drug court in southern California that diverts felony-level substance-using juvenile offenders into drug treatment versus long-term institutionalization. In this court, staff closely monitors youths' efforts in drug treatment, in school, and at home to make sure they are adhering to the treatment plan set by the court. Based on fifteen months of participant observation and 112 interviews with staff, the youth clients, and their parents, this study outlines the detailed processes by which expanded state (social) control works at the court, as well as the effects of such processes over time on the clients' case outcomes.

DIFFERENT PERSPECTIVES ON DRUG COURTS AND THERAPEUTIC JURISPRUDENCE

In viewing noncompliance as an interactively constructed notion, this book offers a unique perspective of drug courts and therapeutic jurisprudence. None of the previous studies sufficiently capture the highly negotiated staff assessments of youth noncompliance; as such, they cannot provide a clear sense of how final case outcomes are established or explore in detail how the court's complicated form of social control works in practice. Some trace the drug courts' type of social control back to the ideas of French philosopher Michel Foucault, who wrote about governmentality in which the influence of the state becomes localized and actualized in individuals' self-regulating actions (Foucault 1991). For example, Dawn Moore (2007) takes a Foucaultian approach in discussing drug offenders as "criminal artefacts" situating drug courts within a long history of social control inscribed and ascribed to the drug offender's docile body. Elsewhere, some studies have taken a more macro or political perspective to study drug courts, such as Dorf and Sabel (2000), who discussed therapeutic jurisprudence as a form of democratic experimentalism, and Mirchandani (2005, 2008), who views these courts as case studies for comparing Nolan's emotion-based therapeutic state to political philosopher Jurgen Habermas's rational deliberative democratic state.[11] While these scholars highlight the idea of therapeutic jurisprudence as an expanded form of the social control discussed in this book, they do so from a theoretical or a static empirical perspective based solely on staff perceptions of their work and front-stage courtroom interactions between staff and clients.

Other research is more policy focused, looking at retention and recidivism rates as well as cost-benefit analyses. Most studies now indicate that adult drug court participants have lower recidivism rates than those in comparison groups. Drug courts are also cost effective, providing an average savings of $2.83 for every dollar spent on drug courts (Aos et al. 2001; Carey and Finigan 2004).[12] A new wave of drug court policy research is starting to address the variation of case outcomes by offenders' race, class, and gender and the impact of specific components to the court model on case outcomes. For example, some have looked at the effect of the court's graduated sanctions on client behavior, finding varying results: one study (Hepburn and Harvey 2007) found little to no effect of sanctions on program retention or completion, while another (Harrell and Roman 2001) found that graduated sanctions did have a deterrent effect on participants' substance use and criminal activity. Yet these studies do not problematize the concept of client noncompliance, nor do they consider the staff negotiations in assessing noncompliant status. They take noncompliance at face value and from there launch their analyses of the drug court.

Even the studies that do take a social constructionist view of noncompliance do not probe deep enough into the staff negotiations of that status. Mackinem and Higgins (2008) attempt to discuss how drug court staff produces client success and failure based on its evaluations of the offenders' "moral identities." Elsewhere, Burns and Peyrot (2003) and Cook (2006) have analyzed how drug court judges and restorative justice facilitators convey notions of accountability to the offenders. While these scholars offer interesting perspectives of the drug court and therapeutic jurisprudence, they focus primarily on staff typologies and front-stage courtroom interactions. Similarly, Whiteacre (2008) raises many provoking questions about drug courts as expanded forms of social control and about the ambiguities in accountability, pointing out glaring contradictions between the juvenile drug court staff and youth clients' perceptions, and between the principles and actual work of juvenile drug courts. However, because Whiteacre relies so heavily on interview data of the youth participants and staff, he only sketches out these ideas without showing how they affect the staff's decision-making process concerning those youths.

This study takes a different approach to looking at drug courts in action, emphasizing the highly contested and unpredictable backstage staff negotiations behind official decisions. These negotiations occur before the frontstage courtroom interactions that are the focus of the previous research. Ignoring this phase of the decision-making process curtails the understanding of how noncompliance is a socially constructed phenomenon in the drug courts. Namely, it limits our view of how youth's ultimate case outcomes in the juvenile drug court result from several staff negotiations about the youths' behavior that are shaped by the various factors mentioned earlier. In going behind the scenes, this study illustrates the fluidity of the drug courts' work, showing how the staff crafts assessments of the youths incrementally over time based on the changing influx of information about them week to week. In addition, previous studies, with the exception of Whiteacre's, largely focus on drug policy and drug courts in regard to adults, not youths. My case study on youths sheds more light on the practical work of noncompliance and accountability: by the very nature of being juveniles, they are not completely responsible for their actions (under the rule of the law and also practically); yet we still hold them to the same standards as adults. So, by focusing on the juvenile drug court the putative nature of noncompliance and accountability is even more exposed for analysis.

ACCOUNTABILITY IN ACTION

To do this kind of analysis, the study looks at what the drug court practitioners do in actuality versus what they say they do in theory. It specifically relies on two analytical frameworks: people-processing institutions (Hasenfeld 1972) and law in action (Manzo and Travers 1998). These frameworks share the view that abstract concepts of law, accountability, and noncompliance must be understood through an empirical focus on staff's daily work routines.

People-Processing Institutions

A people-processing approach (Hasenfeld 1972) looks at how social control institutions, such as courts, governmental agencies, schools, and psychiatric and medical institutions funnel people into and through their organizations and ultimately to different institutional fates. In contrast to private companies whose main task is to manufacture some kind of objective product for a financial profit, people-processing institutions work to transform individual people into clients, students, patients, or other "institutional selves" (Gubrium and Holstein 2001).[13] I use this analytical perspective to highlight three interrelated dimensions of the juvenile drug court: the court as dependent on a network of external agencies, staff decision making as a practical work activity, and the staff's interpretive practices in its decision-making process.

The juvenile drug court has ambitious goals for its youth participants and depends on several external agencies—schools, drug treatment programs, family, and probation—to instill behavior changes. This approach exemplifies Hasenfeld's description of a people-processing agency that merely confers a new status, such as delinquent or drug user, onto individuals before sending them to other agencies who work on getting the youths to change their behavior. Understanding this broader organizational context in which the court operates helps inform the analysis of the staff's decision-making process in assessing youth noncompliance. That is, the drug court relies upon these agencies to be the external parts of its ward system that monitor and limit where youths can go and how they act. An interagency view also provides a way to understand how staff socially constructs youth noncompliance. The drug court staff's assessments of youth noncompliance are built on these external agencies' information about the youths' behaviors. The amount and quality of information provided by the agencies shape the drug court staff's negotiations about youth noncompliance.

I also consider the practical orientation to therapeutic jurisprudence work, relying on the long-established sociological notions (Becker 1963; Garfinkel 1967; Matza 1969) that the court's decision-making process is not a simple application of a legal statute or a direct reflection of ideological intent of therapeutic jurisprudence. Similarly, I consider how decisions are shaped by a variety of practical and organizational factors. For example, current decisions are made with an eye toward future likely outcomes. Specific decisions are concerned with "organizational horizons" (Emerson and Paley 1992), such that staff evaluates how its decision about one noncompliant incident may affect what could happen later in a youth's case. In addition, the decisions are grounded within a "workgroup" culture (Eisenstein et al. 1977), in which the staff members become intimately familiar with one another's work styles and concerns and adjust their own decisions according to their perception of other staff members' acceptance of it.

Finally, a people-processing perspective pays attention to how a staff groups together individual troubles and youths into more generalized categories to assign meaning and to determine an appropriate court response. This approach is akin to sociologist David Sudnow's 1965 study that discusses how public defenders' work is not oriented toward ensuring due process for each individual defendant based on possible innocence. Rather, public defenders' work is organized along a classification process whereby they compare each individual case along the lines of "normal crimes." It is through the repetition of this work that the normal crime framework can develop and be used. Similarly, the juvenile drug court staff views individual youth's troubles or problems within a more general context based on its experiences in working with youths over time. Transforming individual youths into clients, and specific actions into noncompliant behaviors, requires a certain amount of interpretive work. In this effort, the staff employs a variety of interpretive practices, or "the constellation of procedures, conditions, and resources through which reality . . . is apprehended, understood, organized, and represented in the course of everyday life" (Gubrium and Holstein 2000, 94).[14]

Law in Action

At the same time, I propose that interpretive practices are not mechanically applied by staff to make decisions in the juvenile drug court. Therefore, I use a "law in action" approach (Manzo and Travers 1988) to suggest that there is an interactive and reflexive process between interpretive practices and individual decisions. This approach calls for particular attention to how law is *enacted* through staff member discussions.[15] Because the juvenile drug court staff interactively constructs decisions mainly through its institutional talk (Drew and Heritage 1992), in which staff members assess notions of noncompliance or compliance for individual youth, such an approach is crucial to expose the social construction of noncompliance.

This study pays particular attention to how staff members employ descriptions (Frohmann 1991, 1997; Garfinkel 1967; Maynard 1982, 1984) in connecting individuals to normal cases. These seemingly neutral tools to represent people and places contain coded or unstated moral notions that influence the decision-making process. For example, Lisa Frohmann (1997) showed how prosecutors' decisions to pursue rape cases included general descriptions of the defendants and locations of the crime to assess the case's "convictability" or the chance that they would win the case. The descriptions were proxies for the women's race, class, and gender (e.g., a case with a white middle-class female victim is perceived as more "winnable" than that of a poor black female victim). This study looks specifically at how juvenile drug court staff members use general descriptions as coded references to race, gender, or class and how they affect their decisions about youth noncompliance. The descriptions are organizationally defined and can be contested among different staff. To describe someone in the court as a "typical methamphetamine user" conjures up certain images or attributes. How the staff conceptualizes a methamphetamine user exposes the local organizational setting in which it is used; for example, a judge's description of a youth as a "typical meth user who lies" is based on the judge's regular interactions with methamphetamine-using youths in the court. In addition, the successful use of such descriptions depends on both the speaker's and the hearer's agreement as to their meaning in that moment. Staff disagreements over descriptions can prompt contested and negotiated views of a youth's noncompliance.[16]

In sum, *Discretionary Justice* unpacks the complicated nature of assessing youth accountability in a juvenile drug court. Figure 1.1 is a conceptual map depicting the various actors, filters, statuses, and responses involved in a staff's decision-making process.

PLAN OF THE BOOK

The book starts with an overview of the juvenile drug court's work, which is essentially one of supervision and structure. Staff members often described the juvenile drug court as offering more intensive supervision than traditional probation programs. Reminiscent of the original juvenile court's philosophy of *parens patrie*, the juvenile drug court staff firmly believed the youths benefited from having additional structure in their chaotic unregulated lives. Yet the juvenile drug court differs from the traditional court in that it monitors the youths' actions much more closely, and its therapeutic intention is mainly to teach youths to take accountability for their actions versus linking them to outside agencies for treatment.

Chapter 2 describes the court setting, including the network of external agencies such as drug treatment centers, schools, probation programs, and families, upon whose cooperation the drug court staff relies to assess youth noncompliance. It also considers the unique feature to the drug court staff's work: there is a certain unpredictability of the youth clients' case outcomes that makes the staff's work of assessing youths' accountability all the more difficult. Staff members often stated that they never knew which youths would turn themselves around and complete the program. Knowing that, the staff attempted to develop a sense of the youth's workability, trying out different sanctions and rewards to influence the youth's behavior. Depending on how those court responses impacted the youth, the staff readjusted its strategy and honed its idea of the youth's workability.

Chapter 3 expands upon the organizational context for the staff assessments of youth accountability and noncompliance by analyzing the influence of the drug court's three-subcourt structure on staff discussions and decisions. While this seems a simple procedural task in the juvenile drug court, a youth's assignment to one of the three courts directly influences how staff is able to monitor and respond to his or her actions.

Chapter 4 turns to the weekly staff decision-making process, looking at how staff discusses and responds to the incidents of trivial youth non-compliance. This activity is the nuts-and-bolts work of the drug court, because it brings to life the therapeutic jurisprudence philosophy of holding youths accountable for their actions. In addition, the interagency model requires staff members to gather and present information about youths to each other. This information is not necessarily an objective rendering

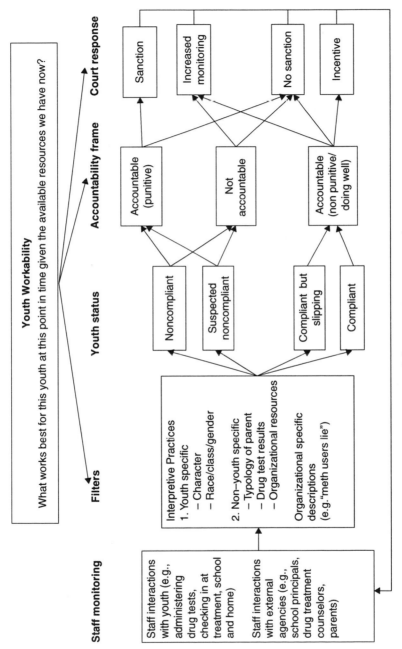

1.1. Accountability-in-action conceptual map

but rather, a strategic presentation. Analytically, this information should therefore be considered a resource, not fact, in understanding the juvenile drug court staff's decision-making process.[17] This chapter specifically looks at the interpretive practices and normal cases staff members use to translate certain kinds of information into different assessments of noncompliance, possible noncompliance, or compliance. These categorizations are specific to the youth's case history but also are compared against a set of other youths that the staff deems similar.

Similarly, chapter 5 discusses the use of new technology (e.g., drug tests) in the drug court to facilitate assessments of noncompliance. In the juvenile drug court, drug testing is a significant measure of accountability, given its scientific "objectivity." For example, a positive drug test "proves" to the court that the client is not telling the truth, even if the laboratory results are potentially disputable. The technology of drug testing creates certainty amidst the ambiguity. This chapter argues that such scientific measures are still subject to the staff's interpretations and negotiations. It shows that drug test results can be determined by the staff's views of the youths, the youths' drug use, and the staff's competency in administering drug tests. The meaning of drug test results is therefore a mixture of scientific "facts" (e.g., laboratory results) and staff interpretive practices.

Chapter 6 focuses on the families' perceptions of the juvenile drug court, specifically the staff's intensive monitoring of their children and its decision-making process. The staff often told the parents they were the court's "eyes and ears" about the youths' behavior. Yet parents were faced with the dilemma of whether or not to report their youths' noncompliance to the staff. Interviews with the parents serve as a counterpoint to the staff's perspective, shedding light on how families view and negotiate court intervention, as well as various "everyday hassles," which are much more influential on youth noncompliance than one might think (Wolf and Colyer 2001).

Chapter 7 considers how the staff's weekly negotiations inform and are shaped by an evolving sense of the youths' workability. It looks at the interactive relationship between the staff's weekly decisions and its long-term notion of the youth's workability. Ultimately, there is tension between ensuring consistent responses among cases and addressing individual accountability.

The book concludes with some reflections on the implications of penal policy and how accountability is a new proxy mechanism for differential treatment based on race, class, and gender. Drug courts place the onus of an offender's fate squarely on his or her shoulders, rather than considering possible social structural barriers affecting offenders' efforts to stay compliant. Moreover, attributing offenders' failure to their lack of accountability erases any racial or gender disparities in outcomes. Drug courts, then, represent a new form of self-driven penal policy in which the offender is viewed as driving his fate to either freedom via drug treatment or additional incarceration.

This study shows how the drug court staff's decision-making process creates uncritical notions of human agency in its assessments of participants' actions. Emphasizing human agency under the rubric of accountability assumes offenders have complete control over their bodies and actions, independent of the organizational influences that constrain, influence, and shape their actions. So, while the concept of accountability is premised upon the person's actions, it is filtered through localized staff constructions of what those actions mean. Put another way, the current system overemphasizes individual accountability, ignoring the ways in which social control institutions go unchecked in shaping an individual's ability to be accountable. The risk the drug courts identify, manage, and seek to change remains localized on the individual level.

CONCLUSION

This book takes the reader inside the juvenile drug court to highlight the multiple and detailed monitoring mechanisms of accountability. It specifically considers the practical work of the court, looking at how the staff presents and then negotiates the meaning of information in its decision-making process. Given the growing emphasis in other settings (e.g., welfare and education) on individual accountability and on new forms of technology to detect any individual deviation from that accountability, this work is increasingly important.[18]

Drug courts and other accountability-based policies can be considered as what Patricia Gray describes as a neoliberal policy of "transformative risk technologies." These policies focus on changing the "bad" behaviors among the targeted group of clients while essentially ignoring "the structural factors that severely restrict their choices" to engage in said behaviors (2009, 447). Gray uses the example of job training programs for at-risk youth in the United Kingdom to state that "in advanced liberal modes of governance, socially excluded young people are held individually responsible to negotiate successfully the risk of unemployment" (2009, 447), with the government allocating its resources toward job preparation and job-ready programs versus job-creation programs. Even "successful" youths in these risk-oriented programs could end up with poor quality education and jobs. The consequence is that we train a new generation of post-Fordist workers to expect nothing stable from the job market. This kind of individualized focus is akin to the efforts by the founders of the original juvenile court who only focused on "correcting" individuals and their families while ignoring the larger social problems affecting those individuals. As Barry Feld writes in *Bad Kids*,

"A century ago, Progressive reformers had to choose between either initiating social structural reforms that would reduce inequality and ameliorate criminogenic forces or ministering to the young people damaged by those adverse conditions. "Child saving" satisfied Progressives' humanitarian impulses without engendering more fundamental social changes" (1999, 9). The question remains: by basing clients' success on their ability and/or motivation to adhere to specific program requirements (e.g., not using drugs, improving school test scores, keeping medical appointments), are we indirectly blaming the victim when the client fails to do so? What often goes unrecognized in this new form of accountability-based justice are the larger systemic barriers for some individuals to be able to decide their fate as equally as others.[19] In short, are we simply individualizing larger social problems?

So, while these accountability-based policies appear to offer a new way for clients to prove their "worthiness" for help, as evidenced by their levels of responsibility, these policies actually help to create further cleavages among the deserving and undeserving clients by pushing those people who fail deeper into the deviant groups. As Gray suggests in her article, the youths unsuccessfully looking for employment in the United Kingdom learn essentially to blame themselves (or be blamed by others) for their low or marginalized position in the economy. In this way, the unaccountable client—whose status has been, in large part, socially constructed by the state—is penalized for his failures not just in the present but also in any future attempts to become more accountable.[20] The unaccountable client is the newest form of the undeserving client, with the state abdicating more and more of its responsibility to its citizens.

CHAPTER 2

Setting and Methods

THE JUVENILE DRUG COURT'S overarching goal to teach accountability to the youths is not an easy task. Rather, it is a complex process for staff that involves gathering information from various external agencies and negotiating how to interpret it. Youth accountability—as found in the juvenile drug court—depends on the youths themselves, as well as many institutional actors, work routines, and organizational contingencies.

INSIDE THE COURT

With its unique countywide model, the juvenile drug court in this study opened in 1998 with the ability to handle up to 150 youths at any given time.[1] As with many other drug courts, this one is post-dispositional, meaning the youths already have been "true found" (guilty) on felony-level offenses. The drug court is one of a few noncustodial dispositions such as probation, work programs, and community service that allows youths to remain in their communities instead of going to juvenile hall, California Youth Authority, or a group home. These youths have all had some prior experience with the juvenile justice system and drug treatment. Probation officers and judges refer them to the court after they have accumulated three noncompliant events while under traditional probation supervision and have substance abuse treatment as a condition of their original probation.[2] The staff describes the youths as requiring intensive supervision. Some state the youths are hard-core kids one step away from long-term institutionalization. They largely base their assumption on the youths' past record, as most have been involved in the juvenile court for some time and have failed in the first-level probation supervision.[3]

Most of the youths are Caucasian and Latino, with a few African Americans and Asian Americans. They range from fourteen to seventeen years old. Eighty-one percent of the participants are male. The Caucasian youths are mainly from middle-class families, while the Latinos, African American, and Asian American youths mostly come from poor families.[4] In general, Latino youths are overrepresented and whites are underrepresented in the court: 51 percent of the drug court youths were Latino,

TABLE 2.1

Sample weekly schedule for youth

Hours	Monday	Tuesday	Wednesday	Thursday	Friday
8 A.M.–1 P.M.	School	School	School	School	School
3–6 P.M.	Treatment	Court (til 4:30–5 P.M.)	Treatment	Treatment	
7 P.M.	Curfew	Curfew	Curfew	Curfew	Curfew

NOTE: The hours for school would vary depending on the type of school (e.g. independent study programs were much shorter than mainstream schools). The youths' curfew also varied based on the youth's age: fifteen year olds had to be home by 6 P.M. versus seventeen year olds whose curfew was technically 7 P.M.

compared to 27 percent in the general county population, and 37 percent of the drug court youths were white, compared to 56 percent of the county population.[5]

If accepted into the court, the youths are expected to go to school every day, be respectful at home, and attend drug treatment after school. Staff frequently monitors youths' actions in these areas. In addition to making frequent appearances in court, the youths can expect to see their drug court probation officers, police officers, and drug counselors between two to three times a week, checking on them at their schools, drug treatment programs and homes at all hours of the day. Table 2.1 shows a typical week for a youth in the beginning stages of the court.

The youths had very little free time outside of the court. Many wanted to work but could not do so because of the rigid court schedule. Here's how Sebastian, a seventeen-year-old Latino, described his schedule in the beginning of the program:

> I was going to school and drug court every week. He'll [drug court counselor] come to my house and test. Actually, I was going to drug classes also. . . . So like Tuesdays and Fridays, because those were my days to go to counseling [treatment], I had to tell my teacher I had to leave so I had to get on the trolley and on the bus. Then after that I'll get out at like 4:30 or 5:00, and then I'll have to get on the bus again and go to the trolley, then go home. So by the time I get home, it's like 6:00 or 7:00, already kind of dark . . . So the only free time I really had was my weekends.

The youths have to complete four phases to graduate from the drug court. Each phase has a different level of court supervision (e.g., random drug testing, interaction with drug court staff), mandated hours in drug treatment of three to nine hours a week, and court appearances (e.g., weekly, biweekly, monthly). The youths advance through the phases based on their "sober day" count, which is determined by their drug test results. To graduate, the youths have to accumulate 365 consecutive sober days,[6] in addition to completing the other requirements related to treatment, school, and home. If the youths test positive for drugs, their sober day count gets reset to 0 days. So, even if they have 364 days clean and then test positive for drugs, they go back to 0 sober days and face at least another 365 days in the drug court before graduating.

If the youths do accumulate enough sober days to graduate, they become eligible for successful termination of their probation, dismissal of all charges, and waiver of all fees except for restitution fines. If the youths repeatedly test positive for drug use, the staff can decide that they require more intensive treatment, found at a residential program. In that situation, the staff temporarily removes the youths from the court docket until they have completed the residential program. If the youths get rearrested on a serious offense or are continually noncompliant with the drug court requirements, the staff can also decide to terminate them from the program and refer their case back to the juvenile court. At that point, the youths may face placement in probation camps or possibly the California Youth Authority.

WHEN DO THE YOUTHS COME TO COURT?

Depending on where they live, youths are assigned to one of three subcourts that meet once a week in the afternoon. Each subcourt is described below:

1. East County (Tuesdays): The catchment area for this court encompasses urban, suburban, and rural communities. It is perhaps the most diverse demographically among the youths, with African American and Asian American youths living in the more urban and poor neighborhoods and the white and Latino youths living in the more affluent rural and suburban communities. These youths had fairly good public transportation options to be able to get to their schools, treatment programs, and court.

2. North County (Wednesdays): This court meets in an off-site court facility about twenty miles north of the mainstream juvenile court building, where the other two courts meet. The youths in this court are primarily middle class and either Latino or white. The public transportation in this area is extremely limited, making it almost untenable for most youths to get to the court without a car.

TABLE 2.2
Staff names and roles

Roles	East County Tuesdays	North County Wednesdays	South County Thursdays
Judge	Hooper	Samuels	O'Reilly
Public defender	Charlie	Charlie	Charlie
District attorney	Jack	Jack	Jack
Clinical therapist	Mark	Mark	Mark
Probation officer(s)	Sarah and Joe	Allen	Julie
Drug counselor(s)	Eva and Jill	George and Bill	Peter and Raul
Police	Andy	Yates	Grant and Andy

3. South County (Thursdays): The youths in this court are primarily Latino and white, and most come from middle-class families. It is perhaps the most urban of all three courts, with treatment programs and schools located on a few main streets that are easily accessible by public transportation.

INTERAGENCY TEAM APPROACH
TO WORKING WITH YOUTHS

Like other problem-solving courts, the juvenile drug court employs a team-based approach to working with youths. Each of the three subcourts has dedicated teams of one judge, prosecutor, defense attorney, probation officer, police officer, drug counselor, and clinical therapist. Table 2.2 is a snapshot of the teams.

The three judges were all Caucasian males who had been working at the drug court for several years.[7] They presided over other dockets since the drug court assignment was not a full-time position. As a result, the south court judge, O'Reilly, knew many of the drug court youths from his normal delinquency caseload. Hooper, the east court judge, handled juvenile traffic court and truancy court. He saw so many youths in all these different settings that he often had a hard time keeping track of who was who. Samuels, the north court judge, handled dependency cases, so he did not see the drug court youths outside of the weekly sessions.

The rest of the staff all had extensive experience, ranging from two to thirty years, in the juvenile justice and/or substance abuse treatment field prior to coming to the juvenile drug court. Charlie, the public defender, was a Latino and had been with the court since its inception. Jack, the district attorney, was a Caucasian who started in the court at the same time I started the fieldwork. He used to be a probation officer and social worker. At least half of the ten drug counselors were former drug users in recovery, and this group was mostly Latino and Caucasian and predominantly male.[8] The four probation officers were all Caucasian and divided evenly in terms of gender. The three police officers were all male, two Caucasian and one African American.

The court's team approach fostered a different kind of legal decision-making process compared to traditional courts. Each juvenile drug court started its team meeting by reviewing the youths' actions that week and deciding together if the youths deserved a court punishment or not. In these meetings, the staff reviewed the youths' progress reports written by the probation officers and drug counselors based on information they accumulated from external agencies (e.g., schools, homes, drug treatment) during the week.[9] The staff would then decide which youths were noncompliant or compliant and the appropriate court responses for each individual youth.

This team dynamic allows for a more flexible and discretionary decision-making process, because the staff members' opinions are not necessarily tied to their institutional roles of judge, public defender, district attorney, probation, or police officer. Rather, the staff members offer various perspectives about the offenders' behavior with the goal of motivating those offenders' progress in treatment. The substantive nature of the court's decision-making process is focused on therapeutic aspects such as the youth's drug test results or attendance at drug treatment versus the legal aspects of the case. The judges become quasi social workers as they consider the treatment issues for each offender. To do so, they rely upon a new key courtroom player, the drug treatment counselor, whose in-house expertise helps inform the staff about the youths' efforts.

The court's team-based model helps the staff develop an intimate knowledge of each person's work styles, allowing a workgroup culture to develop (Eisenstein and Jacob 1977). This culture is facilitated by the fact that all the judges, the public defender, and Julie, a probation officer, have been working at the court since it opened.[10] Moreover, the lawyers and the clinical therapist sit on all three courts, and Judges O'Reilly and Hooper often preside over each others' caseloads. In addition, the probation officers and drug counselors cover each others' caseloads, testing youths assigned to other staff if necessary. Most of the staff had a working familiarity with each other and most, if not all, of the youths in all three courts.[11]

Relationships with External Agencies

The juvenile drug court's work does not occur in a vacuum. As figure 2.1 shows, a drug court client's progress is tied to his or her participation in

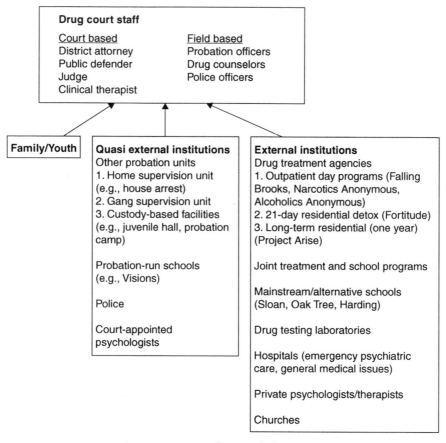

2.1. Agencies working with drug court

several other agencies and institutions. The juvenile drug court operates within a complex and varied institutional environment (Hasenfeld 1972, 1992; Hasenfeld and Cheung 1985), as its personnel develop regular working relations and close ties to several legal agencies, such as the police, probation and juvenile halls, nonresidential and residential treatment programs, and core community institutions like schools. Most of the program names have been changed for confidentiality purposes.

Quasi-external agencies differ from external agencies in that they represent other divisions of the same organizations—probation, police, and juvenile court—involved in the drug court. Operationally, they were closely intertwined with the drug court and provided the actual day-to-day super-vision of the youths in custody or on house arrest. The drug court had a somewhat conflicting relationship with these quasi-external agencies, largely due to the countywide budget cuts that reduced their ability to provide services to the drug court. The most affected was the probation department, which scaled back operations in its home supervision and custody-based units. This greatly limited the drug court's ability to punish its youths.

The external agencies included drug treatment programs, schools, and drug laboratories.[12] Depending on the youth's case, staff could also work with local hospitals, private psychologists, and churches. In general, the court staff worked with a select group of treatment providers and schools, developing close working relationships with their staff. The majority of the drug agencies followed a twelve-step, cognitive behavior modification model. The treatment consisted of mainly group therapy where youths learn to curtail their drug impulses and identity as addicts to maintain a lifetime of sobriety. The court's drug counselors often knew many of the staff in these treatment programs—either having previously worked at those same places or sharing the ex-addict identity.

Most of the youths were behind in school, often by several grades. A significant portion of the youths attended probation schools. These schools were run in partnership with the city's school district to accommodate the youths on probation who had been kicked out of the regular school system. They typically had up to thirty youths in one room and met in storefront locations in mini-malls. If the youths did not attend a probation school, they would most likely be in a continuation school. Very few, if any, youths went to mainstream schools, mainly because by the time they got to drug court, they had been in and out of juvenile hall so often that they fell behind on their schoolwork and the schools had kicked them out.

YOUTH TRAJECTORIES: EXPECTED BUT UNPREDICTABLE USES OF NORMAL REMEDIES AND WORKABILITY

While the drug court states its focus is on the youths' drug use, the youths could end up taking several different pathways in the court that might not have anything to do with their drug use. Those pathways are not preset trajectories. Instead, they evolve over time as staff members work with the youths. The pathways are also influenced by various organizational factors, such as the court's fluctuating resources and contingencies. The ideal trajectory would proceed along the following lines:

A sixteen-year-old youth is referred to the drug court after getting arrested for violating his home supervision, or house arrest. He has been on probation for two years now. The offense that got him on probation is residential burglary. He and his friends, while high on methamphetamine, broke into a neighbor's home for fun. He starts the drug court program in September by getting released from juvenile hall on home supervision. After getting enrolled in school and a drug treatment program, the youth is rewarded by getting off home supervision. He is regularly late to school or treatment, for which he gets a warning from the judge. The following week he is on time to both programs. The youth then gets a positive drug test for methamphetamine use, for which he receives a short-term stint in juvenile hall of three days. After that, he goes back to school and treatment and continues doing well; the staff gives movie tickets to reward him for his progress. In December the youth gets another positive drug test result and receives yet another short-term stay of five days in juvenile hall, with a warning that the next time he will go to the twenty-eight-day program in the probation camp. After he gets a third positive drug test in late January, the court sends him to the twenty-eight-day program. When he is released, he is back on home supervision until he gets back into school and treatment. He does well until May, when he begins to slip in school, gets a series of positive drug tests, runs away from home, and stops coming to court. When he is arrested on the court's bench warrant in August, the staff sends him to the 120-day drug program, also at the probation camp. Upon his release from the 120-day program, he seems to exhibit more direction and determination to do well in the court. He starts to accumulate more sober days, and despite an occasional punishment for a missed school day or treatment appointment, he appears to be set to graduate from the program the following August, almost two years after starting the court.

This scenario shows how staff uses graduated sanctions and rewards to respond to youth behavior.[13] The sanctions become increasingly serious (three- and five-day stints in juvenile hall, 28-day and 120-day programs at the probation camp) as the youth accumulates noncompliant actions (e.g., drug use). In theory, each successive punishment has a greater impact on the youth who ultimately changes for the better. Yet each positive drug test prolongs the youth's time in the court, as it resets his sober time clock; it takes this youth almost two years to accumulate 365 consecutive sober days to graduate from the court.

Most of the youths do not meet this ideal progression for two reasons. One, the staff might know exactly how to respond to the youth but may not have the available resources at that moment, disrupting the ideal flow to a youth's trajectory in the drug court. Second, the staff recognizes that some youths may have other problems besides drug use, but it takes time for the staff to discern if the youth's main issue is one of those problems, such as general delinquency, school and home troubles, or mental illness. So the use and effectiveness of the court responses might vary according to what particular trouble the staff is trying to rectify or remedy, which only becomes clearer over time. Possible sanctions, listed in increasing order of severity, for youth noncompliance are the following:

- Increased drug testing/supervision
- Warning (lecture)
- Community service
- Essay
- Change of treatment program or school
- Work project
- Home supervision (house arrest)/ESP (electronic supervision through an ankle bracelet)
- Short-term custody (two to five days in juvenile hall)
- Long term in-custody drug treatment (28 and 120 days in probation camps)
- Community-based residential treatment (twenty-one-day detox, one year)

This book refers to the court's responses as normal remedies instead of sanctions because normal remedies convey a more naturalistic way to understand the staff's uses of the court's punishments. According to Emerson (1981, 20), "this approach contrasts sharply with those that assume that decisions are directly determined by characteristics of the offense or the offender: it is not the offense and offender per se, but how offense and offender articulate with prior and prospective remedies that provides decision makers with distinctive grounds for choosing or recommending particular outcomes." This helps explain why the staff might vary its responses to the same objective trouble like drug use or truancy over time when the official policy calls for the same sanction. The variation is based on the staff's sense of how to fix or remedy the particular trouble, given its general understanding of how the case might progress. That general understanding comes from the staff's comparisons of one youth or situation to a similar group of youths or situations, versus a formulaic application of sanctions for individual acts of noncompliance.

In sum, the juvenile drug court is a complex organization that involves several moving parts, inside and outside its walls. The following chapters look at how the staff's use of normal remedies affects and shapes its view about a youth's workability—that is, the staff's ideas on how to influence the youth's behavior to adhere to the court's overall goals of individual accountability. If the staff feels like it can continue to work with the youth, it will discuss different normal remedies to have some kind of impact on the youth. If those remedies continually have no effect, the staff may move toward terminating the youth from the program.

The staff's sense of workability evolves within a context of unpredictability, both on the individual and organizational level. While the staff might recognize a particular behavior or type of youth, it also does not proclaim to know which youth will make it or remain workable. As a result, the staff works with youths for a long time, rarely giving up on them and trying different remedies in hopes that something may stick. The idea of unpredictability also applies to the drug court itself, given that its ability to access quasi-external and external programs fluctuated over time. This study argues that the staff's process of deciding normal remedies every week and crafting workability over time is grounded in the larger organizational context in which the staff conducts its work.

METHODS

A brief note about methods is necessary before going into the subsequent analytical chapters.[14] The data presented in this study is based on fifteen months of participant observation and interviews that I conducted in two phases, from October 2003 to October 2004 and from July to August 2007. To get a sense of the naturally occurring staff decision-making process, I attended all the weekly sessions for the three courts. These sessions were where the bulk of the action occurred in the drug court, or, more specifically, where the youth's noncompliant status was determined. The team meetings started between 1:30 and 2:00 P.M., with the court hearings starting immediately afterward with the youths and their families. In the court hearings, the public defender first talked briefly with the noncompliant youths about the issues and proposed remedies. These youths came before the court one by one, with the judge talking on behalf of the team about the court's decision. Depending on what the youths and families said, the judge could change that decision. After these cases were done, the compliant youths were seen as a group. The team meetings lasted between thirty minutes to two hours, while the court hearings lasted between forty-five minutes and two hours. I observed 172 team meetings and court hearings over both fieldwork periods.

I also attended the screening meetings where staff evaluated possible new clients. These meetings occurred weekly, provided there were cases to be reviewed. These meetings were often quite short (fifteen to twenty minutes). In total, I observed twenty-four meetings, in addition to a few more that were held before court if there were only one or two cases to consider.

As I was not allowed to tape record either the court sessions or the screening meetings, I wrote down the staff's discussions as accurately as possible to get a sense of the naturally occurring decision-making process. The staff's conversations presented in this book are based on these written field notes, with most of dialogue being literal transcriptions of the conversations.

To gain a better understanding of how the staff collected information about the youths, I observed staff members as they visited the youths in their communities. I conducted twenty-six ride-alongs with the field-based staff (e.g., probation officers, drug counselors, and police officers) that checked on the youths in their schools, treatment programs, and homes. These ride-alongs lasted anywhere between two to eight hours, with staff mainly visiting the youths to conduct drug tests and talking with school officials, drug counselors, and parents about the youths' behavior.

Finally, I conducted a total of 112 formal interviews of staff, selected youth clients, and the clients' family members during both fieldwork periods to obtain a more nuanced view of the logic behind the staff decisions and the youth's understandings of the court's purpose. In general, I asked them open-ended questions about their experiences and perceptions of the drug court. I interviewed the staff members multiple times during the first fieldwork period to get their feedback on patterns that I started seeing in the court. In addition, I did several informal interviews with staff while at court, especially during the break and after the court hearings, to clarify details or get a staff member's opinion about a specific discussion. Finally, during the second fieldwork period, I interviewed the youths and their parents (twenty-four youths and twenty-four parents) to ask questions about their views about the juvenile drug court intervention and specific court responses to their noncompliance.

This three-pronged approach of court observations, community observations, and interviews provided me with a broader picture of the drug court staff's work from the perspectives of the staff, youths, and parents. More important, it allowed me to see how youth noncompliance was more of a social construction than an objective fact, as staff selectively picked up on bits of information about the youth to present an interpretation of that youth as not being responsible. As the following chapters show, a youth's progress in the court was contingent not just on him but also on the drug court staff and other agencies' interpretations of him, which may or may not have anything to do with what he actually did.

CHAPTER 3

What Court Day Is He?
Intercourt Variations

TO ILLUSTRATE THE SOCIAL construction of youth noncompliance, this chapter takes an in-depth look at one structural factor that impacts the drug court staff's assessments of youth noncompliance: the youth's assignment to one of the program's three court parts. These court parts meet on Tuesdays (east county), Wednesdays (north county), or Thursdays (south county), and youths are assigned based on where they live. In principle, the youth's court assignment should not have any effect on the staff assessments of youth noncompliance, which are supposed to be based on the actions of the individual youths. Moreover, the three courts are part of one program, using the same policies, procedures, and resources—so staff in each court should interpret and respond to the same types of actions fairly consistently. Yet, despite these structural similarities, one of the three court parts—the north court—did appear to have a different impact on staff assessments of youth noncompliance and, subsequently, the youths' overall progress in the court. The north court generally had the lowest number of noncompliant youths each week of all the three court parts.[1] It also was able to process youths faster compared to the east court or south court.

Many possibilities come to mind to explain this difference. One guess is that the north court youths were somehow different in demographic characteristics of race, class, and gender in ways that gave them more advantages or resources to remain in compliance with the court. They tended to be more middle class compared to the east court, which had youths from the poorest neighborhoods in the county and higher noncompliance rates. However, the south court youths were fairly similar demographically to those in the north court but had worse outcomes. Another explanation is that the north court youths lived in more geographically advantageous areas in terms of public transportation networks, schools, and treatment programs, making it easier for youths to comply with court requirements. In actuality, the north court covered the largest geographic area of the three courts, with the worst public transportation options.[2] Youths in the north court had a harder time getting around, depending on rides from family and friends to get to school, treatment, and court, compared to the south court youths, who had the easiest time getting to their schools and treatment programs, which were concentrated on one or two large streets.

It is also possible that the north court staff was more effective in influencing youths to change, compared to the staff in the other two courts. Sociologists James Eisenstein and Herbert Jacob attribute such a difference to a courtroom workgroup dynamic. Their 1977 book, *Felony Justice: An Organizational Analysis of Criminal Courts*, proposes the workgroup concept to characterize the ways that the working relationship between the judge, prosecutor, and defense attorney help shape case outcomes, in addition to the expected factors of the severity of the offense and the person's criminal history. Others have used this concept to compare case outcomes in different courtrooms, either in the same county or across various counties. Jeffrey Ulmer argues in his 1997 book, *Social Worlds of Sentencing: Court Communities under Sentencing Guidelines*, that despite sentencing guidelines based exclusively on legal factors, the workgroup dynamic influenced the application of those guidelines among courts in three Pennsylvanian counties.[3] So, even if the subcourts in the juvenile drug court used the same sanctioning guidelines, the presumption here would be that the north court workgroup was distinct from the other two courts in ways that led to a more favorable impact on the youth participants.

This chapter uses the courtroom workgroup concept to highlight the social construction of youth noncompliance and the multifaceted notion of individual accountability. Eisenstein and Jacob break down the workgroup's influence on the decision-making process as follows: the interdependence, stability, and familiarity among the courtroom actors; the specialization of cases (e.g., the more specialized the cases the more similar they are to one another, which leads to more routinized processing); and the importance of the workgroup's goals (e.g., doing justice, maintaining group cohesion, disposing of caseload, and reducing uncertainty).[4] This chapter suggests that the difference with the north court lies not only in staff familiarity but also in the structural differences such as staffing patterns, caseloads, and types of cases that affect the three subcourts' ability to assess youth noncompliance.[5]

Therefore, it is important to address the ways in which organizational issues that are completely outside of the youth client's control (like the three-court part system) directly influence the staff's decision-making process and subsequent client outcomes. Doing so underscores the need to view client accountability beyond the individual youth's actions. Moreover, the differences in the three subcourts further expose the fluidity and tension in the accountability discourse: each court workgroup could highlight different

TABLE 3.1
Judges' styles

	East Court Judge Hooper	North Court Judge Samuels	South Court Judge O'Reilly
Judging Style	Education	Therapeutic	Pragmatic
Common question in team meetings	"What school is he in?"	"Is he struggling with sobriety?"	"What's going on with this kid?"

aspects of the therapy-punishment spectrum in its assessments of youth non-compliance.

JUDGES' STYLES: THE NORTH COURT JUDGE IS MOST THERAPEUTIC

Recent policy literature on drug courts suggests that a judge's style may have an impact on case outcomes, with some styles being more effective in motivating youth to comply with the court rules.[6] This would make sense even if the drug court staff made decisions as a team, because the judge leads the discussion and communicates the staff's decision to youths and families during the court hearings. He represents the court to the youth, so how he expresses the court's goals and rationales influences how the youth sees the court. It would appear that Samuels, the north court judge, had the most effective style with the youths, since his court had the lowest average number of noncompliant youths per week. Samuels was the most therapeutic of the three judges, inserting drug treatment idioms such as "relapse as part of recovery" into the staff discussions. The other two judges did not use that jargon at all, focusing instead on education or more general notions about the youth. Table 3.1 depicts the differences among the judges.

The policy literature might look at Samuels's style as being more effective in motivating youths to be compliant; however, the judge's style could affect his interpretation and response to the youth's noncompliant behavior. Those different interpretations help shape the variation in compliance rates among the three courts. Consider, for example, how Samuels discusses the case of Tracy, a white seventeen year old. Tracy has just started in the court, and while she has tested clean for drugs so far, she has had serious truancy problems, to the point where the school staff is considering putting her in a specialized program for chronic truants.

SAMUELS (JUDGE): Tracy has twenty clean days and has truancies. . . .
ALLEN (PROBATION OFFICER): The dad said she suffers from migraines. . . . if there are continued unexcused absences the school will put her on SARB [School Attendance Review Board]. . . . She probably would have to have a doctor's note [to excuse any future absences].

SAMUELS: Can we send her for a neurological work up? . . . The migraines could be a trigger for relapse. . . . If there is no physiological reason, we'll know it is something else.

Samuels could have given her a sanction for these absences, even with the father's explanation of her migraines, because they were unexcused. The official drug court sanction would be a day in juvenile hall for every day of missed school. While Allen, the probation officer, does not ask specifically for a sanction, he does infer the court response needs to be serious enough to address the problem before the school refers Tracy to SARB, a school-based truancy program. In SARB Tracy would no longer be able to have her parent call to excuse her absences; instead, she would require a doctor's note. After hearing the warning about SARB, Samuels still does not sanction Tracy. Instead, he picks up on her medical needs, referring her to a neurological evaluation. This could be seen as the ideal therapeutic jurisprudence response, as Samuels sees the connection to drug issues, stating migraines could be a possible trigger for a future drug relapse. Samuels wants to get the health problem resolved quickly to keep Tracy on the path to sobriety. At the same time, he is not purely therapeutically oriented, as he expresses an element of doubt in allowing for the possibility that the staff might have to revise its response if the doctors do not validate her explanation of migraines.

In contrast, Hooper, the east court judge, had a different view of school absences. In the next example, he explicitly states that he wants to issue a normal remedy to emphasize the importance of school, which translates into him assigning community service to Janet, an African American girl in the tenth grade, for two school period absences.

HOOPER (JUDGE): Do we want to sanction Janet for absences at school?
SARAH (PROBATION OFFICER): Nah.
BARRY (DRUG COUNSELOR): She has absences for fifth and sixth periods. . . .
HOOPER: There's gotta be some sanction here. . . .
SARAH: She would be fine with a warning.
JACK (DISTRICT ATTORNEY): I agree. . . .
HOOPER: How about community service?
SARAH: Yeah.
HOOPER: It is not acceptable that she skips school.

No one else on the team wants to punish Janet for these absences beyond a simple warning. The judge first described the absences as if they were for complete days. He is concerned with determining "some sanction" and is dissatisfied with the probation officer's and district attorney's suggestion of a warning. While Hooper wants to give Janet community service, he ultimately yields to the staff's suggestion of a warning, but only because she recently broke her hand, making it difficult to do community service.

Given this view of school truancy, it makes sense that Hooper would not hesitate to hold another youth accountable for being late to school. In this example, Fernando, a seventeen-year-old Latino, was tardy at school, in addition to staying out one night past curfew:

HOOPER (JUDGE): Fernando is not compliant at home.
CHARLIE (PUBLIC DEFENDER): Otherwise, he is compliant at school.
EVA (DRUG COUNSELOR): He was so tardy at school.
CHARLIE: Well that's better than he used to . . .
[*Later in court hearing*]
HOOPER [TO FERNANDO]: What are you doing out at 12 A.M.?
FERNANDO: It was 10:30 P.M.
HOOPER: Not according to your father. You were also tardy for school. All right, uh, four hours community service. . . . Part of this [program] is growing up, is assuming obligation. It is extremely important for your record to try to graduate.

Fernando's father reported his son came home after curfew, which typically would lead to a court response. However, the staff views the father as a difficult, overly harsh, and demanding parent, so it typically does not side with him. At the same time, Eva, the drug counselor, brings up Fernando's lateness to school. This prompts the judge to give him community service, despite the public defender's claims that Fernando's tardiness is not that important and is an improvement from before. In his conversation with Fernando during the court hearing, Hooper does not focus as much on the home trouble as the school issues. To him, accountability involves going to school and graduating.

The south court judge, O'Reilly, is perhaps the most lenient of the three judges. Consider this example with Marisa, a white seventeen-year-old who had school problems the past week:

JULIE (PROBATION OFFICER): Marisa's teacher says she was irritated with her because she was absent so often, almost daily, and that when the teacher looked at Marisa's time card, Marisa was fifteen minutes late, up to an hour and a half late [*her school is only two hours long*]. Marisa stays with her boyfriend, who drives her to school in the morning. . . .
O'REILLY: I want to see a copy of the time card every week.
JULIE: Marisa can manipulate. . . .

[*Later, when Marisa comes into the courtroom with her mother, O'Reilly tells her that if she is a minute late to school, she is going into juvenile hall.*]

O'REILLY [TO MARISA]: I'm not kidding.

MARISA: I know you're not . . . [*she leaves the courtroom*].

GRANT (POLICE OFFICER) [JOKING TO O'REILLY]: You say, "I'm really serious" this week, which is more than last week, when you just said, "I'm serious." She didn't show any proof, and you let her get away with it again.

This is the third week in a row that Marisa has had school or treatment issues. She has yet to get into any trouble for them. This week, O'Reilly just warns her to do better. Unlike Samuels and Hooper, O'Reilly appears to give more chances to the youths before issuing any kind of normal remedy. However, at the next court hearing, O'Reilly does end up putting Marisa in juvenile hall for one day because she continued to be late to school and did not fulfill her treatment requirement of Narcotics Anonymous meetings.

While these four situations are distinct, they all center on school-related noncompliance. Consider the different responses of the judges: Samuels sees Tracy's absence as related to a physical problem; Hooper wants to make the youths do community service; and O'Reilly simply issues warnings that other staff jokes are empty threats. These variations in response do suggest that the youths' case outcomes are affected by the judge who handles their case. Yet the judges' styles still do not account for all the differences among the three courts' decision-making practices on youth noncompliance. That is, the influence of the judges' styles could go in the direction of lessening or increasing the court response. While these examples seem to suggest the north court judge is lenient because of his therapeutic style, he sometimes was harsher in his recommendations concerning drug issues. Given this variation in the impact of the judge's style on staff decision making, there must be other differences between the courts that are affecting staff assessments of youth noncompliance besides courtroom workgroup factors.

STAFFING PATTERNS—OUT OF SIGHT, OUT OF MIND

Each court part had the same composition of staff on its decision-making team: a judge, a district attorney, a defense attorney, a probation officer, drug counselors, a police officer, and a clinical therapist. However, there were variations in that staffing pattern that translated into different levels of resources to supervise the youths, which in turn shaped how staff assessed youths' noncompliance. The most important variation would be law enforcement coverage. While all the courts had dedicated police officers, the north court had a harder time enforcing its bench warrants for its youths compared to the other two courts. The north court's police officers had jurisdiction over just two of the many neighborhoods in that court's catchment area. Only 38 percent of the youths observed during the fieldwork period lived in those two neighborhoods.[7] If a north court youth lived outside the two neighborhoods, the staff would have to call the sheriff and police departments in those areas to ask them to enforce warrants on the youths. That process could take months, since these cases were a low priority for those law enforcement agencies. In contrast, the other two courts' catchment areas were within the unified citywide police department's jurisdiction, so their dedicated police officers had more connections and resources to pick up any of the courts' youths with outstanding warrants.

This difference in law enforcement coverage affected the three courts' assessments of youth noncompliance in that the north court youths with unenforced bench warrants were considered absent without leave (i.e., AWOL, on the run) and removed from the court's weekly docket. This had an out-of-sight, out-of-mind effect on the staff's work in a few ways. It basically lowered the north court's noncompliance rates, which no longer included these youths until they were arrested on the warrant or on a new charge. Moreover, the north court probation officers and drug counselors no longer had to check up on AWOL youths in the community for the court's weekly progress reports. That freed them up to supervise the other youths still on the court docket, focusing only on correcting the more minor instances of noncompliance among the remaining youths. In that way, the north court caseload becomes easier to supervise if the AWOL youths stay undetected for a longer period of time than in the other courts. So the lower noncompliance rates for north court do not reflect a better group of youths or a more effective staff as much as it indicates a selectivity bias of creaming the crop.

Consider how this AWOL issue works for Olivia, a seventeen-year-old Latina assigned to the north court. She went AWOL from the court three months before and returned to the court only after being arrested for breaking her mother's window:

CHARLIE (PUBLIC DEFENDER): Olivia broke her mother's window, so she is
    here on a new offense—vandalism . . . our options are 28 or 120 [days in
    the custody-based probation drug treatment program].
JACK (DISTRICT ATTORNEY): Twenty-eight . . .
MOLINA (SUBSTITUTE JUDGE): She has been AWOL since April 20 . . .
CHARLIE: So 28 or 120? . . .
GRANT: 120 because she's been AWOL for three months and has had no
    treatment . . .
MOLINA: Does everyone agree with that?
CHARLIE: I'll submit [agree] . . .
BILL (DRUG COUNSELOR): She's been approximately seven blocks from my
    house. I see her when I go grocery shopping. We've been struggling to
    get the sheriff to pick up the youths.[8]

Olivia's seemingly persistent noncompliance—as suggested by being AWOL for three months—is not just based on her unwillingness to come to court but also the court's inability to get the sheriff to enforce its warrants. If Olivia had not been arrested on a new charge, she might have stayed away indefinitely. The irony here is that the drug counselor knows exactly where she has been, seeing her regularly in his neighborhood. However, because he is not law enforcement, his hands are tied. In contrast, the other two courts were able to pick up youths on warrants more quickly and respond to the initial reason for the warrant instead of having to wait until a new arrest, as in Olivia's case.[9]

While these different staffing patterns provide some insight to north court's outcomes, they alone do not explain completely how the youths in north court seem to do better than the other two courts. They might simply explain something about noncompliant youths who go AWOL or youths on the verge of doing something wrong.

Lower Caseload and Types of Cases

The most influential court difference in shaping staff assessments of youth noncompliance is a combination of caseloads and types of cases among the three court parts. Table 3.2 provides a snapshot view of the differences.

The north court had the lowest average caseload, averaging fourteen youths per week compared to twenty-one to twenty-two youths in the other courts. Moreover, the three court parts handled different types of cases.[10] The north court was held in an off-site courthouse with no juvenile hall facility to hold detained youth. As such, it could only hear the regular cases of its own youths who had not been arrested that week. If the north court youths get arrested by the police, the east and south courts handle those detention cases. In addition to new arrests, detention cases also include youths released from the custody-based 28- or 120-day probation program. Finally, the south

TABLE 3.2
Caseloads and cases by subcourt

	East (Tuesdays)	North (Wednesdays)	South (Thursdays)
Average number of youths per week	21	14	22
Types of cases	Detention (new arrests, release from custody)		Detention (new arrests, release from custody)
	Regular cases	Regular cases	Regular cases
			New Cases

court had the additional task of orienting new youths into the program. It typically would hold the half-hour orientation before its regular team meeting and court hearing;[11] however, depending on the number of new youths attending this orientation (and if they were being held in detention), the south court staff would sometimes hold impromptu detention hearings for its noncompliant youths in juvenile hall before the orientation, leading to some confusion among the staff members about which youths they were discussing when.[12]

Caseloads and types of cases work in tandem to influence staff assessments of youth noncompliance. The north court's lower caseloads allowed its staff to review each case in more depth. For noncompliant youths, this meant the staff was able to more thoroughly clarify possibly noncompliant behaviors to perhaps return the youth's status to compliant. Consider this next excerpt, in which the north court team discusses Manu, a seventeen-year-old Latino who was suspended from school for two days for allegedly tagging, or writing graffiti on the wall. Allen, the probation officer, discussed the various steps he took to investigate this suspension. That week there were only thirteen youths on the docket, two of whom (including Manu) were noncompliant:

ALLEN (PROBATION OFFICER): I went to the school today and talked to the principal. Manu served a two-day suspension for a tagging incident. When he was confronted about the tagging, it kind of sounded like some kind of miscommunication. The teacher apparently told him to talk to the principal—rather than do that, Manu chose to bail [leave school grounds]. When I talked to him, he said it was presented to him as more of a joking matter. He denies that he did it.

CHARLIE (PUBLIC DEFENDER): Is he back in school?

ALLEN: He is back in school, um, . . . however, he did get suspended. I'd personally rather not put him in the hall. . . .

BILL (DRUG COUNSELOR): One thing concerning me, he said, "I didn't do it," and it seems he was lying. . . .

ALLEN: He [Manu] said he didn't do anything. The principal took me over to see it . . . it was some gang-related reference that didn't strike any chord with me. . . .

BILL: I don't know. . . .

ALLEN: I find it hard to believe that he did it.

CHARLIE: That was just part of it—he didn't handle it right—he took off.

Allen's investigation into the incident appears to explain away the majority of Manu's noncompliance, such that he recommends a less severe normal remedy than the typical two days in juvenile hall for the two-day school suspension. Look at all the steps that Allen takes in this effort. He first goes to the school to talk to the principal in person about it. He also talks to Manu to get his side of the story. While Bill interprets Manu's denial as evidence of lying, Allen adds further proof that he saw the tagging with his own eyes, and it did not seem that serious at all, despite its gang-related reference. Because of this thorough review, Allen is much more lenient than both the public defender and the drug counselor in how he views the situation. The staff ultimately decides to give Manu fifteen hours of community service for not appropriately handling the suspension when he left school.

The probation officers in other courts do not do as much follow-up to reports of noncompliance. That is not because they are less efficient than Allen. They just have more youths to get information on each week. For example, in the south court, Julie, the probation officer, describes a recent fight between Samuel, a seventeen-year-old Latino, and his sister apparently over the use of the TV. He also used the telephone, even though he is on home supervision, which does not allow it. The mother called Julie to tell her about it. That week Julie had twenty-eight youths on the docket, of which twelve were noncompliant.

JULIE (PROBATION OFFICER): Samuel's mother called yesterday and left a message. Actually, I finally ended up speaking to her. Samuel got in a physical fight with his sister, and she called the police on him. The sister ended up with a big knot on her head. The fight was over the TV. The mom also said Samuel is using the phone. . . . She called me on my own time. I gave her Officer Grant's number.

JACK (DISTRICT ATTORNEY): You know what, he is on home sup[ervision]. Why is he on the phone? . . .

JULIE: He came to the probation office Monday to test and that was clean. . . .

CHARLIE (PUBLIC DEFENDER): Samuel has a home sup violation. What do we do?

JULIE: I think he should go in to juvenile hall. . . .

CHARLIE: I think he should do work project. That will bother him more than custody time.

JACK: Yeah.

CHARLIE: Usually we detain if he used, but he hasn't used yet. . . .

LOPEZ (SUBSTITUTE JUDGE): Five days.

CHARLIE: Okay.

JACK: Fine.

Unlike Allen, who talked to Manu about the tagging incident, Julie does not talk to Samuel or his sister to find out their side of the story. This is not due to Julie's lack of effort. She mentions that she talked with Samuel's mother during her "own time," after working hours. But she did have more than two times the number of cases and six times more noncompliant youths than

Allen did the week he investigated Manu's case. Even though Samuel gets a clean drug test, the staff still decides to issue a normal remedy, giving him five days of work project (that is, doing manual labor, like picking up trash or clearing brush on the side of the highway) for presumably both the fight and using the phone. Had Julie been able to investigate as thoroughly as Allen, perhaps the staff would have found out more information to explain Samuel's actions to recommend a more lenient normal remedy or possibly change his status from noncompliant to compliant, as Allen did for Manu. In the end, Samuel does not show up to court, and Judge Lopez issues a bench warrant for his arrest.

The types of cases also affected how the staff members in the different court parts were able to work with the youths. Because it is held in an off-site facility with no juvenile hall, the north court only has to handle cases on its own youths during its court hearing. This alleviates much of the confusion found in the other courts, because Judge Samuels only deals with youths from his own court. He rarely, if ever, asked the other staff, "Who's that kid?" The other judges, however, frequently had to be reminded who the youth was and if the youth was part of their own drug court.

The added task of processing detained noncompliant youths limits the north and east staff from supervising their own caseload as closely. Given that detention reports for new arrests take about one and a half hours each to prepare, the more youths in detention the less time the staff has to go into the field to monitor its caseloads. As a result, youths might feel emboldened to engage in noncompliant behavior. Consider the following excerpt from a south court discussion about Marisa, who O'Reilly warned about school tardiness earlier in the chapter. Julie directly mentions the tension between the time she needs to spend on detention reports and on verifying possible youth noncompliance:

JULIE (PROBATION OFFICER): I had a long talk with her. I don't know what the truth is. She went to the doctor on Monday and told me she has a history of migraines. . . .

JACK (DISTRICT ATTORNEY): She is sick for school but not for NA [her treatment program]?

JULIE: Her explanation is that her headache—she needs time for the medicine to work. Marisa told me she has a virus and a swollen lymph node on the back of her head and she, um—so, and her mom verified, "I'm not lying for her—she was sick." . . . She held the cup [for the drug test urine sample] and said, " 'I just went an hour ago . . . can you come by at 9 A.M. tomorrow at school?" I said I may be busy with the detentions and that is not good for my schedule, so I'll patch her today.

Marisa has a history of not completely obeying court rules regarding school, drug testing, and treatment. So, in this discussion Julie describes the lengths she has already taken to monitor Marisa's behaviors (e.g., a long conversation with her, two home visits, and a conversation with her mother). However, because Marisa could not test that day, Julie was unable to obtain another drug test in time for the court hearing that week, opting instead to use the sweat patch drug test, the results for which would take much longer. In the end, the judge simply talks with Marisa before court, telling her to go to school. One could imagine how the team might have responded differently had Julie been able to administer a second drug test or spend more time on Marisa's case that week.

Multiple organizational factors sometimes converge at the same time to affect staff assessments of individual youths. In the following example, the types of cases and number of cases influence the staff discussion about Enrique, a seventeen-year-old Latino who had a second delinquency case in another court that was recently dismissed. Julie was supposed to monitor that case to make sure Enrique got back into the drug court as soon as possible to continue the drug court supervision if his other case was cleared. That week Julie had four detention cases to handle, with a total of eighteen youths on the docket:

JULIE (PROBATION): I might have forgotten to calendar Enrique. . . . The other court dismissed the petition without prejudice. He got high because he thought he was not in drug court.

CHARLIE (PUBLIC DEFENDER): He got high because of that?

JULIE: He was celebrating. . . . He's so scared.

O'REILLY (JUDGE): I'll tell him, 'cause he is doing well, I decided he will not be in custody.

After Enrique's case was dismissed in the regular delinquency court, there appeared to be some kind of miscommunication where he did not realize he had to go back to drug court. Because he thought he was free from all legal obligations, he celebrated by getting high. When Julie finally got in touch with him, he became worried, probably because he knew drug court could possibly place him in custody for drug use. While Judge O'Reilly promised to not do that, Enrique did not show up to court to hear that promise. When Enrique does not show up for court again the following week, the judge issues a bench warrant for his arrest. He is arrested a month later, and the staff suspends him for a new charge. He allegedly threw a knife at a police officer. While I cannot be sure that Julie forgot because of her four detentions cases on the docket that day, it is possible that they were a drain on her time from her typical workload that week. And while Julie's forgetfulness is not the reason why Enrique did not show up, one could assume that if she had not forgotten, perhaps the bench warrant could have gone out before he committed an offense that would lead to his suspension from drug court. Again, to see the youth's noncompliance as solely based on his actions ignores the larger organizational context in which court caseloads and staff workload also play a role in how noncompliant status is produced.

CONCLUSION

Even though the three subcourts had the same staff familiarity, organizational goals, and external resources, they dealt with information about the youth's actions differently. The variations stemmed mainly from the lack of detention cases combined with lower caseloads in the north court. The youths assigned to the north court were at an advantage to youths in the other two courts. Instead of considering the staff's work environment only as background information from which to study drug courts, it is important to pay attention to how it influences staff evaluations of the nature and extent of youth noncompliance. Individual progress is based not only on the youth's own actions but also on the organizational setting.

While this three-court-part situation is unique for drug courts that typically have only one courtroom, one could extrapolate to see the importance of observing how a court's structure influences its staff's assessments of youth noncompliance and, by extension, the youth's accountability. The policy literature (Marlowe et al. 2006) begins to get at this view, calling for a second wave of drug court research to look at specific components—graduated sanctions and rewards; drug testing; race, class, and gender; and team workgroup cultures. However, there is little attention paid to the practical work issues underlying how those components manifest in any drug court setting. That is, the court's staffing patterns, as well as the types and amount of cases, affect the staff's view of and response to a youth's responsibility for his or her actions. It is critical to see beyond the individual youth or the specific drug court program components to understand how drug court outcomes are created. Youth noncompliance is a product of staff interpretive practices in assessing youth actions, as it is always trying to answer the practical question of "What do we do now with this youth"? Those practices themselves are grounded within a larger organizational context of limited resources and varied relationships with external agencies.

CHAPTER 4

Building Accountability through Assessments of Noncompliance

They make you do so much, and if you don't do it, then you get in trouble really fast. . . . You would think that you only get in trouble if you test dirty, but they get you in trouble if you don't do all these other things, even if you're staying clean. . . . Like if you miss school sometimes. . . . But it's like, if I'm staying clean, then what's the big deal?

> Michaela, a white seventeen-year-old in the east court

You don't do what they tell you, they'll lock your ass up . . . for any little thing, you can do up to like five days [in custody]. . . . It's just they're on your ass, no freedom, no nothing.

> Dominic, a fifteen-year-old Latino in the north court

THE STAFF'S IDEAS about youth accountability are constructed from its weekly discussions about several kinds of youth behaviors. How does the staff's attention to "any little thing" relate to youth accountability? The staff can seize upon—and often counts on—the instances of youths missing drug treatment, failing a drug test, skipping school, or being late for curfew to teach them about accountability, which the staff defines as holding the youths responsible for their actions. So the "therapeutic" orientation of the drug court staff is not just about connecting youths to drug treatment programs; it is to monitor the youths' performance in many areas and to correct their "bad" behaviors through the use of normal remedies such as warnings from the judge, house arrest, and short-term stints in juvenile hall.[1] This combination of therapy and punishment in the drug court model often creates a complicated practical task for staff to accomplish in its weekly assessments of youth actions.

The staff makes its assessments by engaging in an intricate and somewhat improvisational dance among the various members that occurs in their team meetings before the court hearing. The intricacy comes from the voluminous minefield of information through which the staff has to wade to determine the meaningful and actionable bits of information. The improvisation also comes from the informality and sometimes chaotic nature of the staff's team meetings in which assessments occur. A joke here, an interruption there, simultaneous discussions about two different youths—these moments could all steer the staff off the expected course in responding to an individual youth's case.

This chapter breaks down the steps in this complicated dance in which staff evaluates and decides to respond to youth noncompliance. In this dance, there are three overarching parameters that staff follows:

1. Otherwise normal behaviors are now considered illegal
    Through its close monitoring of the youth, the drug court staff inevitably finds out more ways that the youths are misbehaving (e.g., arriving late for school or drug treatment sessions, disrespecting their parents/legal guardians). These incidents of noncompliance are not just bad behavior. As violations of the youth's probation, they are considered sanctionable by the juvenile drug court staff.

2. Staff assessments and responses are unpredictable
    The court's sanctioning decisions are not an automatic process, even if the instances of youth noncompliance seem cut-and-dried. Staff members do not always agree with each others' interpretations of those actions, resulting in a series of negotiations that can sometimes become highly contested. In this sense, all the information generated by the staff's intensive supervision of youths is debatable, and its ultimate meaning is not fixed until its team discussion.

3. Weekly staff assessments are inconsequential yet significant in crafting youth workability
    Because the youths' noncompliance is often based on trivial behaviors, juvenile drug court staff's decisions do not carry the same import or severity as those in traditional juvenile courts, which have fewer decisions with clearly established legal purposes such as adjudication and disposition. This allows for drug court staff to be more flexible in making decisions, using a "let's see what happens" approach to trying different things with the youths. However, at the same time, those weekly assessments build and refine the staff's notion of the youth's workability (its idea of how to steer the youth toward its desired goal), which itself informs the final case outcome. The youth's response to the court's normal remedies informs subsequent staff discussions about the need for additional remedies. So the weekly staff meetings to review youths' behaviors serve a larger purpose than evaluating the youths' compliance in that moment; they help the staff to figure out the youth's workability. That is, the staff's weekly

decisions about a youth's behaviors coalesce to craft its general understanding of the best way to work with that youth over time.

Given the complexity of these steps, a youth's noncompliant status can be seen as a product of staff interpretations of that youth's actions. The therapy-punishment tension in the accountability model underlies these staff interpretations, as staff views of the youth's noncompliance could fall into one of the two poles (or somewhere in between). For example, the staff could view a youth's school absence as a sign of potential drug relapse (i.e., therapeutic) or as an indication of increasing delinquent behavior (i.e., punitive). Moreover, the direction of these mini-decisions could get sidetracked at any point along the way depending on the fluctuating organizational resources to match the staff's interpretations of the youths' behavior.

EXPECTED TYPES OF NONCOMPLIANCE AND NORMAL REMEDIES

The staff constructs notions of youths' noncompliance based on information gathered about five main areas of youth behavior. The first area relates to the youths' attendance and behavior in school and drug treatment. In general, the staff does not punish youths for their school grades or performance in drug treatment, as long as they are attending those programs on a regular basis. The second area relates to the youths' behavior at home, specifically if they are disrespecting their parents or staying out too late. The parents of female clients tend to report more instances of troubles at home compared to parents of male youths. Similarly, Latino parents were more likely to report home troubles, as they tended to rely on the court to help them reassert their authority over their children.[2] This relates to the third area of noncompliant behavior, which is an unexcused absence from a drug court hearing. The fourth area is the youth's drug test results which could be positive for drug use, too diluted for a valid result, or nonexistent because the youths avoided testing.[3] Finally, the staff considers youths' new arrests or contacts with the police. Depending on the severity of the offense, the staff might keep or suspend the youth until the new offense is resolved in the traditional juvenile court.

Staff members consider selective pieces of information as evidence of noncompliance meriting a court response. Table 4.1 outlines the expected forms of noncompliance and subsequent normal remedies. Note that when custody is mentioned, it refers to either juvenile hall or probation camp.

When staff sees a youth committing any of these behaviors, it can pick from a variety of normal remedies to hold the youth accountable for the noncompliance. Common normal remedies are varying lengths in custody (3–5 days in juvenile hall or 28–120 days in probation camps) and home supervision, or house arrest. Once on home supervision, the youth is supposed to be

TABLE 4.1

Typical youth noncompliance and expected normal remedies

Area	Specific behaviors	Typical normal remedies
Drug treatment	Unexcused absence	Day in custody for day missed, home supervision
	Lack of participation or bad attitude	Warning, essay
Drug tests	Failure to test (miss test)	Custody (varying lengths); home supervision
	Diluted test results	Lose sober days; custody (varying lengths); home supervision
	Positive drug use	Custody (varying lengths)
School	Unexcused absences/class periods	Day in custody for day missed, home supervision
	Disrespectful towards teacher	Warning, essay, letter of apology
Home	Disobedience towards parents/legal guardian	Warning, home supervision
	Leave/run away from home (AWOL)	Bench warrant, custody (varying lengths)
	Missed curfew	Warning, home supervision
Court	Unexcused absence	Bench warrant, custody (varying lengths)
General	Violate house arrest	Custody (varying lengths)
	Contact with police	Warning
	New arrests	Possible termination from program

inside the home at all times, unless he is at school, treatment, work, or anywhere accompanied by a parent. The staff uses home supervision more than any other normal remedy in the court because of its all-purpose quality. For example, when youths get out of custody, the staff releases them on home supervision as a motivator to them to reenroll quickly in school and treatment. If staff suspects the youths are noncompliant but has no hard evidence (e.g., possible missed drug test or seemingly unexcused absence at school), it can put them on home supervision as a warning before any custody time. If staff sees the youth engaging in high-risk behavior that could lead to more serious noncompliance (e.g., brewing conflict with the parents for staying out late, general acting out), it can put that youth on home supervision until he shapes up.

To decide which normal remedy to give a noncompliant youth, the staff engages in a series of steps to determine the severity of the youth's noncompliance and appropriate court response. Those steps involve determining:

1. What is the problem?
2. Is it really a problem?
3. What do we do about it?

While one might expect the staff to answer those questions in a routine manner, there is an element of staff negotiation that sometimes results in a different court response. Consider this excerpt about Randy, a white seventeen-year-old in the south court. The south court staff is debating if Randy's decision to leave school without permission is actually a problem.

ALLEN (PROBATION OFFICER): Randy had a problem at school. . . .

PETER (DRUG COUNSELOR): The mom hasn't gotten on Randy, including at school. He is not to leave school without permission. Let the judge admonish him for it.

ALLEN: I wouldn't let it go. He kind of is slipping at school.

CHARLIE (PUBLIC DEFENDER): When he left, it was to go to the interview on 4/20.

PETER: He said he did.

CHARLIE: Let's get proof. If he doesn't, give him some time.

SARAH (PROBATION OFFICER): Interview for what?

PETER: A job.

ALLEN: I wouldn't worry about giving custody time, but tell him to knock it off.

The staff focuses its debate on the nature of the problem but not the severity or court response. Allen first presents the issue definitely by stating he had a problem at school. While Peter agrees that he left school without permission, he suggests the larger problem is with the mother, who has not "gotten on Randy" about other things. Charlie disagrees with both of them, stating it is not a problem because he left to go for a job interview. He suggests it would only be a problem if he did not have proof of the interview. In the end, most agree a warning would be sufficient, when he could be given home supervision or even some time in custody for leaving school.

Even if the staff does not debate the action as a problem, it can question the severity of the problem. Consider this excerpt for Gianna, a fifteen-year-old Latina in the east court who had missed drug treatment two times in the past week.

JULIE (PROBATION OFFICER): Gianna didn't go to treatment Friday or Monday, nor did she call . . . . Sylvia [the treatment provider] suspects Gianna was given child care duties because she has a huge family with ten in the home.

EVA (DRUG COUNSELOR): There are twelve in the household. . . .

CHARLIE (PUBLIC DEFENDER): Admonish her and do it [home supervision] next week if she keeps it up.

JACK (DISTRICT ATTORNEY): She's slipping. . . .

HOOPER (JUDGE) [TO CHARLIE]: I think you're right.

The staff members go back and forth as to how serious the problem is before determining the appropriate response. Julie first states the absences are perhaps due to family issues (i.e., child care responsibilities), implying an ongoing structural barrier to treatment participation. Charlie and Jack offer individual-based views about Gianna's actions that lead to different interpretations about her accountability for those actions. Charlie infers she can improve her attendance by next week if they simply warn her not to skip treatment. Jack sees Gianna's absences as an indication of her lack of effort in that she is "slipping." In the end, the judge sides with Charlie's interpretation of the problem and gives a warning for Gianna.

Finally, the staff could spend most of its discussion deciding the appropriate normal remedy to a youth's noncompliance. In this next case, Paul, a white sixteen-year-old in the north court, got into a fight with his mother when she would not let him go outside to smoke a cigarette. The staff members agree that this fight is a problem that merits a court response, but they have varying ideas on what that should be:

SAMUELS (JUDGE): What happened at home with Paul? . . .

BILL (DRUG COUNSELOR): He was verbally abusive to his mom. Paul wanted to smoke a cigarette outside, but she said no. He then started calling her names. The stepdad intervened and called the sheriff. There was a physical altercation but no hitting, just shoving and moving around. The sheriff told him that if he has to come back, he was taking Paul into custody, not his mom or stepdad. That calmed him down and then he apologized to his mom and stepdad afterwards.

[*Samuels asks if they should order him a psychological evaluation.*]

BILL: I don't think so.

SAMUELS: Everyone agree it would be helpful?

[*Most staff members agree . . .*]

SAMUELS: Any suggestions? [*Adding that he will admonish him . . .*]

SARAH (PROBATION OFFICER): Mark [clinical therapist] could work with him.

[*Samuels summarizes the staff's decision: they will order a psychological evaluation, have him work with Mark, and admonish him.*]

The staff does not question the validity or severity of Paul's incident at home, especially given the third-party involvement of the sheriff who defined the trouble as being Paul's fault. However, there is some negotiation around the staff response. The judge initially questions whether or not there might be any mental health issues, suggesting a psychological evaluation; however, the drug counselor does not appear to think this is necessary. The rest of the team agrees with the judge, like the probation officer who suggested additional individualized counseling with Mark, the court's clinical therapist. In the end, the judge decides to go with both options, counseling and a warning.

These kinds of negotiations are part of the routine work done in the team meetings, as staff members toss around different suggestions and eventually come to some kind of agreement about the court response. In all of the discussions, the main task for staff is to articulate its understanding of the youth behavior, using one or more interpretive practices, and get the rest of the team to agree to then decide upon a normal remedy. Here is where the process can get tricky: while this task often is accomplished with relatively little debate, it can become difficult when staff members do not always accept each others' use of the interpretive practice(s). That is, the staff can employ interpretive practices for cross purposes such as upgrading or downgrade the severity of the youth's action or raising the practical or ideological issues about a proposed normal remedy.

Steps 1 and 2: Interpretive Practices to Define the Problem

Accountability

In their depiction of a youth's actions, some staff members bring up the court's overall goal of teaching youths to be accountable for their actions. As Julie, a probation officer, put it, "I know that people need to be held accountable. That's a huge part of recovery. People don't change when things are going well. So, initially they decide to change because a certain amount of psychic pain and sometimes a crisis has to be precipitated, and custody may be that crisis."

In the following excerpt the north court staff talks about Vito, a sixteen-year-old Latino youth, who recently was kicked out of Project Fortitude, a twenty-one-day detox program, after only a few days. According to the Fortitude staff, three youths said that Vito collected their money to buy drugs for them. Project Fortitude staff kicked out all four youths and also found drug paraphernalia in Vito's room at the program. However, among the four youths, only Vito tested clean for drug use. There is no proof that Vito sold or used drugs, other than the other three youths' accounts and the drug paraphernalia found in Vito's room. Vito's mother is supposed to bring him to court today to address the situation:

CHARLIE (PUBLIC DEFENDER): Well, I'm not going to get into it with Vito if he used or provided the drugs.

SAMUELS (JUDGE): Right.

CHARLIE: He was kicked out and needs to go back to the program.

SAMUELS: It is not a matter of guilt or innocence. He needs to be taking responsibility and needs to be mindful of dangerous signals. But others were kicked out. Did the other youths also have possession of paraphernalia?

GEORGE (DRUG COUNSELOR): I don't know. All have taken drug tests and were dirty except his. . . . He pointed to this kid and said he snitched and ratted him out, which violated his confidentiality.

ALLEN (PROBATION OFFICER): That's just added stuff to the issue of him not taking responsibility.

The staff agrees that Vito's problem is not finishing Fortitude, but they say so for different reasons. Charlie suggests Vito should go back to Fortitude instead of getting a more severe normal remedy for the dismissal. Other staff indicate Vito's lack of accountability. Samuels explicitly disregards the legal issues of guilt or innocence to suggest the more important issue of Vito not taking responsibility for his actions in the detox program. Similarly, Allen agrees with Samuels, dismissing George's last comment about Vito blaming another youth for being a snitch. The staff decides to keep him in juvenile hall for twelve days, until he can go back to Fortitude. Later, when Vito protests the court's decision because he tested negative for drug use, the judge reasserts the accountability discourse, explaining to him that "it is your responsibility to complete the program. That is the issue today. For example, if you were not wrapped up in this, you would already be out of there." As a result, for circumstantial evidence of noncompliance, Vito spends almost two weeks in juvenile hall, with an additional three weeks in the detox program, under the rationale that he needs to learn accountability.

Monitoring Progress

Most of the time, staff does not explicitly invoke the idea of accountability in its negotiations of youth noncompliance. Instead, the staff can situate a youth's action within his performance in the program to date to decide the seriousness of the trouble. This background knowledge about the youth makes the issues of deciding the trouble somewhat easier, in that the staff has more context for it. The staff sometimes considers the youth's overall behavior in the program to downgrade the severity of the specific action being discussed, given the youth's exceptional progress in other areas.

In the next example, the staff discusses the case of Ricardo, a seventeen-year-old Latino youth in the south court who recently got into trouble in another neighborhood and had to call his mother to pick him up.

RAUL (DRUG COUNSELOR): The mom told me he called from Main Street . . . late at night, and she went to pick him up and said he smelled like alcohol. . . . Ricardo said he was in another neighborhood and got in a fight, so he got upset and went to a friend's house and drank . . .

JULIE (PROBATION OFFICER): He told me how much he craves alcohol. Maybe he needs more than five days [in juvenile hall].

[*Julie recommends the 120-day probation in-custody drug treatment . . .*]

JULIE: I always protected him from the 120 because he was doing so well in school and got wonderful grades. . . .

O'REILLY (JUDGE): Let's give him four days in [juvenile hall]. I'll tell him I'm not adverse to pulling him out of school and sending him to the 120, but I'll tell him the only reason he is not in 120 is because of school.

As this example suggests, the staff does not automatically follow the chart of normal remedies to respond to specific actions. Rather, it relies on its sense of the youth's overall performance to inform its understanding of the individual problem to address today. In other words, the staff considers how a youth's good behavior in one area (e.g., school) could mitigate his noncompliance in another area (e.g., drinking). Julie had known of Ricardo' cravings for alcohol before, but she "protected him" from the "needed" 120-day probation treatment program because of his impressive school performance. The judge decides to only threaten to send Ricardo to the 120 program, using fear to motivate him to stop drinking while acknowledging his school compliance. Normal remedies then are to be used not only to react to noncompliance but also to propel youths' progress in the program.

In contrast, the staff could link a specific act of youth noncompliance to a pattern of general behavior to upgrade the severity of the problem. In the next excerpt, Julie, the probation officer, talks about Alicia, a sixteen-year-old Latina who has been in the south court for almost a year but has never gotten past ninety consecutive days of sobriety without testing positive for drugs. Julie connects this latest incident to several past incidents to demonstrate a pattern of risky behaviors:

JULIE (PROBATION OFFICER): Alicia continues to be a grave concern of mine, and she continues to make poor decisions. . . .She took off Saturday [from home] and came back at 5:30 on Sunday and told me and the counselor at [drug treatment] that she drank. She said that she left because the grandmother's sister was bad-mouthing her mother, and the grandmother said, "Don't disrespect the aunts." I think she wanted to see a guy . . .

O'REILLY (JUDGE): What do we do with her today?

JULIE: I think it's time for drug dorm [probation's 120-day in-custody drug treatment].

CHARLIE (PUBLIC DEFENDER): Oh.

JULIE: Her grandmother told me she found a pill in the bedroom that was rochas [rohypnol]. I'm still concerned she's taking these pills, and that she told me she's taking it all through drug court. It wouldn't surprise me if she combines it with alcohol. . . . For her safety, I think the drug dorm is a good idea.

CHARLIE: I don't think the offense warrants it.

JULIE: It's an accumulation of things.

CHARLIE: The accumulation of stuff for what she was punished already . . .

O'REILLY: ESP [electronic home supervision], and the next step is drug
    dorm.

Before stating Alicia's specific noncompliant actions this week, Julie first says a
generalized statement that Alicia continues to "make poor decisions." This
tactic appears to ground Alicia's current actions of leaving home and drinking
alcohol within a broader pattern of misconduct versus an isolated event to be
addressed. Julie also discusses how Alicia does not take responsibility for her
problematic behavior in leaving home by stating Alicia blames her grandmother for not defending her mom. She adds a gendered comment to question
Alicia's statement, suggesting she "wanted to see a guy" to further underscore
the dangerousness of Alicia's behaviors. Staff did not police this kind of behavior as much for boys as with the girls. Put another way, the staff is quicker to
respond to such behavior with girls as a problem, whereas similar actions from
the male youths often go unaddressed for longer periods of time.

    In this way, Julie builds up her case to suggest Alicia requires the drug
dorm, a 120-day program in a probation camp, which is not the typical normal remedy for the offense of drinking (with no confirmed drug test) and
staying out all night. Julie offers more justification for her suggestion, describing additional noncompliant past behavior by Alicia, who admitted to taking
rohypnol ("date rape" drug) the entire time she has been in drug court. Charlie,
the public defender, tries to go back to focusing only on the current week's
actions, but Julie says explicitly that the punishment is for "an accumulation
of things," creating a treatment-punishment tension in the discussion. Julie
thinks that, for "her safety," Alicia needs the drug dorm, where she can learn
to not take such dangerous risks, while Charlie does not think this incident
merits such a severe response, especially since Alicia has already been punished by the court for past noncompliance. In the end, the judge offers a
compromise of electronically monitored house arrest and then drug dorm for
the next time Alicia is found noncompliant.

Situating an Action within a Youth's Character

    To assess noncompliance, the staff can relate a youth's trouble to his or her
general character. Staff members may see a youth as simultaneously "likeable,"
"gang-involved," "drug addicted," or "depressed." Those descriptions arise
from performance in the program, rather than from a deep moral judgment
about the youth's true nature. Because they are tied to how the staff works
with the youths, the staff assessments of the youths' character are temporary
and fluid. Staff mainly invokes an assessment of a youth's character to determine
the youth's workability in the court. At the same time, the cumulative effect

of temporal descriptions may eventually play a role—that is, if the descriptions are used over an extended period of time.[4]

Two descriptions—mentally ill and gang-involved—are partially informed by the youth's race and class. For example, staff did not hold youths accountable for behaviors caused by their mental illness. And while staff suspected many of the youths had mental health issues that affected their ability to stay in compliance with the court, it was primarily the white middle-class youths who had access through their families' private insurance to get diagnosed and treated for mental health problems. Such access translated into the staff excusing the mentally ill white youths more often than their undiagnosed or untreated minority peers in the court.[5] Regarding gangs, the staff tended to view Latino gangs as a more serious threat than other gangs to a youth's workability. Staff remarks about a white youth's membership in gangs often went ignored or dismissed as irrelevant to the youth's workability in the drug court, even though those gangs claimed to be white supremacist groups. This difference in opinion was based partly on the court's resources: the neighborhoods with the Latino gangs had heavier drug court police enforcement, so their activity was more likely than that of white supremacist gangs located in the remote parts of the county to catch the attention of the drug court.

The influence of these descriptions of youths' character is not easy to pinpoint because they are fluid in the staff's decision-making process. Charlie touches on this issue when asked about the drug court's willingness to work with gang-involved youths, regardless of their race: "some of the best kids we've had have been so-called gang members. . . . A lot of the guys . . . aren't really as bad and they need somebody like us to help give them a reason for getting away and breaking that mold. A lot of them have good leadership qualities that we can build on." Charlie suggests the so-called gang member is not that "bad" if he responds to the drug court staff's efforts to help him bring out his "leadership qualities." If the youth is not responsive, the staff could invoke his gang identity to indicate he is no longer a workable client in the court.

The character assessments then are not just innocent descriptions. Staff members use them to present the youths in different lights, either to downgrade or upgrade a particular action and, by extension, to influence the staff's decision-making process. In cases where staff determines that a youth's behavior is noncompliant, staff can talk about the youth as "a good kid" and choose to withhold punishment. The "good kid" label is tied to a youth's current attitude and prior performance in the court.

In the next example, the south court staff discusses how to respond to Tony, a fifteen-year-old Latino who missed one day of drug treatment:

JULIE (PROBATION OFFICER): I called Tony at school about why he missed treatment. He said he stayed after school to help clean and that he finished around 1:30 P.M., but it was too late to go to treatment because he would get there at 3:00 P.M., and he knew that he'd already be turned away. I said [to Tony] have the teacher call treatment to tell them why he would be late, because if not, he will be terminated if he gets three unexcused absences from treatment.

RAUL (DRUG COUNSELOR): Other than that . . .

JULIE: He's doing a super job.

O'REILLY: He's a good kid.

RAUL: He has a better attitude.

JACK (DISTRICT ATTORNEY): We have to give him credit because he told a lie we haven't heard before.

The staff could have technically given Tony one day in custody for missing treatment, which Julie interprets as poor thinking in not having the teacher call ahead to the treatment program. However, the staff's sense that Tony is a "good kid" with a "better attitude" means Tony does not need this normal remedy to "fix" the problem. Even though Jack says he might be lying, the rest of the staff believes Tony and decides not to give him a normal remedy.

A youth's bad attitude can heighten the staff's sense of a youth's noncompliance and subsequent court response. The north court staff is discussing how Jay, a white sixteen-year-old, has shown poor attendance at twelve-step meetings. He was supposed to do three meetings a week but has done only one so far:

SAMUELS (JUDGE): Things are going well except attitude.

ALLEN (PROBATION OFFICER): And twelve-step. . . .

BILL (DRUG COUNSELOR): He's not having a good go of it and has a bad attitude and now is digging his heels in on the twelve-step. . . . He said he had one meeting. . . . He is way behind on his treatment plan. . . . I just wanted to point out he is digging his heels, and to tell him to keep up with the treatment plan.

SAMUELS: Any suggestions? Admonish?

CHARLIE (PUBLIC DEFENDER): Admonish . . .

SAMUELS: How about we let him know one week home sup[ervision] for every meeting missed? Let it pile up.

The staff members cite their opinions of Jay's character to inform their sense of his workability as a drug-addicted youth. Bill describes Jay's "bad attitude" about having to do twelve-step meetings as a sign of him not wanting to engage in drug treatment at all, so he asks for the judge to admonish the youth to go to treatment. After hearing about Jay's resistance to twelve-step meetings, the judge takes it one step further to suggest one week house arrest for every meeting missed. Typically, the staff does not issue such a specific and harsh warning for missing twelve-step meetings. While the judge might have normally asked Jay to make up the meetings for the following week (adding the two meetings missed this week to next week's expected three meetings), he instead threatens to give him two weeks of house arrest for missing two hour-long twelve-step meetings. Again, like the previous example, Jay's bad attitude is tied to the staff's anticipated sense of how it can best work with him now. However, it is a temporary assessment. Once Jay's attitude improves (as linked to his performance in treatment), it no longer becomes relevant in the staff's decision-making process.

Comparisons to Other Youth

Another staff interpretive practice compares one youth's actions to those of other youths to ascertain the seriousness of the noncompliance. Again, Charlie contextualizes this interpretive practice within the staff's everyday work patterns: "We've done . . . every different type of kids over the years, and very few are a new type. And so we'll go back and say, 'Remember that, this is like so-and-so' . . . that's a better way of describing it, like a picture." Staff could use this comparison to downgrade the severity of the act by depicting the trouble as insignificant in the grand scheme of things. Alternatively, the comparison could upgrade the severity, suggesting the need to address the trouble immediately to avoid further and possibly more serious noncompliant actions. Similar to the previous interpretive practice, the issue centers on the youth's workability, with the staff denying or preserving the potential that the youth could actually still benefit from being in the program.

The following excerpt shows how staff can downgrade the severity of trouble by comparing a youth to another youth. Randall is a sixteen-year-old African American in the east court who is in a special school for mentally ill youth. In the following discussion, the staff mentions another drug court participant, Sam, to interpret Randall's recent positive drug test for alcohol use and school truancies:

HOOPER (JUDGE): Dirty?

JOE (PROBATION OFFICER): Yep. The test was positive for alcohol at court. He [Randall] probably drank before court . . .

CHARLIE (PUBLIC DEFENDER): What was the blood alcohol level of the test . . .

EVA (DRUG COUNSELOR): He said it was his cousin who got the drinks. . . . The mother said he took medication.

CHARLIE: That level would be a Nyquil level at 0.02 [below the official level of positive use].

JOE: Did he go to school?

EVA: He didn't go . . .

HOOPER: You're talking about Randall. . . . We gotta give him a little leeway. He's like what's-his-name?

CHARLIE: Sam.

JOE: My whole thing is that he gets his psychotropic medication at school and he is not going to school on a regular basis, so he gets no meds.

Normally staff would focus on Randall's noncompliant behavior or discuss whether to believe the mom's statement about Randall taking medication like Nyquil as the cause for the test result. However, the judge compares Randall to Sam, another youth with mental health issues, to suggest that they need to deal with him differently. This comparison to Sam shifts the staff's focus back on Randall's mental health issues. The probation officer then clarifies his question about the school absence to say he is concerned with making sure Randall goes to school to take his medications.

This excerpt highlights the multifaceted and nuanced influence of race and class in the staff's descriptions about youth noncompliance. Randall is one of the few minority youths to have a confirmed mental health problem that does lead the staff to interpret his noncompliance as caused by his mental illness. So, it is not automatic that the staff would excuse only the white youths with mental health problems. Beyond the issue of diagnosing a mental health problem, race and class differences can manifest in the venues of treatment (e.g., public school versus private therapist) and the families' views of treatment (e.g., white parents were more likely to make sure the youths took the medication versus the minority parents, some of whom did not believe their youths were mentally ill). In Randall's case, the mom resisted the court's insistence that her son take his medication all the time, saying she did not want "the state" in her home and that he only needed the medication to focus better in school.

Staff might also bring up former youth participants as a foreshadowing of the bad things that could occur without early intervention. In the following excerpt, the south court staff links Simon's actions to another youth, Ruben, to suggest Simon's school absences should be considered more seriously.

O'REILLY (JUDGE): What's happening? I don't like this.

JULIE (PROBATION OFFICER): Simon hasn't been to school since August 10 [two weeks ago]. Three absences were excused because of teacher conferences, but the next week he said he lost his bus pass, but he didn't tell anyone. He dressed as if he was going to school. Then miraculously he found his bus pass but still did not go this week. . . . I'd love for him to go with Mr. Lydell to Job Corps at least to explore it. . . . Otherwise, he will fall in like Ruben and others.

The judge starts the discussion with a general statement of displeasure about Simon's recent behavior. According to the progress report, Simon's mom told the staff that her seventeen-year-old Latino son smelled of alcohol and came home at eleven one night, which was after curfew. Julie also discusses his school absences, doubting his excuses about the bus pass. She suggests that Simon go with the court volunteer, Mr. Lydell, to Job Corps, a voluntary residential year-long vocational training program, to see if that program might motivate him to finish the court program with some "positive" future-oriented goals. Julie infers that this is a critical time in Simon's tenure in the court. While he has been testing clean for drug use, he has been slipping for several weeks now in the areas of school and home. She suggests that if they do not respond now, Simon could "fall in like Ruben," a former drug court client who was similarly noncompliant at school and home. Ruben, a seventeen-year-old Latino male, ultimately got kicked out of the court after committing a new and more serious offense where he allegedly almost killed a rival gang member by beating him in the head with a steel pipe. So, while Simon's school absences are not technically a delinquent act, Julie, by associating Ruben's performance to Simon's, attempts to suggest they could lead to that. It is implied that Simon might turn to a "dangerous" Latino gang the way that Ruben did, making him unworkable in the eyes of the staff. In the end, the staff's worries are unfounded. Simon later explains that he is scared his mother will kick him out of the house after he graduates, so he's trying to delay his graduation. While the staff initially decides to send Simon to juvenile hall for four days, it does not end up issuing a normal remedy for the absences.

Working with External Agencies

The network of institutions (schools, treatment agencies, hospitals, churches, and families) working with youths greatly informs how staff assesses and responds to youth noncompliance. There is a wide variability in the external institutions' requirements and supervision. Some treatment programs and schools are longer than others, thereby increasing the chances that a youth may be absent and considered noncompliant. For example, a teen recovery center meets for three hours, whereas a Narcotics Anonymous meeting lasts only one hour. In addition, some treatment programs include a family participation component. If the parents refuse to participate, the youth is subject to termination from the treatment program and subsequently seen as noncompliant by the court. Treatment programs and schools also differed in how they monitored youth compliance. As a result, court staff had to negotiate when it agreed or disagreed with those agencies' assessments of the youth's noncompliance. For example, one school reported a drug court participant was tardy—and thus noncompliant—for being five minutes late to class, whereas other schools do not keep strict records of attendance, making it impossible to determine if the youths went to school at all.

Diversity among external programs in requirements and supervision contributes to the drug court staff's multiple and contested interpretations of youth noncompliance and accountability. Consider the example of Frank, a fifteen-year-old Latino in the north court suspended from school for leaving school grounds with another youth who smoked marijuana. The staff discusses how the school's Latino vice principal overreacted to the situation:

ALLEN (PROBATION OFFICER): Frank was suspended from school Monday after he and another person left the campus. . . . Frank came back reeking of marijuana and the vice principal found drugs on the other youth but not Frank . . .

BILL (DRUG COUNSELOR): I went over right away to drug test Frank, who didn't have a great attitude, but the guy [vice principal] had a worse attitude. . . . The vice principal told me if he was clean, they wouldn't suspend him. I came back to the office and said he was clean. The VP was not happy. He wouldn't come out and say it, but it was on his face . . .

JACK (DISTRICT ATTORNEY): Frank is not making any effort at school . . .

BILL: All the kids who they have sent there and gotten into trouble are Hispanic. . . . I will say we are slowly making progress with Frank, who did talk to me more than he ever has before.

ALLEN: Frank does things he is not supposed to do, which makes it worse because this [vice principal] guy's not going to lay off.

CHARLIE (PUBLIC DEFENDER): Quite often this is what happens. The officials of color are harder on their own kind.

GEORGE (DRUG COUNSELOR): When I tested him Tuesday, I came across an attendance clerk who sang the praises of Frank, saying that he participates more and he had a great attitude . . .

SAMUELS (JUDGE): I will let him know to follow the rules.

ALLEN: How about three days of custody?

CHARLIE: Admonish him and give him three days later.

SAMUELS: Three days stayed?

ALLEN: Yeah.

CHARLIE: For how long?

SAMUELS: Sixty days.

CHARLIE: Whoa, that's tough—a lot of pressure.

SAMUELS: He can't leave the campus. This is in his control.

Frank gets suspended from school for three days even though he did not have marijuana on him and he tested clean. The variation in schools is apparent here when one compares Frank's situation to Randy's from earlier in the chapter. Randy did not get into trouble for leaving school early. The drug court staff recognizes Frank's school, especially the vice principal, is much harsher on students compared to other schools. Bill states that the vice principal promised not to suspend Frank if he tested clean, but when the results came back negative, the vice principal ended up suspending him anyway.

While Jack suggests that the reason for his ire is more about Frank's lack of effort (and thus meriting a normal remedy), Bill suggests a more race-based interpretation by noting that the only youths who get in trouble at that school are Hispanic.[6] Charlie further underscores that statement by saying officials of color like the vice principal are more severe on "their own kind." Moreover, the drug court staff feels Frank is improving. Bill says they are "making progress" with him, and George cites the attendance clerk who noticed his increased efforts in school. Even despite the staff's critical view of the vice principal and its sense that Frank's performance is improving, the staff discusses the need to respond to the suspension, if only to explain why he is not getting the usual normal remedy of a day in custody for the one-day suspension. Samuels notes it is within Frank's control to not leave the school grounds, suggesting there is still some element of individual accountability that Frank must see and accept for this situation. He gives Frank three days custody—one day custody for every day suspended—but "stays" it, meaning the court will enforce that decision only when Frank commits another noncompliant action.

External agencies also affect staff assessments by the information they provide to the court staff. Any of these agencies could withhold, transmit, summarize, or reinterpret information about youths' behavior and subsequently impact the staff's ability to know if the youths are compliant or not. For example, the staff members of some probation units, treatment programs, and schools were more proactive about informing the drug court staff about youths' performance, either by calling on a regular basis or attending the drug court team meetings. Other agencies never returned the drug court staff's phone calls or provided the requested information in a timely manner. This varied interagency information flow fosters the negotiated and contested decision-making process in the juvenile drug court, as staff shares different pieces of data and challenges the accuracy of each other's knowledge about the youths. For example, staff often discusses the credibility of a probation home supervision violation mainly because there is no official report to review.

In the next excerpt, the drug counselor states that Leon, a seventeen-year-old Latino in the east court, violated his home supervision, but the public defender questions the accuracy of that report to lessen the apparent severity of Leon's noncompliant action:

HOOPER (JUDGE): Leon is doing all right? . . .

EVA (DRUG COUNSELOR): Yes, Your Honor, he violated from home sup[ervision].

CHARLIE (PUBLIC DEFENDER): What does that mean?

EVA: He wasn't home.

CHARLIE: [For] how long?

EVA: I don't know.

CHARLIE: You don't know where he went? how long he was away?

HOOPER: What do we want to do?

CHARLIE: It [the drug court summary report] says he took off without permission.

HOOPER: Let's find out . . .

CHARLIE: If he goes in to custody, it should be overnight.

JACK: What if he was gone for less than three and a half hours?

CHARLIE: I say not overnight . . . who told us [about this violation]?

EVA: I believe home sup.

SARAH (PROBATION OFFICER): I'll try to get the home sup report.

By questioning Eva about how long Leon was gone and where he went, Charlie is suggesting she is too quick to assess the situation as a home supervision violation. Often times, the drug court staff hears from the probation department's home supervision unit that a youth has had a violation, only to find out later that the parent took the youth somewhere, or the youth was not really out that late or that far from home. This distinction has real consequences, as a home supervision violation could lead to custody (e.g., overnight in juvenile hall), whereas the other situations are not considered noncompliant. The discussion with Leon also reveals staff's concern with who provided the information. That either adds or detracts from the credibility of the information; for example, a field home supervision officer may not have checked with the main probation office to see if the parent had called to excuse the youth. As a result, Sarah says she will try to get the home supervision report to get the "official" version. Staff finds out later that Leon was right outside his house, which technically is still a home supervision violation, since he is supposed to be inside his house. The judge gives him a more intensive type of home supervision, electronic monitoring, instead of the originally proposed normal remedy of custody. The staff's questioning of information then serves to mitigate or dismiss entirely the assessment of a youth's behavior as noncompliant. While the staff's skepticism usually works to the youth's advantage, that is not always the case.

STEP 3: INTERPRETIVE PRACTICES TO DECIDE A RESPONSE

Even if the staff is able to move with relative ease through the first two steps of determining the nature and severity of the youth's noncompliance, it also faces myriad possibilities to answer the last question of "what do we do?" In that effort, the staff brings up many different issues, either ideological or practical, to steer the team toward a particular normal remedy. For example, the public defender raises practical concerns to argue against another staff's recommendation of what the youths "should" be given. In contrast, the probation officers state these practical issues with a more begrudging acceptance, as they would often like to give the youths a more severe court response. All of these moments are strategic and occasioned moves, since the staff selectively invoked certain interpretive practices to achieve its desired normal remedy.

Purpose of Sanction: Consistency or Individualized Justice

There is a general tension between staff members who believe the court's normal remedies should be issued consistently among all the youths and others who argue for issuing them in a more individualized manner. Judge O'Reilly explains the rationale behind the consistency efforts:

> I go to these drug programs all around the country all the time, and they emphasize that each kid needs to be treated individually and they need to discuss the sanction as to how it fits into that kid's treatment in life. I don't agree with that . . . the day for a day rule is real simple, they [the youths] know it, they know what the sanction is and that's it. . . . They know and talk amongst themselves, as to what goes on and they're going to figure it out. And then pretty soon you've got all of them lying to you . . . or they're going to be mad about the program because so and so didn't have to go into custody.

He notes two reasons for maintaining consistent sanctions, or normal remedies: One, it makes it easier for youths to remember the rules and thus to stay in compliance. Two, it fosters the youths' perception of fairness and equal treatment in the court, which also helps to keep them in compliance if they are not mad about the differential staff responses to various youths. In contrast, Charlie notes the need to have a more individualized approach, stating, "They're people, they're kids, and they differ. . . . You have to look at it. You can't just say that this equals $A + B = C$. You have to look at what A is there and what B is there and then it works out to C, but let's change the answer and make it a C- or something." The staff alternated between these two ideological extremes. O'Reilly often did "make it a C-" in deciding the normal remedy for a particular youth, and Charlie did not always object to a normal remedy based on the consistency perspective.

Both extremes are apparent in the following example with Ricardo, who was discussed earlier. Some staff members state the need to individualize the normal remedies, while others advocate consistency among youths in discussing Ricardo's recent drug testing sweat patch. It recently fell off, which staff technically considers a positive drug test result:

RAUL (DRUG COUNSELOR): These kids see that we respond differently to the rules and it's okay to tamper with the patch.

CHARLIE (PUBLIC DEFENDER): This is different. This kid called and there were three [urinalysis] tests around it, so it was not just a patch . . .

JULIE (PROBATION OFFICER): He was negative on the UA [urinalysis] from the thirteenth and the creatinine levels were thirty-four.

RAUL: Nothing is really happening. He just loses his [sober] days.

CHARLIE: We're not supposed to consider the youths as a group . . .

JULIE: That's a problem. Other peoples' sanctions are different on the same day.

CHARLIE: They are different situations.

O'REILLY (JUDGE): I say overnight, right?

CHARLIE: That's fine. . . .

JULIE: As long as we make clear the rules.

Instead of discussing how to motivate Ricardo more in the court, Raul suggests treating his patch issue as a noncompliant incident. Raul warns that, otherwise, as O'Reilly warned earlier, the consequence will be that all the youths will see that it is "okay to tamper with the patch." However, Charlie points out that the particulars in this case are "different" than other situations. After Raul repeats his opinion that Ricardo is not getting a strong sanction, Charlie states that "we're not supposed to consider the youths as a group." Julie then articulates the tension between the need for consistency versus individualized treatment, as "other peoples' sanctions are different on the same day." O'Reilly, who stated before that consistency matters, offers a compromise of one night in custody, to which both Charlie and Julie agree. This excerpt demonstrates the negotiated nature of youth noncompliance: the same action could mean different things to the staff members, who each propose a different court response.

Making Do

The staff raises specific practical issues surrounding the court's response more often than the ideological purposes of those responses. Many issues regarding age, lack of placement options, and budget limitations affected the staff's stated desire to provide individualized treatment plans for youths. For example, certain sanctions are not possible if youths are too young or too old. If they are young (sixteen years or younger), the staff has more difficulty placing them in highly desired vocational programs. But if the youths are older than seventeen years and six months, the staff faces different obstacles, as it can no longer send them to the 120-day drug treatment program at the probation camp or the one-year residential treatment program. Diego, a seventeen-year-old Latino in the east court, recently turned himself into the court after using drugs and missing school for a few weeks. The team is debating what to do, since he is turning eighteen in two weeks, limiting their ability to send him to long-term drug treatment programs. Diego was almost a third of the way through the program before admitting this most recent drug use to the staff.

BARRY (DRUG COUNSELOR): Diego is in custody.

JACK (DISTRICT ATTORNEY): He has three sober days now and has not been in school since November 24 [twenty-one days] . . .

BARRY: He did admit he did use, and the mom brought him in on the fourth [of December].

CHARLIE (PUBLIC DEFENDER): The eleventh of December . . .

KELLEY (JUDGE): He's been here for a year and fell off the wagon. He used meth[amphetamine]. . . . How many sober days does he have?

BARRY: 111 . . .

SARAH (PROBATION OFFICER): He is turning eighteen in two weeks.

BARRY: We have already tried the 28 and 120 programs . . .

KELLEY: What do all of you think about it?

CHARLIE: He did turn himself in on the eleventh [of December] to court . . . He's too old for Project Arise [the year-long residential treatment program] . . .

BARRY: We could do the twenty-eight again . . . By the time he finishes we could terminate him after he is eighteen.

CHARLIE: If we do the twenty-eight, we could bring him back to decide what to do. We should make him a deal to tell him to sign up for school . . .

SARAH: If he does that and shows positive change, we can terminate jurisdiction successfully, but not from probation . . .

KELLEY: We are doing a backwards sanction, and the only reason is because of his age. [*To Mark*] Maybe you can get him to work on goals.

MARK (CLINICAL THERAPIST): Okay.

KELLEY: Then he can share them with us. . . . Twenty-eight.

Diego's workability is essentially defined by the upcoming deadline of his eighteenth birthday. While the court could legally keep jurisdiction over him until he is twenty-five years old, it loses most of its normal remedies after he is eighteen. He is too old for the most likely normal remedy of the 120-day probation treatment program and the year-long program. In the end, the team decides to send Diego to the 28-day program, which Judge Kelley describes as a "backwards sanction," since it was chosen solely because of the age constraints on the other available normal remedies. Diego then is no longer tenable in the court based on the organizational limits to working with him.

The external agencies' fluctuating resources also compromised the court's ability to work with youths. They occasionally had waiting lists, depending on the time of year and location. It could take between one day to several weeks to get youths into drug treatment and schools. This delay, in turn, affects how long a youth remains on home supervision, increasing the probability of home supervision violations and financial burden on the parents, who are charged for a portion of home supervision costs (about thirty-five dollars a day). In addition, during the peak of the county's budget crisis, the only short-term residential treatment option available to the drug court staff was the 21-day community-based detox program, since the 28-day probation program closed. At that time, there was only one provider, Project Fortitude, who ran three of these programs. A long waiting list subsequently developed, during which time the youths either stayed in juvenile hall or were on home supervision. Here the east court team discusses what to do with Cruz, who has been sitting in juvenile hall for over two weeks while waiting for a spot in Fortitude:

HOOPER (JUDGE): Cruz just went in [to juvenile hall] . . .
JOE (PROBATION OFFICER): He's been in for a while.
CHARLIE: Fifteen days.
JOE: He has been screened for Fortitude.
CHARLIE: He's been accepted?
JOE: He has been, but there is a waiting list . . .
HOOPER: I don't think detox will do it for him. He should do long-term.
JOE: Want to release him?
HOOPER: There is not much we can do. He's in [juvenile] hall for two weeks.
    I'd rather have him work with Mark [clinical therapist].

Here we see how the court's inability to provide the suitable and desired treatment program affects Cruz's workability. Cruz has been in juvenile hall for two weeks after admitting to using marijuana. When he was first brought into juvenile hall, Cruz told Charlie he wanted to go to detox. Joe, the probation officer, said at that point, "I spoke to him. He said he needs help and that he has a lot of problems." But because of the unforeseen delay in getting him into the facility, the staff releases him from juvenile hall on electronic house arrest until a bed opens up. He runs away to Mexico right before he is scheduled to enter the program, over three weeks later. By not sending Cruz to treatment when he appeared ready to stay clean, the court lost an opportunity to capitalize on his motivation to engage in treatment. The drug court itself limited his ability to complete drug treatment, which is one of the primary conditions to remaining compliant in the program. Cruz's compromised workability is due to his efforts and the court's hampered ability to work with him.

Another obstacle is the limited availability of normal remedies during the county's budget crisis, which impacts the quasi-external agencies upon which the drug court relies. In the next excerpt, the north court staff discusses how to make do in the case of Rita, a white fifteen-year-old who stayed out all night. The probation department recently eliminated all short-term custody options in juvenile hall to cut costs:

SAMUELS (JUDGE): Rita has eight [sober] days and needs to bring in four twelve-step [meetings].

ALLEN (PROBATION OFFICER): Yeah, she had a little trouble where on a couple of nights she went out without Mom's permission. Mom called this morning, after Rita was told not to go . . .

BILL (DRUG COUNSELOR): She presumpted [drug tested] clean but was out all night . . .

SAMUELS: How about a weekend?

CHARLIE (PUBLIC DEFENDER): We can't . . .

SAMUELS: That's right [because of no more short-term custodies] . . .

BILL: Home supervision.

The probation department's budget cuts significantly affected the drug court staff's decision-making process that relied upon short-term stints in juvenile hall as normal remedies for youths' noncompliance. The staff previously would have given Rita a weekend in custody for this kind of behavior, but now it is forced to give her a lesser sanction of home supervision as its next best choice. This discussion raises the question: How can the court expect youths to be accountable for their own actions when it has to deal with these kinds of organizational issues limiting its ability to hold them accountable?

Finding Creative Responses

Faced with these compromised and limited resources from the quasi-external and external agencies, the drug court staff figured out creative ways to respond to youth noncompliance. The staff has few alternatives at its disposal if the youth has a bad home situation. As such, the staff agrees upon certain normal remedies used for other types of noncompliance if they help address this placement problem.

The following excerpt shows how the staff debates whether to keep Lewis, a seventeen-year-old Latino in the south court, in juvenile hall while waiting for a spot in Project Fortitude. The underlying question is not if Lewis needs detox but where he can live, since his mom does not want him back in the house. Finding a group home for boys is extremely difficult. Lewis has been in the program for over eleven months:

O'REILLY (JUDGE): Okay, what's with Lewis? . . .

CHARLIE (PUBLIC DEFENDER): We detained him. He is going to be screened [for Fortitude], but we don't think he's going to get in soon . . .

O'REILLY: That is the problem. The mother doesn't want him back.

CHARLIE: If we are going to hold him 'til we know if he is not in Fortitude, what if they don't want him. We will need to find him a place. . . .

O'REILLY: I want to hold him 'til he gets in Fortitude. Remember, we don't really want him in Fortitude, but more 'til the mom will take him back.

The judge clearly states that the reason he is keeping Lewis in juvenile hall has nothing to do with detox. He is counting on the delay to give the mother more time to "cool out," so that she will eventually allow him to come back home. This shows the practical orientation to the staff's decision-making process. While the official record would show "detain pending Fortitude," the impetus behind that decision is more "detain until home placement becomes available again."

A similar technique is used when staff deals with a youth's decreasing custody time. Custody time is the maximum amount of time youths can be incarcerated for the offense for which they have been true found (i.e., guilty). The drug court staff draws from this bank of custody time to send youths to juvenile hall and probation camp for noncompliance. The amount of custody time then becomes a crucial factor in how staff works with the youth in the program. If the youth is running low on custody days, the staff might classify the noncompliance in a more formal legal fashion to add time to work with the youth. In the next example, the east court staff discusses how to respond to the recent arrest of Roger, a sixteen-year-old African American:

CHARLIE (PUBLIC DEFENDER): Roger is in custody for resisting arrest . . .
HOOPER (JUDGE): This whole thing is funny about how he was on his bicycle and that escalated to resisting arrest.
SARAH (PROBATION OFFICER): Well, he was hiding.
HOOPER: I know, why don't we handle it there.
CHARLIE: Is there a petition? Why don't we release him on home sup[ervision] until the petition is filed?
SARAH: I think Joe [probation officer] told me there was a petition. . . .
CHARLIE: How many [custody] days does he have?
SARAH: Ninety-five.
CHARLIE: He needs more time.
SARAH: We could use the new charge to add more time.
JACK (DISTRICT ATTORNEY): If it is a misdemeanor, my office is not going to file it, since I'm the one to file it, and there is a six-month backlog to filing in my office.
HOOPER: We can handle the probation violation today. What about this more time comment?
SARAH: Well, if we have a true finding on the new charge, then we can have more time to work with the youth.
CHARLIE: Well, I didn't say this, 'cause I'm his lawyer.
SARAH: It would add six months.
CHARLIE: It would be more than six months . . . Jack?
JACK: It's a year. . . .

The staff uses this incident to be able to work more effectively with Roger. While the judge thinks the latest incident with the bicycle is not serious enough to merit a resisting arrest charge, and the district attorney states he would not normally have done anything with it, the team discusses processing the offense formally to add more time on the books to work with him. The public defender agrees with the idea, believing Roger "needs more [custody] time," even though he technically could have advocated for getting the charge dismissed or handled merely as a probation violation. For therapeutic purposes, the defense attorney cedes his traditional role of advocating legally for the youth.[7]

This decision raises an important point about creative responses. In deciding the most effective normal remedy for Lewis and Roger, the staff essentially extends the court's reach over them. To help maintain the home placement for Lewis, the staff places him in juvenile hall until his mom agrees to take him back. He ends up spending two weeks there until the staff lets him go back home. The staff also could add a year of additional custody time to Roger's case under the guise of helping him to do better in the court. In that situation, the meaningless charge of resisting arrest would become a reality, as Roger would have to admit to it (i.e., plead guilty). If Roger fails, then that year could be added to his final disposition in mainstream court on his original charge and the new one.

Conflicting Uses and Limited Acceptance of Interpretive Practices

Sometimes negotiations become heated as staff members form conflicting perceptions of a youth's actions. While the staff members worked as a team in the court, there are clear tensions along two interrelated lines. First, the field-based staff (probation officers, drug counselors, and police officers) have a deeper knowledge of the youths' actions, since they interact more with the youths than the court-based staff (attorneys, clinical therapists, judges). This difference can lead to debates in the team meeting where the field-based staff feel the youths are conning the court-based staff. Allen, the probation officer, describes this tension, noting that the probation officers and drug counselors "are out working with these kids almost daily. And when we make a recommendation, it's not just an off-the-cuff recommendation . . . This is based on what a kid's doing or, you know, what's going on at home, in school, in treatment, and everything else, whereas a lot of times [the ideas of] other members of the team seem to be an off-the-cuff recommendation." Second, the public defender and the probation officers often clashed philosophically. The former felt the latter was solely out to punish the youths unnecessarily, while the latter felt the former was too aggressive in the team meetings just to win the argument. While the staff described these tensions to me in the interviews, its decision-making process was not necessarily always shaped by them, as the judges and public defender often agreed with the probation officers' recommendations. The extreme differences occurred more when the staff's interpretive practices were not in alignment with one another. Moreover, these disparities did not always fall along court-specified roles.

The most heated staff discussions occurred when one member's use of an interpretive practice was not accepted by the rest, or when the staff members employed interpretive practices that were incompatible with one another. In the following example, the east court staff discusses Victor, a sixteen-year-old Latino youth who has been arrested with two other drug court youths for breaking into cars. Victor has been in the court for several months already and has been sent to the 28-day and 120-day programs for drinking alcohol and going AWOL. The question today is whether to keep him in drug court or to terminate his case and send him to the probation gang supervision unit. The staff employs various interpretive practices to establish his workability as either drug or gang-focused.

JACK (DISTRICT ATTORNEY): Victor is a gang member and is violent.
CHARLIE (PUBLIC DEFENDER): It was Sebastian [another drug court youth] that did something stupid. Victor was just the lookout guy.
JACK: No.
ANDY (POLICE OFFICER): No.
HOOPER (JUDGE): What happened?
JACK: It was gang behavior.
RICHARD (PROBATION OFFICER): I recommend to terminate and send the case to GSU [gang unit] for screening . . .
CHARLIE: What gang affiliation is here?
RICHARD: He admits to it.
CHARLIE: He was with Sebastian . . . and another drug court kid.
HOOPER: They are part of some gang.
CHARLIE: No.
RICHARD: According to him, Victor, Sebastian claims one gang.
CHARLIE: This wasn't a gang thing. They hang out.
HOOPER: It seems to me I warned him before about hanging out with the wrong kinds of people.
JACK: They broke into two cars.
CHARLIE: I'm not saying he didn't do it.
JACK: These are three gang members.
CHARLIE: This was not a gang thing.

The staff members disagree immediately about Victor's character and the nature of the crime. The district attorney describes him as a violent gang member, given the new arrest charges. In contrast, the public defender tries to downgrade the severity of the situation by comparing Victor to Sebastian, the other youth involved in the car theft, to suggest Victor was merely a "lookout," a nonviolent participant. The police officer and probation officers side with Jack, continually referring to Victor as a gang member, a characterization that Charlie refuses to accept. Hooper then brings up Victor's past performance, recalling his warnings to Victor to avoid these kinds of people, as further evidence that perhaps Victor is a gang member since he is refusing to stop. Jack returns to talking about the initial problem for today—that they broke into two cars—which Charlie does not dispute until Jack inserts the added descriptor of "three gang members." This debate has implications for how they will respond to the incident. If he is guilty and violent, he does not belong in drug court, which in theory does not accept violent youths. If he is simply guilty but not violent, then he can stay in drug court. The issue of gang membership seems to tip that scale, as it serves as an indicator for violence. Given the import of this decision, the staff continues to debate whether or not Victor is in a gang by looking at other possible clues:

HOOPER (JUDGE): I'm not trying to defend the kid, but I think to put it in context—this is not . . . [a] prep kid. The kid lives in the roughest town that is Hispanic, where the code of behavior is "don't be a bitch," and you have to go along with the others . . . But there are certain things you just don't do. . . . Was he there or just a go-along guy? . . . The question is—is he salvageable at fifteen? He has shown us he can stay clean, but he has the habit of hanging out with the wrong people. I say give him one more shot.

JACK: He should be in the gang unit because he is by association a gang-related person. The parents say he has associations with gang members, especially Sebastian, who is one who keeps coming around to have him do things . . .

HOOPER: I've heard enough. He has one last chance. We need to monitor him closely. . . I haven't seen too many kids come out of [gang unit] as exemplary kids.

Hooper seems to be almost debating with himself as he sorts through the various possibilities to explain Victor's behavior. While the judge initially appeared to lean toward the district attorney's view of Victor, he now cites Victor's age, race, and neighborhood as signs that he is probably not violent. At the same time, he raises the importance of youth accountability, stating, "There are certain things you just don't do." The way he resolves the discussion is by summarizing Victor's past performance in the court as staying clean but hanging out with the wrong people. Jack still insists on sending him to the gang unit, adding that the crime was not drug related and that the parents know of Victor's gang membership. The judge makes the unilateral decision to keep

Victor in drug court because he still thinks of him as "salvageable." He also mentions his distrust of the probation gang unit's ability to help youth. This same debate continues over the next several months, as Victor has some additional, yet more minor, brushes with the police. Eventually, Victor starts to accumulate enough sober days to advance to the last phase of the program. By the end of the first fieldwork period he had 225 sober days and had almost completed drug court.

Victor's case encapsulates the complicated interpretive dance of assessing youth noncompliance and the long-term consequences of each weekly discussion. The informality of these discussions lends a certain unpredictability to the outcome. Had the judge not given Victor a chance, he would have been sent to the gang supervision unit. Had the probation officer and district attorney been more insistent on transferring him, perhaps the judge would have yielded. Had Victor been older, not Hispanic, or living in a different neighborhood, perhaps the gang issue would never have come up. Also, this discussion brought up issues that continue to be raised during Victor's career in the court.

SILENT VOICES: YOUTHS' PERSPECTIVES OF THE COURT AND STAFF DECISIONS

This chapter has yet to address one critical actor's voice to understand the social construction of youth noncompliance: the youths themselves. The youths' views of the staff's decisions provide even more insight into the therapy-punishment tension in the drug court and how it affects their subsequent actions.

One point that comes across clearly is the staff's accountability message for youths' behaviors, drug-related or not. According to Charles, a sixteen-year-old African American in the east court, "They [the drug court staff] want to—they want to see you succeed. I mean, they don't wanna see you come back. . . . But, if you continue making the wrong choices . . . you will be in custody again." Ben, a biracial sixteen-year-old in the north court agrees with Charles, saying that drug court "keeps me clean. . . . Personally, I don't want to get sent to juvie [juvenile hall], so if I don't want to go to juvie, then that means don't pop a dirty, or, you know, don't use, so, basically, that's like the motivation." Kevin, a white sixteen-year-old in the north court, recounts how he got five days in custody for receiving a five-day school suspension for having a lighter on school grounds, because it was his responsibility to know the school rules.

KEVIN: I had a lighter at school and then, um, I was just playing with it . . .
    And, I guess one of the security guards saw it. And then, cause I guess

it's so bad to have a lighter that you're suspected [for] . . . smoking, like cigarettes or something . . .

LESLIE: When you told them [the drug court] the reason . . . why you're suspended, what did they say?

KEVIN: They were just like, "That's your fault. If it's school policy, then we can't do nothin' about it."

The staff places the locus of responsibility completely on youths' shoulders for a variety of behaviors. If the youths do well, then the staff rewards their behavior with incentives. If they fail, then it is based on their wrong choices and it is their fault.

Alicia, the fifteen-year-old Latina discussed earlier, adds a more nuanced perspective to the staff's decision-making process. She says the staff looks at all the possible reasons behind her behavior to figure out a way to motivate her to do better. She explains:

> I've had a lot of chances in drug court. . . . They give you a lot of breaks. . . . They really look at . . . "is she doing it on purpose, is she doing it to get back at something?" They look at "Is she doing it because she doesn't care what happens to her?" . . . Julie told me, "I don't think you deserve [drug dorm]. I don't think you deserve Project Arise. So, I'm just going to give you a couple days [in juvenile hall], because I know you can stop. You've done it before." That's true. That's why I'm stopping [using drugs]. I'm going to have to do it sooner or later.

Alicia understands that the staff's emphasis on individual accountability should translate eventually into her making better decisions. But what appears to motivate her to stop using drugs is not the incentives for good behavior or the threat of juvenile hall and other normal remedies for noncompliant behavior. Rather, her motivation comes from the chances she gets and Julie's words that "I know you can stop."[8]

Others echo Alicia's sense of the individualized approach to each youth's cases. The youths I interviewed did not interpret the different staff responses among youths as unjust or unfair. They attributed those differences to the particularities of each youth's case. Greg, a biracial seventeen-year-old in the east court, described a situation in which both he and another youth had similar problematic drug tests: "He didn't get locked up for it, and I think if that would've happened to me, I would have probably got locked up . . . because of what, h-how I got dilutes [ambiguous test results] in the past." So the staff's debate about the deleterious effects of inconsistency in its use of normal remedies among the youths appears to be unfounded.[9]

The youths do appear to understand the court's philosophy of individual accountability, acknowledging that it is their actions that dictate the staff's decisions and that they must accept whatever punishment the staff decides. However, the ways in which the youths views the staff's practical application of that message become a bit more muddled. For example, many youths saw the staff's responses as punitive, not therapeutic. George, a white sixteen-year-old in the east court, sees the court as almost like a boot camp: "I don't really feel like they're trying to teach us anything. They're just basically trying to whip us into shape. . . . I just see it as a program where it's like, 'this is your last chance. You smoke, you're locked up.'" Even the youths who wanted to see the therapeutic side of drug court had some confusion about the actual program. Luke, a white sixteen-year-old in the east court, characterizes the court's treatment approach as follows: "I thought it [drug court] was going to be like everybody sat around and just talked like a therapy kind of a thing, but you just go there, and they check up on you and let you know how many clean days you have." Perhaps James, a seventeen-year-old Latino in the south court, sums it up best when he says, "It's good that they focus on the good things, you know, but, like, they emphasize a lot on the bad things. . . . They're trying to catch you." James does not elaborate as to the underlying therapeutic purposes of catching youths; rather, he suggests the court is simply monitoring their behaviors.

Sometimes staff members compromise the drug court's accountability message by holding a youth responsible for situations in which they are also complicit. For example, Austin, a sixteen-year-old Latino in the north court, describes how staff put him on home supervision when it couldn't find him to do a drug test at school. Part of the mix-up was that the staff did not remember he had changed schools for the summer. He says,

> I was tripping out, 'cause when the summer started they didn't test me for like over a month . . . my PO [probation officer] is calling over here [at home], and I wasn't even here. I was at summer school. And, um, they told me, "Where you been at?" And I'm like, "Well, I been in school." [They said] "You should—you're supposed to be responsible." . . . I told them I gonna be at school. I mean, they knew about it. They knew everything. They had a paper, everything, and they're all blaming me. I, like, uh—I just left it like that. I didn't say nothing.

Austin could have been more insistent about clarifying his noncompliance status with the staff, since he states that it did know about his new school. Technically, he does not need to be on home supervision, because it was the staff's responsibility to go the right place to drug test him. But he says nothing, leaving the door open for subsequent staff discussions about his lack of responsibility for not testing.

Ignacio, a seventeen-year-old Latino in the south court, describes a similar situation in which the staff blamed him for getting suspended in school after allegedly throwing a spit wad at his teacher. He claims it was his friend who did it:

IGNACIO: They blamed it on me, and the teacher said basically I hit him [with the spit wad]. . . . I talked to my PO [probation officer]. I told her right away, and then, um, she made a deal. Like, I have to do community service. I have to go to school. I have to write him a letter . . .

LESLIE: Okay. Did you feel like that was a fair response?

IGNACIO: Yeah, 'cause I told myself I don't want to get locked up again or, like, get suspended and stuff.

LESLIE: So, even though you didn't do it, you still wrote the letter and all that stuff?

IGNACIO: Yeah.

Both Austin's and Ignacio's situations indicate a flaw in the accountability model: for whatever reasons, youths will sometimes not clear up or admit to noncompliant actions, exposing them to being held accountable by staff without cause.[10]

In addition, the staff's constant monitoring and normal remedies can sometimes make youths want to be noncompliant. Sean, a white seventeen-year-old in the south court, states,

It could help you, like, if you, if you follow the program, and they, they keep you clean, 'cause they, you know, you'll get a test the next day, so that'll really help you. . . . They even want you [to] go get a job, get your education. So they, they kinda push you to good . . . they also got good advice all the time. But, on the other hand, just, there's so much stuff that you have to do for them, like get a job and all that, it's just, it's sometimes you get frustrated and want to relapse.

Rita, a white fifteen-year-old in the north court, agrees with Sean. While she does state that drug court is a good program, she also says the normal remedies are having the opposite effect in more ways than simply making her want to use drugs. She explains,

It's too hard, you get locked up for everything, and that's stupid. Let's get locked up for this long and come out and do the same shit, and then get locked up again. . . . For me, getting locked up makes me want to use. So, the more they lock me up, the more I'm going to probably use, because that makes me want to. It's not helping us, it's just making shit worse. . . . Locking you in a cell doesn't do nothing. . . . It makes it very unhealthy in there, it causes depression, doesn't help nothing . . . just locked in a little cage and they feed you disgusting food. It's so sad, because I know when I was in there, I was really depressed. I wanted to seriously hurt myself.

Sean and Rita reveal the interactive nature of youth accountability in two
ways. According to Sean, the youth could actually crumble under the weight
of the staff's expectations for him to "do good." Rita suggests that staff
responses to youth noncompliance affect her future choices to be accountable or not. She also notes the other negative side effects of locking youths
up: it leads to making them feel worse, physically and mentally, which in
Rita's case could drive her back to drug use.

Youths also recognize the limits to the staff's approach of using noncompliant moments to instill accountability in them—namely, because the
staff had only a partial understanding of their character. Hector, a fifteen-
year-old Latino in the east court, said, "I think the staff [members] are like
most people. They judge me by my cover. They judge me by my record."
Dominic, a fifteen-year-old Latino in the north court, also noted that the
court staff saw only one side of him: "They just know what you do for treatment and school and that's it. . . . They don't know who you are pretty much
and where you're coming from, what you've been through. . . . They don't
know what's going on in your house or anything like that. They just know
you from treatment and coming to court." These comments further underscore
how the staff's sense of a youth's character is tied more to his interactions in
drug court than to the youth himself.

On a related note, some youths described how their individual accountability is shaped by staff's comparisons of them to other youths. Henry, a
white seventeen-year-old in the east court, said, "They see me just like they
see every other kid: 'This is a kid who's got a problem with drugs. . . . He
does way too many drugs, and we need to fix that before he hurts himself or
others.'" Dominic described how this comparison to other youths might
have hurt his case when he tested positive for marijuana. He says he didn't
smoke but was just in a car with friends who were smoking. He explains why
the staff did not believe him: "They locked me up, and I tried to explain to
them. . . . [I was locked up] just five days, but like they can't understand.
I guess 'cause they have a lot of liars." While he knows he isn't guilty in this
instance, he also recognizes that staff's views of his accountability are tied to
other youths' performance, many of whom are "liars."

The extent of drug court monitoring sometimes seems overreaching to the
youths, particularly when not related to drug use. Greg, a biracial seventeen-
year-old in the east court, describes his feeling about a recent court decision
that required him to attend anger management classes after getting into a fight
with his stepdad at the court: "I think that the smoking . . . is somewhat relevant, but I don't think the anger management is. I mean, I personally don't
think that I need to take anger management, but the judge thought it was
necessary in the situation." In perhaps an extreme example, James, who
earlier noted the court's emphasis on "catching" youth, describes a recent

situation where his parents told the staff that he was out past curfew. He states he left because of their fighting and his desire to protect his little brother from the discord:

JAMES: They would get really mad, like, over each other. And they [the staff] would be like, "Hi, how's James doing?" [My parents would say] "Well, he comes home pretty late." I don't know. Like, the whole thing that would, like, if the problem with them wasn't going on, they wouldn't like, not ratted me out, but just let them know the truth . . . that affected me a lot. . . . I wouldn't want to be at home, 'cause of whatever drama was happening with them, and I would take out my little brother . . . And, like, they would tell that to them, like, "Yeah, James would leave at 3 A.M., and, like, not come back 'til the next morning." . . . And then I had to go to court, and there's no way I could explain anything.

LESLIE: What happened in court? . . .

JAMES: Um, they gave me . . . a warning. They wanted to lock me up for three days, and I was just like, "You know what? This isn't gonna work, because you're not gonna lock me up over this. It's pathetic. Like, if you were gonna do it, like I'm gonna bounce right now." I told 'em, "You are not gonna lock me up for trying to take out my little brother, of a house, like he could be in danger." It's just bullshit . . . It worked out . . . I just felt like, they're not, they weren't pretty understanding, you know? I expected them to, like, I thought they were gonna be like, "Yeah, we support you, and it's fine that you had to get out and get some air." . . . Um, they were, like, really, they weren't human about it.

While James managed to convince the staff not to hold him accountable for this curfew violation, he came away from that interaction with a view of the staff as not being "understanding" or "human." One can imagine how feeling invalidated might affect his subsequent motivation to adhere to the court's accountability message.

This brief exploration of youth perspectives suggests a more complicated picture of accountability in the juvenile drug court. The youths realize that they set their own paths. At the same time, they suggest that there is a lot of noise in the court's accountability message. For example, while some youths might understand the court's punishments as helping them face their drug problems, others might not see the connection. Youths like Rita or Sean might react to the court's normal remedies in completely opposite ways to their desired effect, such as feeling the urge to use drugs after being locked up for their last positive drug test result. Other youths might begin to feel more alienated or disconnected from the court if they feel the staff is meddling too much in their lives or making decisions without truly knowing them. All of these issues are not helped by the youths' sense that the court is not focused on treatment as much as locking them up for any little thing. It begs the question: How much treatment is happening if the youths view the court intervention as "catching them" in bad behavior?

CONCLUSION

Every facet of youths' performance in the drug court is subjected to staff scrutiny. In team meetings, staff negotiates the meaning of troublesome behaviors based on a set of interpretive practices to decide how to respond in nonstandardized ways. In contrast to the literature on drug courts that takes offender noncompliance at face value, the practical orientation of the staff's work shapes the definitional process of compliance. The array of staff interpretive practices employed in the team meetings in the juvenile drug court reveals a more expansive set of negotiation tools geared toward answering the following questions: what did this youth do now? How bad is it? How do we want to respond? The first two questions focus on the extent of the youth's accountability—in the sense of adhering to the drug court's expectations and showing willingness to take responsibility for noncompliance. The last question involves the staff's ability to hold the youth accountable for noncompliance.

The weekly decisions affect youths' outcomes because they build up staff notions of workability. While the magnitude of each weekly decision is not large, the drug court staff's decisions collectively build upon one another to craft a view of the youths as being a drug addict, a gang member, or just a delinquent. How those workability paths evolve is unpredictable. The staff's use of interpretive practices for each specific weekly assessment is variable and sometimes highly contested. Even the most mundane discussions involve some kind of negotiation, if only for the staff to agree upon which interpretive practice to use to describe the situation. When an approach is not widely accepted, the dance of negotiating noncompliance takes a different turn. As demonstrated in the case with Victor, the team resorts to the traditional fault lines of adversarial justice.[11] In comparison, no one contests the view that Vito, who allegedly sold drugs in a detox program, was irresponsible. Yet, had someone raised more of an objection to the interpretive practices used in his case, perhaps his outcome would have been different.

Finally, while therapeutic jurisprudence is seen as a new form of justice, it involves similar decision-making processes to traditional juvenile court, which Bortner characterizes as a "matrix of fact, experience, bias, professional ideology, personal preference and intuitive knowledge" (1982, 101). Even with the more detailed accounts of youth behavior, the staff's decision-making process is not necessarily more informed than in traditional courts. In fact, one could imagine it is like a sieve: what filters down into the decision-making process is completely dependent upon the staff's sense of its importance, its continued persistence about the information over time, and the other staff's views of the information.

In this sense, the juvenile drug court follows the garbage-can decision-making model (Cohen, March, and Olsen 1972). Cohen et al. argue that this kind of decision making develops in "organized anarchies," such as universities or public institutions that operate "on the basis of a variety of inconsistent and ill-defined preferences" and have unclear technologies upon which to base those preferences. The decision makers dump a lot of problems into the garbage can of "choice opportunities," or what Mohr (1976) describes as organizational "behavior that can be called a decision" within the context of available resources and "energy load," or how much time staff is willing to devote to try to solve the problem. In the juvenile drug court, the staff seems to dump many issues (e.g., behavior at school, home, and treatment; drug test results; court appearances) in the choice opportunities of weekly decisions in assessing compliance.

The increased attention enables the staff to find out more ways in which the youths are noncompliant. So, while the drug courts might maintain that this increased detection is the strength of the program, since it provides more opportunities to hold youths accountable, the accumulation of noncompliant events could build up a more negative view of the youths as unworkable or troublesome. Bosk sees this phenomenon among surgeons in medical hospitals. He describes it as the "deviance amplifying effect of monitoring: the actual rate of unacceptable practice may not increase, but the number of discovered instances may rise" (2003, 98). Turner and Petersilia (1992) also found that increased attention in an intensive probation supervision program led to higher rates of probation violations compared to traditional probation supervision programs.

The ultimate paradox lies in the realization that the more staff knows and the more it finds out, the less it is able to do anything about it. The staff simply cannot respond to all the violations it detects, let alone the ones that go undetected, given its limited time and resources to issue normal remedies for every missed period in school, diluted drug test, or drug treatment counseling session. Instead of slipping through the cracks because no one is paying attention, the youths in the juvenile drug court can fly under the staff's radar, which is overloaded with information about all the ways that the youths are noncompliant.

CHAPTER 5

Social Construction of
Drug Test Results

WHILE THE DRUG COURT staff spends a significant amount of time evaluating youth actions in the school, home, and drug treatment programs, drug testing remains the staff's principal measuring stick of noncompliance and accountability. This reliance on drug tests reflects a long-standing practice in the justice system of monitoring defendants' drug use through random drug testing. In this light, drug tests can be seen as a contemporary intersection of science and law. A positive drug test result "proves" peoples' guilt or criminality because they were supposed to abstain from any drug use as part of their court obligations. Courts no longer need defendants to attest to their compliance; rather, they can determine compliance biologically through urine, sweat, or hair. Drug tests, in short, enable courts to see what could not be seen previously, extending the court's surveillance inside the body and for more periods of time.

In addition to being considered the objective measure of the defendant's drug use, drug testing offers a standardized way to measure the defendants' progress in drug treatment programs. It is often difficult to measure the effectiveness of legally mandated drug treatment that is varied in intensive and program modality.[1] Drug testing then becomes more than simply an intersection of science and law; it can be seen as representing the intersection of science, therapy, and the law. It provides the scientific proxy, or bridge, that helps the drug court staff to evaluate peoples' efforts in drug treatment programs and to determine whether they are legally in compliance.

The staff's understanding of a youth's drug test results involves much more than laboratory results. Not all positive test results are seen by staff as proof that a youth is using, nor are all negative results understood as evidence of not using. Varying staff interpretations subsequently affect how they respond to test results. Figure 5.1 charts test results possibilities, staff interpretations of results, and staff responses to interpretations.

The drug court staff moves from the left to the right side of the chart, using a specific set of interpretive practices to attribute meaning to drug test

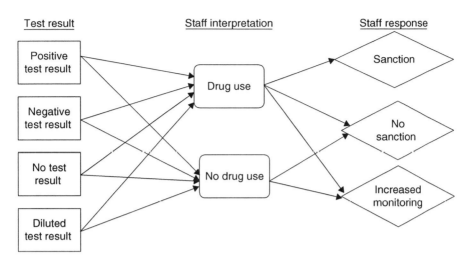

5.1. Staff uses of drug test results

results. The interpretive work includes a reflexive component. The staff's negotiations of each drug test result are based on a set of interpretive practices, and those negotiations simultaneously serve to redefine, reinforce, and reshape staff's understandings of those practices. Moreover, the staff may use the interpretive practices discussed in the previous chapter to understand the drug test results.

This social process to understanding drug test results then involves its own set of everyday work issues that construct the drug test's potential to monitor peoples' drug use. Michael Lynch's (1985) research about a brain science laboratory similarly explores the "social accomplishment of natural scientific order," in which the meaning of "scientific fact" is situated within the scientists' talk and work. Lynch analyzes this knowledge production process as "achieved agreements," which he defines as "something which speakers make happen on occasions of interaction . . . where interactants are oriented to 'facts' which have yet to be determined, or procedures which are in the course of being designed. In such situations, agreement has a different consequentiality, as it becomes synonymous with collaboration on 'fact' or 'procedure' at the scene of an inquiry" (189, 190). In this study, the juvenile drug court staff works to achieve agreement about drug test results, or "facts," as informed by their everyday interpretive practices. These issues are important to explore, given the following paradox: while practitioners recognize that drug testing is frequently problematic, they often base their decisions on the test under the premise that it is the only objective way to determine drug use.

The juvenile drug court staff uses drug tests to monitor the following drugs: marijuana, cocaine, opiates (e.g., heroin), amphetamines (e.g., speed), methamphetamine, and alcohol. The most common administered drug tests are done through urinalysis. One kind of urinalysis test is the presumptive test, otherwise known as the immunoassay test, where a treated strip of paper is dipped into urine and provides instantaneous results. If the test result is negative, the staff does not pursue further testing. If the result is positive, the staff sends the sample to the laboratory for a more scientifically rigorous test called the gas chromatography/mass spectrometry (GC/MS). Another form of testing is a skin patch that measures drug use through the person's sweat. After the person wears the patch for a week, the staff removes it and sends it to the laboratory.

Each of these tests has advantages and disadvantages in helping staff to measure drug use and, by extension, noncompliance. The urinalysis test is the most affordable and commonly used test in the court. However, it has its drawbacks, both in the presumptive and GC/MS forms. The main flaw in urinalysis testing is its time sensitivity in detecting drug use. Methamphetamine and alcohol are difficult to catch because their traces in the urine disappear between twenty-four and forty-eight hours after use. As Narcisco, a seventeen-year-old Latino in the south court, explains, "If you drink today and get tested tomorrow, you can still come out clean." Marijuana, on the other hand, stays in one's system for up to ten days. A second issue arises if the urine is too diluted to have a confirmed test. Diluted samples do not have enough creatinine to measure use.

The advantage to the presumptive test is its immediate results, which allow staff to obtain instant snapshots of youths' compliance. The staff often orders a presumptive test to tip the scales of issuing a normal remedy or not. However, the presumptive test is not completely accurate, as it only indicates some presence of a certain drug in the urine. If the presumptive test result is positive, the staff asks the youth if he or she used drugs. If the youth admits to drug use, the staff issues an immediate but often lesser sanction (three days in custody), than if the youth denies drug use and the laboratory report comes back with a positive result (five days in custody). The youths' admissions are similar to plea bargains. Some youths admit to the test result, even if they did not use drugs, to get a more lenient normal remedy.

The final test, the patch, is the most sophisticated form of testing for court. It is a continuous measure of drug use, eliminating the urinalysis's time-sensitive issue in detecting drug use.[2] The patch also solves the gender staffing problem in urinalysis testing where only female staff can observe the girls testing and only male staff can observe the boys testing. The main drawback of the patch is its long turnaround time. After being on a youth's skin for at least a week, the patch takes an additional two weeks to be analyzed by the laboratory. So, any detected drug use occurred at least two weeks before the staff finds out. As a result, the staff is unable to respond immediately, which the drug court model reportedly claims to do. Judge Hooper referred to this delayed response as "rubbing a dog's nose in the dirt long after he peed there."

Perhaps the main issue with all of the tests is that some youths try to beat them. The youths I interviewed shared different techniques they had tried: taking niacin (vitamin B3) pills, drinking vinegar, and submitting other peoples' urine using equipment like the Whizzinator. Dominic, a fifteen-year-old Latino in the north court, described another common technique: avoiding staff. "You can dodge them easy . . . if you know you're dirty . . . you don't go to school . . . you don't go to your program. You just call it in . . . you're sick or something." Another common technique is to dilute the urine sample. Rebecca, a white seventeen-year-old in the north court, says, "I would like drink a whole bunch of water and like dilute the test . . . dilute to me is better than dirty, because they couldn't prove that I was dirty. "Finally, youths would also time or change their drug use. Consider this interview excerpt with George, a white sixteen-year-old in the east court:

LESLIE: Have you started . . . doing other things like drinking or other types of drugs?

GEORGE: Um, actually, yeah. It made me start drinking.

LESLIE: So have you drank before or . . . ?

GEORGE: Yeah a little bit, not really those, not really my thing, but—

LESLIE: So pot was mainly your thing?

GEORGE: Yeah.

LESLIE: But now they're testing for it, so—

GEORGE: So, yeah. It's the only thing, pretty much, you can get away with.

At the same time, the youths also recognized that they could not really beat the tests. While he tried to avoid testing, Dominic noted that the staff eventually caught up to him. He said, "It ain't worth it, though, 'cause you're in a lot of trouble." Moreover, there was no way that the youths could contest the positive results. James, a seventeen-year-old Latino in the south court, describes a recent incident where he tested positive even though he didn't use: "I tried to fight every way. Like, once you go to court and they tell you you're dirty, you're gonna get locked up. There's not really much to fight it . . . , I tried to call me [sic] real attorney, and, like, he was like, 'There's nothing I can do, we can't just schedule another testing, unless you wanna pay for, like, another testing, but that's after you get out.' " He ended up spending two weeks in juvenile hall waiting to get screened for a twenty-one-day detox program; after the staff found out that the program had a two-month waiting list, it let him out of custody. Greg, a biracial seventeen-year-old in the east court, described a similar example of getting locked up for diluted drug test results, even though he didn't use. He says:

> I've been locked up twice for diluted tests. . . . [I] saw a doctor to see if it was, someone said that it's a form of diabetes, where your urine's always diluted. . . . The reason I was getting them was 'cause I wasn't eating a lot of food during the day, because at my school, the school lunches, I just didn't like eating those lunches. And so I wouldn't eat, and I'd drink, like, two bottles of water, and when I'd get tested it was diluted. And if you eat more food, and drink the same amount of water, then it's not diluted.

Greg's parents ended up taking him to a doctor to explain why he kept getting diluted tests. Even though he appeared to be getting dilutes because he was not eating enough solid foods to absorb the amount of fluids he drank, the staff still sent him to juvenile hall. As James's and Greg's experiences show, the staff is unlikely to change course once they believe the student has used.

Because the staff knows that youths try to beat the drug tests, it often faces the dilemma of sorting "fact" from "fiction" in analyzing drug test results. The staff could assume a youth has used drugs if the participant receives a positive or diluted test result, avoids the test, or, depending on the drug, receives a negative test result, but after the time frame in which drug use can be detected (e.g., alcohol or methamphetamine). How the staff understands and responds to results shapes the meaning of those results. In other words, it uses interpretive practices to situate a specific drug test result within one of four normal case categories to make decisions about suitable sanctions, or normal remedies, for those test results.[3]

INTERPRETIVE PRACTICES

Staff uses several interpretive practices to identify the meaning of drug test results. This section outlines three: patterns of drug use and testing, types of drug users, and staff competency in administering drug tests. The first interpretive practice is particularized to an individual youth's case history, while the other two are more generalized, based on the staff's experiences in working with many youths over time in the court.

Typical Patterns of Drug Use and Testing

Staff often situates a drug test result within a pattern of drug use for a particular youth. The following excerpt demonstrates how the staff utilizes its knowledge of a specific youth's drug use patterns to explain seemingly nonsensical results. The staff discusses how to handle conflicting drug test results from a sweat patch and urinalysis tests for Julio, a seventeen-year-old Latino in the south court:

JULIE (PROBATION OFFICER): Julio does not demonstrate signs or symptoms of meth[amphetamine] use.

CHARLIE (PUBLIC DEFENDER): He denies.

JULIE: His brother and another one who was arrested did get high. . . . The test showed only a small amount of the drug, at sixty-four nanograms per milligram . . .

RAUL (DRUG COUNSELOR): I agree with Julie. Between the time I took the patch off, I tested him three times. All three [urinalysis tests] are negative. I talk to him a lot . . . the symptoms of drug use are not there . . .

JACK (DISTRICT ATTORNEY): There is evidence going both ways, and there is reasonable doubt here . . .

RAUL: This kid, if he used, he would be bouncing off the walls.

Staff normally does not question a positive sweat patch result from a laboratory report, even if the urinalysis test result is negative, because staff considers the sweat patch to be a more rigorous form of drug test. But in this instance, Julie and Raul believe Julio is not lying about the positive sweat patch, as informed by their sense that he usually uses excessive amounts of drugs, to the point of bouncing off the walls. By situating the specific test within a broader pattern of the youth's drug use and other drug tests, the staff comes to interpret this positive test result as false and does not issue a normal remedy.

The staff also looks at the youth's patterns of drug testing, not just drug use. Because the staff members administer between two to three drug tests a week for each youth, they often say they can tell if the youth is clean or not by the way he tests. In the next example, the north court staff talks about a recent positive test from Nelson, a sixteen-year-old Latino, who appeared dirty based on the way he tested:

SAMUELS (JUDGE): Poor Nelson. So this was Monday?

GEORGE (DRUG COUNSELOR): He only gave a quarter inch of urine.

ALLEN (PROBATION OFFICER): Yeah, just enough to test. . . . Bill [drug counselor] was concerned he gave just the bare minimum—usually he has no problems testing. . . . He denied using. This is the second time now in two weeks . . . he had been straight up before. I think Nelson must have used on Saturday if he was positive on Monday but clean on Tuesday . . .

GEORGE: He was really deceptive about this. I was there for one hour, and he peed less than an eighth of an inch. I gave him every opportunity to tell. He didn't buy it. He flat out lied.

While Nelson did test positive on Monday, he tested clean on Tuesday. However, the staff does not view those different results as a discrepancy because, as Allen notes, if Nelson used methamphetamine on Saturday, he would have been clean by Tuesday. The staff appears to focus on the suspicious way Nelson tested on Monday to conclude that the positive test is valid. Nelson gave only the bare minimum of urine to be tested (between an eighth and a quarter inch). In the past, he has had no problems submitting a full urine sample, as Bill, his primary drug counselor notes. So, while Nelson insists that he did not use drugs, the staff views his Monday test as positive and puts him in custody for five days.

Type of Drug User

Staff members rely on their general sense about different types of drug users to provide context for a specific drug test result. The next example shows how the judge's view of methamphetamine users influences his interpretation of Molly's recent claim to be unable to provide a urine sample for a drug test. The court allows forty-five minutes for the youth to provide a sample, after which time the youth is classified as having a "failure to test," which staff treats like a positive test result. After stalling for almost an hour, Molly, a white sixteen-year-old in the east court, ultimately did provide a sample, which turned out to be positive for methamphetamine:

SARAH (PROBATION OFFICER): Last week she was failing to test. You [Judge Hooper] had ordered her to stay and test, but she had trouble producing [a sample]. She finally did fifteen minutes to 5 P.M., after court was already dismissed. . . . One of the problems was that the water fountain broke . . .

JACK (DISTRICT ATTORNEY): She could have gone to the water fountain upstairs.

SARAH: The youths can't go up there unescorted.

HOOPER (JUDGE): Meth[amphetamine] people all seem to fall in the same category, lie, lie, lie and cry, cry, cry. It's the same thing, every one.

JILL (DRUG COUNSELOR): Molly also left the house and violated home sup[ervision] . . .

CHARLIE (PUBLIC DEFENDER): I told her [Molly], "it looks like you're dirty."

SARAH [TO HOOPER]: I told her [Molly], Your Honor, "I work late every night." At that point, she tested.

The excerpt reveals how the staff's general perception of methamphetamine users shaped its interpretations of Molly's inability to test. Hooper uses his knowledge of methamphetamine users as liars to shoot down any other possible explanations, like the broken water fountain. The other staff largely falls into line with the judge, citing additional areas of noncompliance and opinions of how suspicious Molly's behavior toward the test appeared. The excerpt also highlights the staff's assumption that if the youths have problems with testing, they probably are using drugs.[4]

Similarly, the east court staff responds to Morgan's positive drug test with more intensity because it suspects this white fifteen-year-old is an IV drug user. Because it is rare to see an IV drug user in the court, the staff considers Morgan's test result to be a serious problem:

CHARLIE (PUBLIC DEFENDER): He's got a positive test last week.

JUDGE HAUSER: Oh.

BILL (DRUG COUNSELOR): It was really high.

AMY (DRUG COUNSELOR): It was 78,000 . . .

BILL: It could be IV use.

CHARLIE: I don't think it was IV.

BILL: He would have had to smoke a lot to get that high of a level.

CHARLIE: I don't think so, because the dad is really strict.

HAUSER (JOKING): The dad is strict about the type of drug his son uses.

AMY: The levels are really high.

HAUSER: I don't know if I ever have seen it this high in regular delinquency court, where I have seen levels usually in the forties . . .

CHARLIE: He's been here and cooperates with us and has no indication of being high . . .

JULIE (PROBATION OFFICER): This kid is probably a good candidate for a [sweat] patch.

HAUSER: How much [custody] time if he admits?

CHARLIE: Well, he didn't admit.

JACK (DISTRICT ATTORNEY): Five days.

HAUSER: Yeah.

JACK: And then the patch.

Charlie refutes Bill's claim that Morgan was using drugs intravenously, depicting the youth's character as being cooperative and coming from a good family with strict parents. But Amy and the judge both cite the high levels of drugs in the urine sample to bolster Bill's claim that Morgan is an IV drug user, and that his drug problems are more severe than the typical youth. Julie uses the drug test result as a therapeutic tool, suggesting a more intensive form of drug testing, the patch. This exchange demonstrates how the staff's supervision practices can further propel its view of a youth's noncompliance. That is, a problematic test result can inspire more rigorous testing, which can lead to more results, which can be positive. The staff decides to put him into juvenile hall for five days because he did not admit to the drug use.

One final note about this interpretive practice: while it appears to evolve mainly from the staff's interactions with the youths, it also is shaped by the court's drug testing practices. Since staff does not test often enough to catch alcohol or methamphetamine use, it is easier for youths who use those two drugs to lie versus those who use marijuana, which lasts in system much longer.

In addition, the level of drugs in Morgan's test result is seen as exceptional only as compared to those of other youths' tests. While this interpretive practice involves the actions of the staff, as drug testers, and the youth, as drug test takers, the staff only invokes the practice to explain the *youths'* actions, not its own limitations in testing frequency.

Staff's Competencies

The staff's perspective on drug testing can vary, depending on how it views the competency of the person administering the tests. Court-based staff members (e.g., attorneys, judges) mention inconsistency among field-based staff (e.g., probation officers, drug counselors) in performing drug tests. For example, after I asked the public defender when he would challenge drug test results, he responded, "It all depends . . . Who took the sample? How was it collected? If I know this guy's sloppy in the collection—." When I asked how he knew if staff was "sloppy," he said youth participants have told him, and added, "I've gone in several times [to the court bathroom where the testing is done], and I've seen the way the guys write on the youths' [lab sheets] for testing. It's not supposed to be there. You gotta watch." He suggests that not all staff members follow the drug testing protocol, since they are filling out the drug testing paperwork instead of observing youths while they submit urine samples.[5]

In contrast, the drug counselors and probation officers often said that they can tell, independent of a drug test, when youths are using drugs. This knowledge is based on their experience in working with youths. Peter, a drug counselor, articulates this notion in an interview, "If my kids are doing drugs, there are a thousand other signs that are going to point to that before they get a positive test. . . . They're not going to school. They're skipping treatment. . . . They're avoiding me. They have a reason to miss court two weeks in a row. . . . They're more irritable to see me. They're more paranoid. Their behavior is slightly different than normal." Peter articulates a commonly shared notion among the staff that the drug test result is not the only factor in making a decision about youths' drug use. Rather, the staff situates the drug test result within a greater context of locally defined notions of compliance based on the youths' attitude and behavior in school, treatment, and court. George, another drug counselor, states it a slightly different way: "Just how they hold themselves and just don't look you in the eye and when you ask them specific questions, they're evasive with their answers. It's a feeling, too. . . . Before I worked here, I worked with another company where I . . . did fifty tests a week, not fifty people, but fifty different tests a week. So, I've got to the point where I test a lot, and while I'm testing I'm always questioning them." George is not as concerned as Charlie with the preciseness of the collection process. Instead, George bases his interpretations about clients' drug use on his experience and the "normal" behavior that clients exhibit during drug testing. All of these different views toward drug tests emanate from the everyday work processes and concerns of the staff.

NORMAL CASE CATEGORIES
OF DRUG TEST RESULTS

Staff often raises issues about drug test results either to confirm or question the test result's validity. One cannot assume a negative drug test result proves no drug use that justifies no sanction, or that a positive test result indicates recent drug use that merits a normal remedy. The major task in staff discussions involves using interpretive practices to place the test result within a particular normal case category, or "organizationally sanctioned devices for assessing 'what is going on'" (Emerson 1992, 19). Four normal case categories for questionable drug test results in the court are false positive, false negative, ambiguous results, and no results. These categories represent knowledge gleaned from the routine processing of several tests at once. This knowledge also includes the staff's sense of how other members might interpret and respond to certain results.

False Positives

Staff sometimes determines that a positive test result is a false positive, suggesting that a youth did not really use drugs, or that it is not new use and thus does not merit any court sanction. Several situations fall into this normal case category. First, the staff's knowledge about different types of drug tests could lead it to treat a positive result as false. For example, presumptive test results are merely suggestive of drug use and are not laboratory-confirmed GC/MS results. They are technically not proven assertions of drug use, yet some staff members view presumptive tests as truth. As a result, staff often disagrees as to what the presumptive test results indicate and how to respond to them.

In the following example, Raul, a drug counselor, comes into the courtroom with a questionable presumptive test result for Brent, a white fifteen-year-old in the east court.

BILL (DRUG COUNSELOR) [LOOKING AT THE PRESUMPTIVE TEST RESULTS]: We will have a fight on this one because there is a thin line. . . .
SARAH (PROBATION OFFICER): Your Honor, the presumpt is a possible positive.
CHARLIE (PUBLIC DEFENDER) [INCREDULOUSLY]: How is it possibly positive?
SARAH: Because there is a fine line.
CHARLIE: The rule is, a line is, however faint, means a negative test.
BILL: The test will probably come back positive.
HOOPER (JUDGE): If there is a line, send it out [to the laboratory].

Staff members challenge each others' competencies to negotiate the meaning of this presumptive test result. Bill uses his familiarity with drug test results to suggest Brent is using drugs. However, Charlie, the public defender, and Hooper, the judge, employ legal terms to suggest this result cannot be accepted as positive. This disagreement highlights the greater tension about whether to respond legally to the test or to respond therapeutically to the youth participant. Legal staff sees presumptive test results as not legally binding, whereas the treatment staff looks to respond as soon as possible to a youth's drug use, to teach him to take accountability for his actions. The therapeutic intention would be that the next time Brent considers using drugs, he may think of this instance where staff immediately punished him with a sanction for his drug use and decide it is not worth it to use drugs again.

Staff also views a positive test result as false if the levels of the drug in the urine sample are below the legally defined limit. In the following example, the east court discusses Perry's recent positive drug test result for marijuana. The level is four points below the legally defined cutoff of twenty nanograms.

HOOPER (JUDGE): Um, positive, huh?

SARAH (PROBATION OFFICER): Yeah.

CHARLIE (PUBLIC DEFENDER): Well, I believe the cutoff mark was . . . twenty. This is sixteen.

BILL (DRUG COUNSELOR): It was for THC [marijuana].

JACK (DISTRICT ATTORNEY): Anyone have an argument for the positive test?

CHARLIE: The cutoff is twenty . . .

JACK: We have this cutoff because of the error of margin.

HOOPER: I'm not disagreeing with you.

CHARLIE: The way to handle this one is to ask him.

[*Later in the discussion.*]

CHARLIE: I'll talk to him, but I will not trick him into admitting.

SARAH: It [the test] is showing some kind of use.

CHARLIE: Possibly, but it is not a valid test.

JILL (DRUG COUNSELOR): It does show some kind of use.

CHARLIE: If it was a valid test.

This excerpt demonstrates how drug test results intersect with science, law, and therapy. While everyone acknowledges that the drug levels in the urine are below the cutoff of the federal guidelines for a positive test, some staff members still view it as a positive test.[6] The judge, Sarah, and Jill all state that the test is positive and that Perry, a sixteen-year-old African American, was using. So even though it does not meet the legal standards, the test result serves as a therapeutic tool for Jill and Sarah. They can use it as a warning sign to pay more attention to Perry in the upcoming week. Charlie focuses instead on the legality of the drug test result that is "inadmissible." Like the presumptive tests, this test result could be considered legally a positive test if Perry admitted to using, which is why Charlie says he will "not trick" Perry into admitting. In the end, Perry doesn't show up for court and was later excused because of a separate medical issue.

Another false positive test result could stem from the court's own policy of administering several drug tests in a short time frame. Such frequent testing could lead to multiple positive test results for the same drug use. In the following example, the staff talks about Eddie, a sixteen-year-old Latino in the south court. The probation officer considers the positive results for Eddie's marijuana drug test as invalid, given the timeframe in which it was taken:

JULIE (PROBATION OFFICER): Eddie is a new kid, and he had a positive test . . . but he has diminished results, so that means it is not a new use . . .

HOOPER (JUDGE): The results are going down, up, or sideways?

JULIE: The ratio is 1.04, when you do the division, and not 1.50 [the court cutoff for new use].

Julie and Hooper recognize that the court's frequent testing could lead to two consecutive tests detecting the same instance of marijuana use. Staff uses two specific methods to determine new marijuana use. First, two positive marijuana drug tests are considered distinct uses if they are not taken within ten to fourteen days of each other, a timeframe that the court considers to be long enough for marijuana to clear out of the body. Second, if the two tests for marijuana do fall within that time frame, the most recent test result must have levels of tetrahydrocannabinol (THC) that are one and half times higher than those of the first test to be considered new use. While the science behind the drug test result is unquestioned, both the time frame and the ratio are indicative of the court's local interpretive practice imputing meaning on a drug test. For example, the staff often said that it could take longer than fourteen days for marijuana to clear out a person's system, depending on his age or body fat. Other courts use the ratio of one to one, versus one and a half to one. The staff ultimately decides against giving a normal remedy to Eddie.

Staff can also categorize a test result as a false positive after considering alternative and acceptable explanations that could have interfered with the test results. In the following example, the north court staff accepts what Rebecca, a white seventeen-year-old, says about her positive test result because she was taking painkillers after recently having surgery. The staff's response is largely situated within its favorable assessment about Rebecca's overall performance:

SAMUELS (JUDGE): Rebecca has 152 sober days, needs to bring in proof of attendance at four twelve-step meetings, and is doing well.

BILL (DRUG COUNSELOR): I'm not sure if she is going to bring in the meetings because she had a medical problem—a cyst on her ovaries—and has been given narcotic pain medication. She's bringing a note in to state that, so she'll test positive for opiates. It was all confirmed by the mom.

SAMUELS: That sounds pretty serious . . .

BILL: She tried to not take the pain medication, but then the pain was too much, so she did take it. Her parents were monitoring the medications. It was something like an emergency, where it almost was at the point of bursting.

SAMUELS: We should ask if she wants to go early and go home.

Technically, Rebecca could be seen as noncompliant because she should have gotten approval from the staff before taking the pain medication and she did not provide documentation for attending the twelve-step meetings. However, the staff accepts her excuses without any hesitation, considering how she is doing well in the program. Samuels notes her long period of sobriety, and Bill highlights her honesty about her illness and medication use with her parents and court staff. Furthermore, since the staff generally trusts Rebecca's parents, Bill's comments about her parents monitoring the medication support Rebecca's explanation of the positive opiate drug test result.[7] Finally, Bill highlights that Rebecca tried not to take the medication, implying that she is trying to maintain her sobriety by not taking any drugs whatsoever (as encouraged by twelve-step types of treatment programs). Rebecca avoids getting a normal remedy, and this test result reflexively influences the staff's sense of the interpretive practices. That is, the staff's favorable assessment of Rebecca is reinforced by how she tried to avoid taking the medication (type of drug use) and responded to the test result with honesty (general behavior).

False Negative

Conversely, even if a youth's drug test result is negative, the staff can still suspect drug use. The importance of organizational context is apparent here, as staff and youths both recognize the weaknesses in the court's testing system. Joe, a probation officer, says, "You don't get a lot of alcohol tests unless we go out on the weekend, or we've caught a few kids with alcohol. I think a lot of them are probably drinking on the weekends and that we are not knowing about [it]." Several youths agreed with that statement, telling me in their interviews that they used on the weekends or ended up switching from other drugs to alcohol. Hector, a fifteen-year-old Latino in the east court, describes this flaw and how it creates an overinflated view by staff of his sober time being four months, when in actuality it was only two months:

HECTOR: I drank because I just wanted to see what it felt like . . . I got tested the next day, but I came out clean.

LESLIE: Were you nervous?

HECTOR: Yeah, pretty nervous.

LESLIE: What about another time that that happened?

HECTOR: I got high off of meth on Friday, and I went into court on a Monday, and I thought that I was gonna come out dirty, but I didn't.

LESLIE: So . . . the time when you were four months clean [according to the court's records], was [this drug use] during that time, or was it after that time?

HECTOR: I would have to say it was during that time, so, basically, I wasn't exactly four months clean, but I was a couple of months clean.

With this knowledge, the staff can reinterpret past negative drug tests as positive. In this next example, Bobby, a white sixteen-year-old, has accumulated six months of sober time. However, after testing positive for alcohol, doubts arise among the north court staff as to whether Bobby actually was clean during that time:

CANDACE (BOBBY'S TREATMENT PROVIDER): He claims six months of sobriety before the positive test. He's either been using or he has been clever in how he was using.

BILL (DRUG COUNSELOR): It is a possibility, because it was a Monday morning test. . . . I suspect he used a couple times—testing negative, which is my fault because he had such a time clean—and Visions [a probation-run school] said he was never positive, so he was only being tested once a week the first month of drug court. I switched up after I heard problems. Then we got him on Monday.

In this instance, Bill backs up his professional opinion about Bobby doing well by saying the staff at Visions, the probation-run school that Bobby attends, also said "he was never [testing] positive." At the same time, Bill does not say Bobby is drug-free; he merely says that "he was testing negative." This excerpt also shows how the staff's views of drug test results are affected by the interpretive practice of the youths' general behavior. If the youths are doing well, none of the staff question the negative drug test results as suspicious. Some drug counselors like Bill may begin to test the youths less frequently. This, ironically, allows for some youths to hide their drug use more easily. The staff uses positive test result as grounds to reconsider treatment options for Bobby and adds weekly individual counseling sessions on top of his intensive outpatient treatment program.

The staff also discounts negative test results if a third party informs them that the youth is using drugs. In the following excerpt, staff thinks Tom, a sixteen-year-old Latino, is slipping, even with no positive test result. Staff bases this assessment on information gathered from Tom's mother, as well as his noncompliance in other areas:

PETER (DRUG COUNSELOR): Um, I'm a little concerned for Tom right now. He's doing well, but he needs just a few things to do to finish up at treatment, which he hasn't done. His mother said he admitted using to her, but if he didn't say anything to me and test positive, then I can't say anything, and also he's been testing clean. I just get the feeling—I don't know the word. He's slipping. I want the team to say something. . . .

JULIE (PROBATION OFFICER): How many unexcused absences from treatment does he have?

PETER: Two so far.

JULIE: Home sup[ervision] . . .

CHARLIE (PUBLIC DEFENDER): Test on a presumpt.

This excerpt shows how staff can interpret a negative drug test as not necessarily proof that a youth participant is clean, given interpretive clues from his performance in other areas. Peter, the drug counselor, says he is suspicious of Tom's negative drug test results, based on the mother's statement that Tom admitted using drugs. The other staff starts to look outside the drug test to other aspects of his behavior to inform the negative test results. Even though Peter starts the discussion by saying that Tom has almost completed treatment, Julie focuses on Tom's unexcused absences from treatment to support Peter's sense that he is slipping. As Peter stated earlier in his interview, this warning sign is more of an indication that Tom is using drugs than a positive drug test. As a result, the staff decides to put Tom on home supervision. Charlie, the public defender, also asks for an additional drug test, perhaps hoping to clarify this ambiguity and not put the youth on home supervision if the result is negative. At the same time, Charlie's request highlights another organizational response to false negatives, in that the youths are tested more often if the staff suspects they may be using. With each new test, the likelihood increases that they could get a positive result and a court sanction.

Diluted Tests

The situations discussed up until this point mainly have involved laboratory confirmed (GC/MS) drug test results. Staff must also discuss test results that are neither clearly positive nor negative. Staff relies on the same set of interpretive practices to attribute meaning to these test results. Perhaps the most common area of ambiguity is when the urinalysis test result cannot be verified because the sample is too diluted, meaning it does not have enough creatinine to test for drugs. Staff sees diluted test results as red flags that the youths could be using drugs and trying to avoid detection by flushing out their system with excessive amounts of fluids. When asked about this issue, Jack, the district attorney, says, "If they do a dilute . . . they intended to dilute the sample." Similarly, the drug counselors and probation officers generally believe that diluted tests are indications that the youths are using drugs. As Bill, a drug counselor, says, "In my mind, it is positive." Joe, a probation officer, says, "I think a diluted test is worse than a positive test because that kid purposely tried to tamper with the test and deceive the court." At the same time, the public defender may look for plausible explanations for why the test may be diluted, such as a youth drinking fluids to recover from an illness.

With these differing opinions, staff members often debate whether youths intentionally diluted the sample to avoid getting caught for using drugs. If the staff decides the test result was diluted, the staff would treat it as a positive test result, reducing a youth participant's sober days to zero and putting him in short-term custody. The next two excerpts show how the staff arrives at different decisions for diluted tests. The following excerpt about Angel, a seventeen-year-old Latino in the east court, highlights the most common outcome for a diluted test result. While the staff does take away Angel's sober days, it does not put him in custody. It also allows him to earn back those sober days after he accumulates another ninety consecutive days of sobriety.

HOOPER (JUDGE): What happened? He had a diluted test . . . How many [sober] days did he lose?

CHARLIE (PUBLIC DEFENDER): 114. He gets it back in 90 days.

JOE (PROBATION OFFICER): Says who? I don't agree with that.

CHARLIE: The policy is if they give us ninety days clean, they can get their days back . . .

EVA (DRUG COUNSELOR): I spoke with the father. The minor turns all of his checks to the parents, and the check was for $589. He gave $500 of it and kept $89. . . . He is compliant at home and is helping out the parents . . . He's working over forty hours a week.

HOOPER: He's doing really well. I was kind of surprised to see it [the dilute].

Angel is almost a third of the way through the program, with 114 sober days, when he gets this diluted test result. Joe does not agree with Charlie's recommendation to allow Angel to earn back that time. While Charlie retorts it is policy, there is no official policy stating youths can earn back their sober days. The other staff appear to side with Charlie, based on their positive sense of Angel's performance in the court. Eva mentions that he is working more than full time and, more impressive, he is giving most of his paycheck to his parents. In the end, the staff does give Angel the informal policy option, taking away his days but allowing him to get them back after accumulating another ninety consecutive sober days.

On the other hand, staff could use a diluted test as further proof of noncompliance. Alicia, the sixteen-year-old Latina who was Julie's "grave concern" in the last chapter, has had a series of diluted tests over the past few weeks:

JULIE (PROBATION OFFICER): Well, you'll notice the reports of diluted speci-
mens. Alicia is on the verge of being discharged from treatment. Alicia's
explanation for the diluted tests was that she had just been drinking a lot
of water. Alicia said she missed school because she slept over at a friend's
house and woke up late. The grandma called school to say she was ill, so
it was excused. That already shows her lying. She needs to go into custody
for the unexcused absence and dilutes.

O'REILLY (JUDGE): Four days in juvenile hall . . .

CHARLIE (PUBLIC DEFENDER): I have a letter from her school, from the teacher,
saying she is doing great and getting ninety percent of her work done.
That should be worth something.

O'REILLY: It is, but she still gets four days.

The staff had previously given the ninety-day deal to Alicia two weeks before
for a diluted test result, but this time Julie asks for custody. To further justify
her recommendation, she adds that Alicia lied about the school absence.
Charlie tries to counter Julie's interpretation by saying Alicia's teacher is com-
mending her performance in school. However, the rest of the staff sides with
Julie and sends Alicia to juvenile hall for four days. At the next court date,
she gets a positive test result and then gets sent out to the twenty-eight-day
probation program. While the positive test might serve as further proof that
she intentionally diluted the tests, it could also be a response to the staff's
treatment of the diluted tests. Some youths told me they were angry about
the staff taking away their sober days or locking them up for diluted tests
when they had not used. As a result, they began using again.

No Result

Staff can presume youths are using drugs even if no drug test is
conducted. That is, staff suspects youths of using drugs if they avoid testing
altogether. Staff often makes this assessment based on the type of participant.
For example, if there are no tests because staff cannot locate a youth at school,
drug treatment, or home, staff assumes the youth used drugs. If the youth is
on the run, staff also assumes he or she is using drugs and will need to be
tested immediately after being arrested.

The no-result test is a possibility when staff suspects a youth of deliber-
ately tampering with the test. For example, while sweat patches are supposed
to stay on the skin for at least a week, they frequently fall off before staff can
remove them appropriately. As with diluted results, staff must decide if the
youth is trying to hide drug use. If so, staff treats no-result tests as positive

tests. In the following excerpt, the south court staff interprets Julissa's disintegrated sweat patch as a tampered test.

CHARLIE (PUBLIC DEFENDER): Tampered patch, recommend weekend . . .

AMY (DRUG COUNSELOR): Julissa said the patch must have disintegrated down the drain. We did a presumpt test, but it was difficult to get a sample, but twenty minutes later, the presumpt came back negative. My gut is telling me the patch didn't disintegrate.

O'REILLY (JUDGE): No.

AMY: The story changed twice . . .

JULIE (PROBATION OFFICER): She did call me—I have to say that—on my cell phone, but didn't leave me a number . . . so I didn't call her back.

AMY: The story was that she was babysitting her niece and nephew, who were picking at it [the patch] while she was sleeping. I question why she didn't wake up . . .

CHARLIE [TO JULIE]: When did she call?

JULIE: Sunday, but the fact that the whole test disappeared seems suspicious.

RAUL (DRUG COUNSELOR): And she knows we don't go out on Sunday.

JULIE: Another issue is that she didn't go to drug treatment on Monday, because she assumed it was closed due to the holiday. I said you should never assume—but Mr. Horn [treatment staff] called and didn't want a punishment [for her], because he was not real clear about it.

O'REILLY: What do we do?

CHARLIE: A weekend [in custody]. That's the request.

Julissa, a seventeen-year-old Latina, presents a plausible explanation for the missing patch: while she was babysitting, her niece and nephew picked at the patch, loosening it, and it washed down the drain when she took a shower. Julissa also demonstrates responsible behavior by calling Julie, as per the court rules, to inform her that the patch was coming off. Moreover, she does test clean on the presumptive test. However, the staff does not believe her. Amy thinks Julissa is lying about her niece and nephew, while Raul questions Julissa's sincerity in calling, since she knows they do not work on Sundays. Julie looks to other behaviors to further bolster their claims, stating unequivocally that she missed treatment, even though it was a holiday (Presidents' Day) and the treatment staff did not want her to be punished for the absence. Julissa ends up getting an overnight sanction in custody. She also loses her sober time (twenty-one days), but the judge makes a deal for her to get those days back if she accumulates another ninety consecutive sober days.

The next example shows how the staff can respond completely differently to the same situation. Kelly, a sixteen-year-old white girl in the east court, had a sweat patch that came off before staff could remove it, and she called the staff to let them know. Unlike with Julissa, the staff does not consider the scenario a problem.

SARAH (PROBATION OFFICER): Kelly's doing fine. The patch came off while she was on the trip . . .
JILL (DRUG COUNSELOR): I'm not concerned about it being tampered, because she called as soon as it happened.
MOLINA (SUBSTITUTE JUDGE): So, it really came off and she's not trying to lie?
JILL: I tested her.
MOLINA: She's doing okay, 142 days [sober].

The staff situates this instance within a broader pattern of Kelly's good behavior to suggest it was not a tampered test. Instead of poking holes into Kelly's explanation like Amy and Julie did with Julissa, Sarah, the probation officer, prefaces the bad news of the sweat patch with a positive assessment that "Kelly's doing fine." Jill also characterizes Kelly's actions as responsible, stating that she "called as soon as it happened," in comparison to Raul's view of Julissa calling on Sunday as suspicious. The judge remains skeptical. Only after Jill mentions that she did another urine test that came out clean does the judge accept that Kelly is "doing ok." Had the judge questioned them more about Kelly, perhaps the decision would have gone more like Julissa's case. The staff does not issue a normal remedy for Kelly, and as with the case of Rebecca, the test result reflexively reaffirms the staff's perception of Kelly as "doing well," in that she proactively contacted Jill about it.

When a youth fails to test, this is considered a no-result test as well. In the following excerpt, the south court staff discusses how to handle a no-result from Christopher, a white sixteen-year-old. The staff told him to come to the probation office for a drug test, but he never showed up. Since many staff members see Christopher as noncompliant in all areas, they are eager to use this particular no-result as an opportunity to sanction Christopher for his general noncompliance:

JOE (PROBATION OFFICER): He had a failure to test yesterday . . .
RAUL (DRUG COUNSELOR): Has he shown proof of [Narcotic Anonymous] meetings? He never has proof before, nor a pay stub, even though he says he is working.
CHARLIE (PUBLIC DEFENDER): He's on Phase Three—when's the last time he was here?
JACK (DISTRICT ATTORNEY) [READING FROM THE WEEKLY PROGRESS REPORT]: He owes fifteen [Narcotics Anonymous] meetings.
CHARLIE: First of all, we haven't seen if he has meetings or talked to verify if he didn't come to test yesterday. . . .

LOPEZ (SUBSTITUTE JUDGE): Continue till next Thursday so he can provide proof of everything.

JULIE (PROBATION OFFICER): There is a hard copy of the dilute, which is being totally ignored.

Staff uses a youth's response to drug testing to confirm its sense of his overall progress in the court. Joe's interpretation of Christopher's no-result as a failure to test is bolstered by Jack and Raul's sense that Christopher is not complying with any court condition. Charlie offers plausible explanations to challenge those statements, suggesting they need to verify that the first test was indeed a failure to test. He points out that Christopher's advanced status in the program (Phase Three) was the reason the staff has not seen proof of Christopher's compliance, since he was expected to come to court monthly versus weekly. Julie, the probation officer, brings up another problematic dilute test result as further evidence that Christopher is noncompliant. The judge ultimately decides to postpone the decision until the following week, giving Christopher a chance to provide all the necessary documentation. When Christopher does not have that documentation, he ends up going into custody for five days, thus reaffirming the probation officers and drug counselors' sense that Christopher was trying to avoid detection by diluting his urine sample and missing the next test.

In contrast, the same team discusses Mark's case and how this white seventeen-year-old has not been tested in a long time. While he did not have a failure to test, like Christopher, Mark recently was caught with niacin, a pill that youths take to clean out their system, which some staff consider evidence of drug use. While he is not drug tested often, the staff considers him to be doing fairly well since he has a job and high school diploma.

PETER (DRUG COUNSELOR): He told me he didn't want to go to treatment at all. He has a job at Subway. He said working and coming home is all the treatment he needs. [*They talk about a bag with niacin in it.*]

CHARLIE (PUBLIC DEFENDER): All niacin does is color the pee.

JACK (DISTRICT ATTORNEY): He got his high school diploma and is working. That is success.

JULIE (PROBATION OFFICER): He only has thirty days.

JACK: [How about] NA meetings.

PETER: He is showing proof of his meetings. My concern is he is still using.

ANDY (POLICE OFFICER): He is.

JULIE: That may be why he dodges treatment. There is more frequent testing . . .

PETER : So what is the decision?

O'REILLY (JUDGE): No treatment, but he needs to make his work schedule available to them.

PETER: Okay, sounds good.

As it did with Christopher, staff could interpret Mark's behavior as resistant to treatment and the court, especially since he did have evidence (niacin) of trying to tamper with drug tests. However, Charlie refutes that evidence, stating niacin does not work, to depict Mark as unsophisticated in trying to avoid detection. Peter and Jack also note his other positive behaviors (a job and a high school diploma). Julie, Andy, and even Peter remain suspicious that Mark is using, but ultimately they do not dispute the judge's recommendation not to issue a normal remedy for Mark.

These four excerpts demonstrate the highly contingent character of drug test results. Presented with objectively similar situations, the staff could arrive at completely different decisions. In the case of no test results, the differences are based on the staff's sense of the youths (Julissa and Christopher as untrustworthy versus Kelly and Mark as doing fine). Those character assessments evolve from the staff's interactions with the youths and its view of their workability—that is, the staff's sense of how to keep influencing the youth. All of these evaluations, though, are subject to the staff's interpretive practices, which filter and shape how the staff understands the facts of the situation.

CONCLUSION

Instead of being a fail-safe measure of drug use and by extension, youth noncompliance, drug tests provide more uncertain verdicts than expected. Staff anticipates, recognizes, and treats a certain number of drug test results as false positives, false negatives, or ambiguous, with some other instances of no test results as proof of drug use. To reiterate how malleable and negotiable drug test results can be, consider the following scenarios that commonly occurred at the court. If the youths tested negative, the staff remained suspicious that they were using drugs, based on their general behavior or the flaws in the drug testing system. The staff then tested troublesome youths more often until presumably they tested positive. Conversely, if the test results were positive, the staff potentially determined the youths were not using drugs, depending on the type of test. In other words, a negative test result did not automatically or practically signify no drug use, and, likewise, a positive test result did not necessarily mean new drug use.

Given all these possibilities, the juvenile drug court staff understands drug testing results using a set of interpretive practices: the youths' individual patterns of drug use and drug testing, general characteristics of youth drug users, and staff's perceptions of each others' competencies in administering and reading the tests. In short, the meaning of drug test results is located not just in the scientific laboratory results, but also within the interactional and institutional process of the court hearings. Local understandings of drug test results are therefore not based on preestablished or static categories. Focusing on how staff negotiates these understandings is important, given that they have serious implications on the youths' trajectories in the court. Their graduation is based on their sober-day count, which continues to be reset with each positive test result. Indeed, this kind of analysis would be relevant for many other settings than the drug court. Institutions now require people to submit to drug testing as a condition of their employment, participation in sports, schooling, public housing, probation, and parole. So, while it is seemingly innocuous in intention and deemed constitutional by the U.S. Supreme Court, drug testing can have quite severe implications, as a failed drug test could lead to a loss of employment, suspension from school, loss of government entitlements (e.g., welfare, housing), revocation of parole or probation status, or, in some instances, termination of parental rights.

This analysis reveals how drug test results represent the intersection of law, science, and therapy. Drug test results can inform the staff's therapeutic approach, suggesting the need for increased supervision or revision to treatment program requirements. On another note, drug testing as a component of drug treatment could be seen as an inherently compromising and futile endeavor. One must question what kind of counseling can be done while drug counselors and probation officers are observing youths urinating into plastic cups. One final irony to note is the anti-therapeutic influence of drug testing on a youth's drug use. Some youths said they switched from marijuana to methamphetamine, which is a much more harmful and addictive drug, because it was easier to avoid detection in the drug tests. Other youths, like Aidan, a white seventeen-year-old in the north court, told me that the drug court is "turning us all into alcoholics." Staff recognized another irony to drug testing: it might provide more motivation for the youths to use. That is, if the youth knows he has a positive drug test, he might use more drugs since he will be locked up anyway.

Finally, it is not just the custody-based normal remedies for positive drug test results that negatively affect the youths. Taking away their clean time was also demoralizing. For example, Anna, a seventeen-year-old Latina in the south court, got a positive test result for marijuana. She denied using, insisting the result came from her hanging out with youths who were smoking. Anna was not as concerned about having to spend three days in custody as she was about losing thirty sober days and having to start over. She says, "I had like thirty days clean, and then they locked me up. So I had to start all over. . . . I would have more days right now . . . on my way to completing the program." Similarly, Orlando, a seventeen-year-old Latino in the north court, describes his feelings about losing his sober days after getting a diluted test result: "It pisses me off when they take away our days because it's hard enough getting to one day, and then it's like they take away 50 days, and then some. In some cases, they take away a hundred and something days . . . at one point they took away 140. . . . I wasn't using." The staff recognized this problem. Peter described how Christopher, the youth discussed in the last section, gave up when they took away his clean time: "You know, Christopher was so close to the end . . . and they put him all the way back at zero . . . that kid gave up . . . he literally gave up." The question arises: At what point does frequent drug testing do more harm than good in trying to teach accountability?

CHAPTER 6

It's Not Just His Probation, It's Mine: Parental Involvement in the Drug Court

IN NEGOTIATING THE EXTENT and severity of youths' non-compliant behaviors when deciding to hold youths accountable, the juvenile drug court staff commonly encountered the following dilemma: what to do when family members prevent their own children from staying in compliance. For example, staff expected families to help youths stay in compliance with the court's rules (e.g., make them go to school and treatment), but many parents occasionally asked their children stay home to babysit their younger siblings instead. While staff debated who to hold responsible in those situations—the parents or the youths—legally it could only punish the youths. Families are also expected to inform staff about youths' noncompliant actions. The staff asked parents to be its "eyes and ears" for additional supervision. Judge O'Reilly often told parents in the orientation for new youth participants, "we can't watch them twenty-four hours, and you see them every day."[1] However, most parents did not inform, or only selectively informed, the staff about their youths' noncompliance; alternatively, other parents gave information that the staff saw as irrelevant. Family involvement, therefore, can directly impact the staff's sense of a youth's accountability, either in the parents' expectations for the youth that ran counter to those of the court or in the parents' lack of communication with the staff about the youth's noncompliance. Both ways limit the staff's ability to assess the youths' noncompliance and to hold them accountable. By extension, parental involvement (or lack thereof) affected the staff's sense of a youth's workability, or its strategy in getting the youth to adhere to the court's rules.

The irony here is that staff told parents and legal guardians that they were equal members of the team and that their input in the decision-making process was always welcomed. Yet, many parents did not feel an equal partnership existed. Consider the following typical staff-parental interaction in a north court hearing compared to the parents' perspectives of the same hearing:

JUDGE SAMUELS: Rita, the reports are that you are doing very well. . . . [*To the mother*] How is Rita doing at home?
MOTHER: She is doing great.

Judge Samuels always asks parents how their youth is doing at home in front of the entire group of drug court youths and parents. Some parents see this routinized questioning as insincere, while others see it as limiting their willingness to speak up, especially if their comments contradict the judge's assessment. Ben's mother, fifty-two and white, says, "After he's [Judge Samuels] praised him for doing so well in school or whatever, and then to really say the truth, 'No, he's not doing that great at home' . . . everybody hears it, I think it's a little intimidating . . . I just say, 'I'm working on it,' 'cause he isn't doing that great at home." While the staff may feel that it provides opportunities for parents to express themselves, these opportunities may not be as inviting or open as it imagined. When the staff asks for what parents perceive to be superficial mechanical responses, parents might get the sense that their input is not really wanted.

Erving Goffman's ideas in "Insanity of Place" (1969), can help illuminate the variations in parents' responses to staff. Goffman describes how families typically try to adhere to the "family information rule" of not telling others outside the family about their particular family dysfunction. However, when a family member is too disruptive to the family's "internal economy," or that family's own ways of doing things, the family will tell others outside the family, in the "external economy," to control the problematic family member. In this light, parental involvement in the court could be understood as instances when they want help getting their youth back in line with their internal economy. If they don't need that help, parents might not be as likely to align with the staff. Yet at the same time, families in the juvenile drug court face another dilemma. Typically, families have complete authority over their internal economy, deciding what constitutes a problem in their family and when to share that problem with others. However, the drug court's jurisdiction over the youths usurps that parental authority, and families must cede that discretion to the staff, who tells them when and how to break the family information rule. In this instance, parents might be less likely to align with the external economy in the juvenile drug court intervention if parents do not agree or are resentful of this newfound limit to their authority.

Moreover, the court's expectations sometimes go beyond usurping parental authority. They lead some parents to feel like Austin's mother, who says, "this probation is not only his but also mine. It has really affected me because it is like living, but not freely. . . . It is a lot of stress. Not only is it the stress of having your son in probation, it is stress for parents and for all those in the family who are at home." Austin's mother raises an important point about parental involvement: the court intervention itself affects the families in more ways than staff might imagine, to the point where families who might otherwise want to be involved start to withdraw from the process. This lack of engagement could negatively affect the staff's views of the youth's noncompliance. Seen in this light, the influence of parental involvement on staff assessments of youth noncompliance underscores how the youth's ability to learn individual responsibility is contingent upon many actors outside of his actions.

STAFF TYPOLOGIES OF PARENTS

Most staff viewed parents as the biggest barriers to youth progress in the court because they did not reinforce the court's message about individual accountability. While some staff offered legitimate reasons, such as parents having to work two to three jobs or take care of other children, the court still had to deal practically with youth who are noncompliant because of the parents' actions.

The Good Parent

Staff described the ideal drug court parent as being supportive of the court's goals. Allen, a probation officer, says, "Ideal is a parent that understands the issues involved with the kid, that is willing to hold the kid accountable at home as well as, you know, at school, treatment, court, what have you. And a parent that is willing to work with us in using our sanctions, our incentives, as well as their own." Andy, a police officer, says youths with involved parents have the best chance of succeeding, because those parents help "keep their kid in line." He says,

> The majority of these kids who have their parents' support, even the worst ones, that have their parents come in every week and, you know, they're making recommendations with the court, and they're helping keep their kid in line. And they're calling and saying, "Hey, my kid did this today. My kid did that today. I want you guys to come and pick him up." If you're there and you're supporting your kid, he's gonna be successful or she's gonna be successful, either later down the line or earlier. You know? But, all in all, at the end, that person's gonna be successful.

Allen and Andy both indicate a working partnership with the parents is crucial to youths' success in drug court, even if they have serious problems. The staff tries to communicate this message to the parents, as Judge Hooper does with Morgan's father after his fifteen-year-old son left the house without permission to go to his mother's house:

> The thing you need to understand—we have rules and you have rules but they need to be consistent. We can't be stepping on each other's toes. He [Morgan] has a curfew . . . before he goes [over to his mother's house or anywhere else], we have to know more about it so we can make sure it does not interfere with his recovery. . . . [You] should sit down with him to go over the house rules. If those are violated, you have to punish him, not us. If there is a special thing, have him call his PO [probation officer]. . . . It requires a lot of patience all the way around. . . . Addiction—it's a sickness, not a crime and we know most addicts, on the way to recovery—he's going to slip.

According to Allen, Andy, and Hooper, a good parent is present at court hearings to show support, works with staff to set consistent rules and expectations, and communicates with staff about the youth's actions. Moreover, a good parent is willing to accept and learn about their youth's addiction, which Hooper describes as a sickness that requires much patience from everyone involved.

On the opposite end of the spectrum, bad parents are incompetent, uncooperative, unreasonable, enabling, and uninvolved.[2] These parents all share the underlying issue of inappropriate parental control. In the staff's eyes, the parents had lost, did not have enough, or had too much control over their children. More important, the staff viewed them as unable or unwilling to enforce the court's goals of teaching their children to take accountability for their actions.

The Incompetent Parent

According to some staff, even if parents are involved in their youths' lives, they still may not have the adequate skills to be effective parents, which in turn prevents them from helping their children meet the court's expectations.[3] Joe, a probation officer, says, "Generally, I think most of my parents care about their kids and want their kids to do well, [but] a lot of them don't have the parenting skills." Sarah, another probation officer, gives an example of the parents who "don't know" how to be parents: "It is amazing to me when I taught the parents about parenting, the basic parenting skills that they don't have. They don't know that you wake up with your child in the morning when they go to school. . . . They don't know that if your child has to stay up late doing homework, you stay up with them, because it is easier for them knowing that somebody is up with them and is there to help them and support them when they start going crazy because they don't understand the homework they are doing. . . . They don't understand those things."

These staff views raise one important complication for youth's accountability: the staff admits that the parents' ignorance about "basic" tasks plays a direct role in the youth's ability to stay in compliance with the drug court rules. The staff expects the parents to actively support the youths in this process, somewhat contradicting the individual accountability message that it wants to instill in the youths.

The Uncooperative Parent

Staff viewed parents who openly or covertly resist the court's expectations of the youth and the family as uncooperative. The staff described a few reasons for this lack of cooperation. Joe notes that it could be related to the financial costs of the court's normal remedies for youth noncompliance, given that parents are billed by probation every time the staff puts youths on home supervision or sends them to juvenile hall or probation camp. Staff suspected some parents covered up their youths' bad behavior to avoid having to pay for these normal remedies. Staff also stated that some parents resented the court's involvement in their youths' lives and the court mandates. Whatever the reason, the staff was faced with the dilemma of how to handle the youth's case if the reason for his noncompliance stemmed from his family's resistance to the court.

The Unreasonable Parent

Staff considered some parents as unreasonable if they were overly controlling of the youths (e.g., a mother telling staff that her daughter violated curfew when the curfew was only 4 P.M.) or were just mean to their children. In short, staff saw these parents as trying to have too much authority over their youths and not allowing the court to enforce proper expectations of the youths.

The Enabling Parent

Staff defined enabling parents as those who covered up their youth's drug use, thereby allowing their drug addiction to continue and possibly worsen. Staff also applied this typology to parents who did not let their youths do things by themselves (e.g., coddling their children). Staff saw an enabling parent as an impediment to youths' learning how to take responsibility for their actions. Many times, these parents were recovering drug addicts themselves, or spouses of current drug users, who did not want to get their children into trouble.

The Uninvolved or Disinterested Parent

Staff saw other parents as not supportive of their youths in the court at all. Allen, a probation officer, describes uninvolved parents as those "we

hardly ever see. . . . They don't participate. They don't come to court. . . .
you have to pull teeth to get them to go to treatment programs." Peter, a
drug counselor, puts it more bluntly: "The ones that just drive me absolutely
crazy are the ones . . . who just flat out, point blank, don't give a shit." Peter
adds that some parents might simply be exhausted from having their youths
in the juvenile justice system for so long, to the point they expect probation
officers to do all the work. He says, "A lot of parents just have to put their
hands in the air, more out of self-preservation than anything."

These staff types of "bad" parents affect how staff works with youths, as
it readjusts its normal remedies to address familial problems.[4] Consider the
repercussions of the uninvolved parent in the following excerpt about Ralph,
a sixteen-year-old Latino who has been detained in juvenile hall for forty-six
days. In early June the court ordered him to stay in juvenile hall until he
could get into Project Fortitude, a twenty-one-day residential detox program. In the next discussion, in early August, the staff cites his mother's
inability to get to Fortitude to sign paperwork as the reason for the long delay:

JUDGE HOOPER: He's been in the hall already forty-five days.
CHARLIE (PUBLIC DEFENDER): Forty-six days—waiting, and we still have no
    idea when he'll get into Fortitude . . .
MARK (CLINICAL THERAPIST): He did more time than the actual program he is
    waiting for . . .
EVA (DRUG COUNSELOR): Your Honor, the only problem . . . the reason he's
    waiting a long time is that they [probation] have been trying to make
    phone calls to the family but got no response until two weeks ago. Julie
    (probation officer) finally did and they went over to fill out the paper-
    work. That's why it took so long.
HOOPER: We need to get on the same page about this and it will be a court
    order from now on that if we don't hear from the parent in two weeks
    and the parents don't get back to staff, then I'll sign any forms . . . I am
    not going to punish kids for parents being an idiot . . . I'm going to send
    him home.

The staff primarily blames the mother for this delay, as her apparent refusal to
return staff phone calls has compromised the court's ability to respond quickly
to the youth's noncompliance. Mark notes that Ralph has spent more than
twice as long (six and a half weeks) in juvenile hall than he was supposed to
spend in the treatment detox facility (three weeks). While the judge claims it
is the parents who are "being an idiot" in this situation, he does not recognize
or mention the staff's complicity in that situation. The judge had already told
the probation staff he would sign the paper on behalf of the parents two
weeks before. So, part of this delay is the staff's fault for not making sure the
paperwork was completed in a timely fashion. They could have gone to Ralph's

house with the paperwork to get it signed, or they could have delivered a message to the mother to go to the detox program to sign the paperwork. Ultimately, Ralph is the one who is most affected by this delay as he sits in juvenile hall for forty-six days. He does go into detox the following week but gets arrested on a new burglary charge shortly thereafter. The staff suspends Ralph from drug court until that charge is resolved.

CONDITIONS OF PARENTAL INVOLVEMENT

Parents do tell the staff information about their children under certain conditions, and that parental involvement affects the staff's views of the youth's noncompliance. While these conditions are not deterministic, they offer some ways to consider how and to what extent parents share information with the staff. The conditions represent a continuum of parental involvement—starting on one end with parents who use the courts as their "added weapon" in dealing with their children and swinging to the other end, where parents ignore the court's authority as much as possible. Parents often vacillate between the different points of the continuum, depending on how they view the court at any given point during the youth's case. A major element in this continuum is control: are parents trying to keep control over their children, to share control with the court, or to cede control completely to the staff? Parents' movement along the continuum also gets shaped by their frequent interactions with the staff and the staff's views of the parents. That is, if the staff agrees with the parents' interpretations of the youths' behavior, parents might be more likely to continue informing on the youths. If staff rejects their assessments, parents might feel more disenchanted and disengaged with the court, to the point of limiting or stopping their involvement altogether. Orlando's foster mother, a fifty-nine-year-old Latina, discussed the initial difficulties in "letting go" during a conversation with a probation officer in the early stages of her son's drug court case. She says,

> You have to get used to how they run it and what they do so that you can know what to expect. . . . I was very upset the first time that they, that I went there. I think it was the second week that I went there to court with him. And he, he was dirty. And I-I didn't know. Nobody told me . . . And she [the probation officer] says something like, you know, "Well, you know, we don't have to tell you," or something like that she said. I says, "Well, then I don't have to bring him." [*Laughter*] But, it, like I said, it took a couple of weeks for me to just let go . . . And let them handle it.

Orlando's mother describes her adjustment process in the beginning of drug court, citing one upsetting instance when the court did not inform her about her son's positive drug test. While she tried to assert her control to the probation officer with a threat not to bring her seventeen-year-old son to court, she eventually realized that she needed to hand that control over to the staff. This exchange reveals the interactive quality of parental involvement. Had another parent reacted differently to the probation officer's statement, he or she might not have chosen the same path as Orlando's mother to "let them handle it." In this sense, parental involvement in the court is a reflexive, fluid, and situational process, in which the staff and parents engage in their own side bets about youth noncompliance. Yet it is the youths watching these staff-parent interactions from the sidelines who face the consequences of those interactions as the staff holds them accountable for their noncompliant actions.

Maintaining or Reestablishing Parental Control

Parents might align with the staff if the anticipated court response would help address a problem they see with their child, such as risky behavior or challenging parental control. In these instances, parents frame the court intervention as helping them, versus helping the staff, work with their children. This view preserves parental authority, perhaps facilitating the parents' ease in sharing information with the staff.

Parents may tell staff about their youth's noncompliance if they feel the behavior was dangerous. Parents viewed informing on their children not as an act of disloyalty but rather as an attempt to save them from danger. Both Austin's and James's mothers said they would rather see their children safe in juvenile hall than out on the streets or using drugs. Austin's mother, a thirty-four year old Latina, spoke of an instance with her sixteen-year-old son: "for example, when I see that he is misbehaving, like two or three nights that he did not sleep here, I told the probation officer . . . I would rather have him locked up than having something bad happen to him outside." Similarly James's mother, a thirty-seven-year-old Latina, explained why she called the probation officer about her seventeen-year-old son: "for my security and because I love him. . . . If I see him getting drugged, I will call. Like I have told him, I'd rather see him locked up than dead because of drug abuse. . . . It is hard, but a son's life is more important." Both mothers characterize telling on their sons as tantamount to sentencing them to juvenile hall. They do so because they see incarceration as the lesser of two evils. James's mother views his drug use as life threatening, which trumps her hesitation to criminalize him further. Austin's mother, however, does not mention anything about drug use. Her concern was that he stayed out all night. These comments suggest some parents have no qualms telling staff about certain kinds of behavior, but they may selectively withhold information. They still maintain a certain level of discretion in interpreting the level of danger in the youth's behavior and the desired outcome of the court's response (e.g. ensuring the youth's safety more so than the youth's sobriety).

Parents also align with staff to exert control over their children. In this study, almost all the parents who told staff under this condition were Latino. James's mother views the court as helping to maintain the family order in her home. She and her husband call the probation officer so that James understands and obeys his parents' rules. For example, James's father once called staff when James fought with him.[5] According to James's mother,

> The probation officer came because my husband called him. He and my son got in a fight because he had been coming home late, and we noticed something rare in him. He was more aggressive and showing symptoms of drug consumption. So he tried to disrespect my husband, and he immediately contacted the officer. They came quick, warned him about the consequences of his behavior, performed an anti-doping test, and he came out positive. They took him to court with the positive test results and he got locked up . . . [for] fifteen days.

The catalyst for James's parents appears to be an instance of disrespect toward his father, more so than James's drug use. And while he does test positive for drugs, James's mother focuses more on his disrespectful behavior toward his father than on his drug use. Even though the court's response is based only on drug use, parents like James's mother can have a different view about the staff's intervention and intended use of its responses.

Hector's mother, a thirty-eight-year-old Latina, also relies on the staff to keep her fifteen-year-old son in check—well beyond what is actually mandated by the court. She says, "When Hector misbehaves, I immediately get the phone. I call his PO [probation officer] and tell him, 'You know what? Hector is doing this and that.'" She does not appear to have any hesitation in calling, because it allows her to exert more authority over her son at any given moment. When asked to give a specific example, she says:

MOTHER: Right now . . . I was mad at Hector because he did not want to help me fix the bed. He said that he needed to take a shower. I told him that he just took a shower. . . . I told him, "I need your help, Junior. Please help me." He did not want to do it, and I got angry at him. . . . I got the phone, and he told me, "No, no, please, Mom. Please, please. I am sorry, Mom." He knows that if he yells at me. . . . Here I am, his mother. He is not my father. I can raise my voice as many times as I want. He knows that if he raises his voice, I'll call like this. I immediately call his probation and let him know that Hector is misbehaving. I cannot tolerate that he yell at me. At all.

LESLIE: And do you feel that through this program you can control him?

MOTHER: I have Hector here [*signals to the palm of her hand*].

There is no action here that would merit a court response. Hector's mother is intent, though, on using the court as an added way to demand respect from her son, even for something as simple as getting him to do household chores and speak to her in an appropriate tone. Hector's mother uses the threat of alignment with the court to reassert and reestablish her view of the family hierarchy with Hector, in which she is the only authority figure who can raise her voice in the house.

Similarly, Gemma's mother, a thirty-seven-year-old Latina, described how she uses the staff to increase her control over her daughter. She says, "They [staff] always, uh, um, listen to us. . . . I look at this like extra help for me." When asked about what she tells the staff, she says, "She [Gemma] don't even know that we request it [home supervision] . . . . We like if she [has] home supervision, so she just has to stay at home . . . . We talk to them and everything, and everything was confidential." This secret request highlights the idea of the court as parents' extra tool for controlling their child. They see the staff's actions as responses to their wishes for their sixteen-year-old daughter. Gemma's parents moved to the North County area, thirty miles from the city, because they wanted to get Gemma away from her friends there. They used the court's home supervision sanction to curtail her ability to leave home. There is no mention of Gemma's use of drugs or any other kind of noncompliant behavior. The parents wanted home supervision simply so that she would stay at home. And while the parents do not think she knows of their secret conversations with the staff, Gemma admits she does, saying she gets into trouble "just for stuff that my parents tell them . . . like, just little stuff that would get them mad . . . like my curfew violations. I get three days [in juvenile hall] for it."

In all these situations, the staff does appear to take the parents' complaints seriously, as youths like James and Gemma can get locked up or put on home supervision after their parents call the staff. However, the reasons that parents call are not necessarily the official reasons of youth noncompliance for which the staff issues normal remedies to hold youths accountable. James's father called after James disrespected him, not because of his drug use. Parental use of the court to reassert authority can lead to harsher outcomes and require the staff to take more control over the situation. For example, Gemma's parents' request for home supervision makes it easier for the staff to know when she is violating curfew and can legally lock her up for those moments. Over time, the staff can start to view each subsequent curfew violation as more problematic and in need of more serious normal remedies.

Submitting to Court Control: Partial or Complete Cooperation

Parental involvement in the court can also be characterized as cooperation with the staff. Parents understand the staff has the ultimate control over their youth. The varying levels of cooperation stem from the parents' view of the court and their interactions with the staff, which in turn shapes the types of information that parents will share with the staff about the youth's noncompliance.

Some parents cooperate completely with the court, because that is what the law requires. Orlando's foster mother explains why she tells the staff about her son, "All I do is give the information. I don't conceal information for him. I just give the information and pretty much leave it up to them." The thirty-eight-year-old Caucasian father of George, a sixteen-year-old, sees the law as "larger than the parental rights," adding later, "I expected that there's things that I can't do anything about if they . . . wanna put it into effect." These quotes suggest some parents expressed their collaboration with the staff with a passive acceptance, stating they had little power to object to what the court expects.

Parents also said they would cooperate and share information if they felt the staff had a fairly good sense of their children and them. Sydney's mother, a forty-one-year-old Latina, explains that it took a while before she became comfortable calling the staff about her seventeen-year-old daughter. She says, "Now I could call and, um, say, 'I'm having a little problem with Sydney going to school, waking her up for school, you know, what should I do? . . . Before I wouldn't have called them for that." This shift in thinking took some time: Sydney's mother said it was six months before she felt comfortable calling staff. At the time the interview was conducted, Sydney had been in the program for over two years. Sydney's mother later stated that she did not call because she did not want Sydney to get locked up for missing school. After she saw the staff trying to work with her daughter to resolve the truancy issues (e.g., changing her school, allowing some leniency in the tardiness/truancy), Sydney's mother was more likely to call the staff.

Parents might only partially cooperate if they disagree with the scope or extent of the staff's expectations and rules. Many parents admitted to withholding some information that they interpreted as not that important or not falling under the court mandate. Dominic's mother, a thirty-eight-year-old Latina, says,

> If his curfew is 6:00, and sometimes he takes off, he comes back, 8:00, 9:00 . . . he's playing soccer or something, I'll remind him, "Don't forget your curfew" . . . Now, I'm not gonna go tell 'em [police officers], "Yeah he's gone, he's, um, violate, violating probation," because he's playing soccer. He has to play . . . And, and I know he's doing fine, he's not doing anything wrong. . . . He's off the streets. . . . I mean, he told me, whatever he does wrong is gonna come down on me, but if he doesn't get caught, then he doesn't get caught.

Even though Dominic's mother knows it is against the rules to have her fifteen-year-old son play soccer after curfew, she does not tell the probation officer because she views this activity as positive. Dominic's mother is still preserving some aspect of her parental authority—in deciding what and when he can engage in positive activities like soccer. Her sense that "he's doing fine" overrides her concern about the staff finding out about his noncompliant behavior of violating curfew.

Similarly, some parents completely disregard the parts to the court mandate that they do not believe are relevant. Kevin's mother, fifty-five and white, says,

> I don't want to tell them anything . . . because they'd use it against me. . . . I don't think it's [what her son did] so bad. You know, I mean, I'm kind of stuck. " She later says that she only tells them "what he is legally responsible to them for—otherwise, it's not their business. He's in here for drug and anger. . . . That's what he's there for, and that's what he should be in trouble for. . . . And, that's what he has to kowtow for . . . what legally he's responsible to them for is what I will legally tell them. . . . I don't have to tell her [probation officer] he was a bad boy today. It's not her business.

How Kevin's mother views the court affects what she tells them about her sixteen-year-old son. Since she only sees the staff as dealing with drugs and anger, those subjects are what she discusses with them. She does not mention Kevin's performance at home, even though technically that is part of the court's business. She views the staff as making a bigger deal over Kevin's misbehaviors than is necessary, and she does not buy into the court's interpretation of Kevin's dysfunction in the home. Part of this resistance is due to her long involvement with the juvenile court before Kevin even started drug court. In her interview, Kevin's mother discussed the difficulties she had with various programs and staff who did not listen to her and sometimes unfairly punished her son. Her resentment and distrust of the court may stem from those previous experiences, which have impacted how she addresses and interacts with the juvenile drug court staff now. This brings up another interesting issue: while the juvenile drug court staff constantly states how it is different from mainstream courts, some parents view them as one in the same.

Even when parents fully cooperate with and adhere to court expectations, the staff still needs to validate those efforts before agreeing to help the parents. If the staff does not do so, it risks possibly alienating parents from holding their youths accountable in the future. Consider how the court handles the complaints from Ben's mother about her sixteen-year-old son. At the beginning of this chapter, she described the difficulty of being open with the judge during the court hearing. She says her problem is that her son does not listen to her. She wants the staff to help her encourage Ben not to hang out with friends using drugs, a central message that the staff tries to convey. In the following interview excerpt, she describes how she has repeatedly called the probation officer to ask for help:

> I called three or four times the last two, three weeks to ask her to speak with him about his behavior at home. . . . I called her today because Ben gave me hell on the way to school 'cause I won't let him hang out with his drug friends. . . . I told her . . . I want some private time with the judge and you today. . . . And so she said okay . . . because, see, from me, Ben doesn't get it. . . . I'm the bad guy. . . . I needed an intervention with the probation officer . . . Then she said, you know, you need to have the power. But then they said . . . basically, you know, I have to answer to you.

She wants to prevent Ben from seeing his friends who smoke marijuana, especially since the last time he did that he got a positive drug test and spent five days in custody. His stay in juvenile hall led him to get kicked out of his regular school and placed into a probation school, where he is totally unmotivated. She describes the irony of what the drug court staff asks of parents: they tell her that she has the power with her child, but then they reiterate that the parents have to answer to staff. She does want to assert her authority, but she needs the court's backing in that effort, which she does not find is happening.

On the surface, Ben's mother seems like the ideal drug court parent—informing on the youth when he is not doing well at home and putting himself in potential relapse situations such as hanging out with drug-using friends. Also, as Hooper instructed Morgan's father earlier in the chapter, Ben's mother is willing to set the rules instead of depending solely on the staff to punish the youth. Yet in her situation, the staff views her as unreasonable, overbearing, and not a good role model for Ben. This discussion took place in court on the same day as my interview with her:

MIRANDA (PROBATION OFFICER): Ben is doing okay. . . . I had a pep talk with Mom this morning. She said she is being disrespected and the court needs to do something. . . . I told the mom, "You need to step up and be a parent and get your son to know that he cannot disrespect you." She said she understood but asked the court to clarify with him and the ex-husband about the expectations.

BILL (DRUG COUNSELOR): She doesn't let Ben do anything. . . . The dad says, "Go ahead." . . . He's [Ben's] kind of going crazy."

MIRANDA: He wants to go out with [his friends and] use drugs. She's trying to keep him from going out. . . . All she wants is for him to come in early to the court to be admonished . . .

BILL: I talked to him today. I did remind him he could get in trouble for hanging out with youths who used and that he knew how hard it was to not hang out with them. I had a good long talk with him today. I think that's enough.

MIRANDA: Yeah. . . . I think she needs to be brought in by herself and get admonished with "You need to be a parent."

BILL: He [Ben] said, "My mom is f-ing crazy." . . . I told him I have a little bit of understanding, since I talked with her a bit.

SAMUELS (JUDGE): She's pretty much a helicopter parent when she is around, and the dad is laissez faire.

BILL: Yeah.

MIRANDA: The dad doesn't want anything to do with drug court.

SAMUELS: The dad is the more rational of the two.

The staff seems to have the completely opposite view of the situation from the mother. It takes Ben's side about her being unreasonable. While the staff agrees with the mother that Ben is putting himself in risky situations, it does not agree with the mother's proposed solution to the problem. Instead, the staff describes her contributions as indications of being a helicopter parent who hovers too much over her son and views the father, described as an uninvolved laissez-faire parent, as the more rational of the two. The staff ignores her request for a private conference to present a united front to Ben; at the same time, it also fails to tell her that Bill spoke to Ben about the actual concern of him hanging out with his drug-using friends. The question remains: if the staff wants to get the parents involved, telling them to be its eyes and ears and to set up their own rules, where exactly did Ben's mother go wrong here?

Ceding to Court Control—Giving Up

The first two conditions represent situations where parents attempt to maintain some control over their children while trying to meet the staff's expectations of the youths. There is also the condition where parents begin to see the staff as more capable than they are themselves to help their children, and so they give up control altogether. As a result, the staff is able to make decisions about the youth's accountability with relative freedom, knowing the parents will support them or, at the very least, not interfere. The instances for this condition represent more extreme noncompliant behavior, such as repeated drug use or new arrests. This leads parents to report their children and let the court handle it, especially when they feel they are at an impasse or have no new ideas of what to do. Greg's father, fifty-one years old and white, justifies the court's intervention because his seventeen-year-old son's problems are beyond any parent's ability to handle. He states, "You know, especially when you get older and you want to retire and you're dealing with these teenage problems that are not normal teenage problems, you know, because they're of that nature, and it's—that's nice." Henry's father, forty years old and also white, agrees about his son's problems being too much for him to handle, especially the drug use issues. He says, "I have no way of knowing when he's using and when he's not. I can only have suspicion. . . . I can test him, but at the same time, um, when a kid is seventeen, going on twenty-one, um, my control is pretty much out the, out the door. . . . So the drug court has the, the authority to, uh, to do the discipline, as far as the use of the drugs, the violation of his probation." Even if Henry's father did test him for drugs, he sees the court as being able to impose more discipline than he can. Orlando's foster mother echoes this sentiment: "He's [Orlando] always saying, 'Are they gonna lock me up?' . . . I say, 'I don't know, Son. You tell me.' . . . If he's dirty, if he did something, it might show up, and they might, he might get locked up. I have no, you know, I can suspect it . . . He knows what the deal is. I, I don't, and they don't know. I mean, they, they're gonna find out." Both Henry's and Orlando's parents express their limited ability to handle their youth's drug use: while they might suspect that their children are using, they are not able to address it in the same way that the staff can.

Beyond the parents' belief that the staff can better respond to their youth's drug use, parents also talk about accepting that the staff is more capable of making the right decision for their youth's well-being. James's mother says, "The most difficult part has been to turn my son in . . . telling probation to come and get him because I am unable to control him. It is tough, but it is for his own good. It was hard on me when the lawyer told asked me if I wanted him home or at boot camp. It was hard because as a mother, I want him here. . . . But it was for the best to have him at boot camp for six months."[6] Similarly, Greg's father accepted the court's decision, even though it felt like a challenge to his authority as a parent. When I asked him if he agreed with the court's decision to make Greg take an anger management class after he fought with his stepfather, Greg's father said, "Again that's the parent thing taken away. You know, I'm not gonna say, 'No you can't,' because it's like, you know, something needs to be done." While both parents express ambivalence about some court decisions, they ultimately cede control to the staff, trusting it to make the decisions to help their children.

Parents will also give up all control if they are fed up with dealing with the youth. Joe, a probation officer, explains, "You have the parents who will tell you everything because it kind of appears that they don't want to deal with their kid, and they don't want their kid in their home anymore, so they are looking to us to take their kid away and lock them up and take them out of there so they don't have to be bothered in their lifestyle, whatever that may be." Fidel's mother is the perfect example of that sentiment. When speaking with the judge about her son's latest gang-related graffiti incident, she said, "When he is off home sup[ervision], he's high, stoned, bringing alcohol to the house. . . . I don't need this at my house. I've done this since 1999, and I can't do it anymore." Another source of parent frustration comes from the perceived ineffectiveness of the drug court, as noted by Todd's father, who tells the judge, "Your Honor, I have a screen busted, my change drawer has been raided, people at my house I would never imagine. I'm fed up . . . I want something out of this room [the drug court]. I'm running out of patience." This overt relinquishment of control underscores the fluidity of parental involvement—and, by extension, the staff's views of youth's non-compliance and accountability—as parents' frustrations were never permanent states. For example, Todd's father did not always feel this way about his son, stating in other weeks that his son was doing better and advocating for his son to be excused from certain normal remedies.

Again, there is a tension hidden underneath this type of parental involve-ment, as staff might view it as evidence of parents shirking their responsibilities. Joe describes how they come to rely on the drug court, specifically probation (which helps youths get into school and treatment), as a "crutch." He says,

> I think that a lot of parents use probation as a crutch, and they think, "Oh, the probation officer will handle it." . . . All these parents are going, "What are you going to do to get my kid in school?" Well, it is like, what do you mean? You are the parent, get your kid in school. . . . If you are having problems doing it, and you need my help, I will defi-nitely be there to help you, but, you know, you are the parent. You get your kid in the school or get him in here, in treatment. Here is a couple of treatment programs . . . whichever one you think would be best, you know, go ahead, get your kid in.

Joe's comments raise an interesting quandary for parents: if parents cooperate too much with the court, they may not be seen favorably by staff because they are seen as using the court as a crutch. Yet when parents do try to main-tain some amount of responsibility, like Ben's mother, the staff might view their suggestions as inappropriate. Many times, the parents brought up school or treatment options, which the staff rejected for a variety of reasons. The balancing act of control between the parents and staff, then, is not so obvious and fluctuates depending on the youth and the situation.

Avoiding Court Control: Open Resistance and Organizational Barriers

Parents avoid or try to curtail the court's control over their youths for four reasons: financial costs, distrust of the court's efficacy, perceived staff disregard of their input, and lack of meaningful communication with the staff. The families' resistance to the staff's efforts made it more complicated for the staff to effectively convey the accountability message to the youths. This resistance is an interactional and fluid process, developed over time based on the parents' encounters with the staff and their perceptions of the staff (and vice versa).

Many parents mentioned financial issues shaping their involvement. Each time the youths appeared in the court, they were charged a fee. Many normal remedies also involved some kind of charge (e.g., about thirty-five dollars a day for home supervision, thirty-seven dollars a day for juvenile hall), and each offense often came with a restitution fine (fifty dollars minimum). The fees and fines did not have a significant impact on the staff's decision-making process beyond an occasional mention by the public defender trying to advocate for a more lenient normal remedy. In contrast, most of the parents discussed the financial strain created by the court. Of the twenty-one parents asked about fines, only two reported having no problems with them. The amounts owed to the court ranged from $200 to almost $30,000. For example, Narcisco's sister, a twenty-four-year-old Latina, explains why she does not call the probation officer about her seventeen-year-old brother. She says, "When I tell him [Narcisco] that I'm going to call the probation officer, he says: 'Call him.' This upsets me. . . . Does he even know how much it costs when he gets locked up?" In addition, James's mother, who earlier avowed she would call the staff to report any misbehavior, also stated she wished she could ask for more home supervision, but the cost was too excessive given his existing fines. She says, "As a parent they ask you if you want home supervision. I would like to have it, but I can't be paying $100 every time they come. If it was $100 per month for a total of eight visits per se, it would be fine, but $100 each time is too much." Given that his current tab is over $6,000 and her husband just lost his job, James's mother was less likely to request what she wanted because of the cost. While the cost of home supervision is not $100 a visit, her perception of the cost is what matters here, since she actively rejects the idea of it for that reason.

This example represents another lost opportunity for staff to engage the parents' input. The hesitation here is purely for a misguided understanding of the cost. While staff did recognize this financial issue as a problem, it also largely characterized parental concern for it as not a good enough reason to avoid court control. Sarah, a probation officer, criticizes one father for wanting to get his son out of drug court for financial reasons, even though his son, in her eyes, still needed drug court supervision. Joe, another probation officer, sees the irony in parents not alerting staff to the youth's initial noncompliance because of the costs, saying "It gets to the point where they can't handle it anymore [by themselves]. Then they will let me know, and it is, wow, I wish you would have told me this earlier, it would have been better, but I can definitely understand it." James's mother exemplifies Joe's description.

She will not request certain sanctions—even if they might help her—because of the cost.[7]

Parents might also not tell staff about their youths if they perceive the court's response to be ineffectual or impractical. Narcisco's sister explains, "In the first place, I do not like him to be locked up. It doesn't help him at all. He needs to be here at home, he needs to go to school and get his education, and helping me here at home, because I have other kids to look after. What does he get from being locked up? Nothing." Narcisco's sister has a different view from the staff about how to get her brother back on track, even though they both want the same result for her brother (i.e., go to school and behave at home). The added irony is that, because she does not believe in the staff's strategy to hold him accountable, she does not tell the staff when Narcisco misbehaves, effectively limiting both the staff and her ability to try to correct his problematic behavior. Because she does not tell the staff members how she feels, she cannot share with them her ideas on how to influence his behavior. Later in the interview, she shares that instead of locking the youths up, the court "should have more activities for them. Like special interest courses; things that they would like to do." But the current (lack of) communication between Narcisco's sister and the staff limits all of their intentions to try to help Narcisco. Her silence might also lead the staff to start to characterize her as an "disinterested" or "uninvolved" family member, further distancing her from it.

In addition, parents might resist the staff's efforts to solicit information because they do not feel like an equal part of the team—something the judge suggests to them in the orientation meeting. This disenchantment arises when parents do not feel that the staff truly hears their complaints or issues. Kevin's mother said, "They have no clue about this family. . . . I tried when he was first on this probation thing with the hitting . . . thing. . . . I tried to tell this probation office woman and, uh, I didn't get much feedback from her."[8] Orlando's foster mother shares a similar experience, stating her greatest frustration comes when the staff does not take her seriously. She says, "There's been a few times when I tell them [staff] that I can't keep him no more. . . . Been times when I just can't do it no more. And I don't think they take me very serious. . . . It's like they think, they feel, 'Oh, yes, you can' . . . I don't think they can really see. I mean I don't want them to, I don't expect them to, but when I tell them, 'I am tired,' you know, it's, I'm, I'm not bluffing, I'm not, as I am, I am exhausted."

Other parents note the hypocrisy in staff not talking more to parents. Ben's mother says, "I've never had a say or choice. Well, actually I take that back. I think I had a choice in what twenty-one day detox he could go to . . . which is odd, 'cause they're always talking about wanting to work with the parents." Henry's father adds, "If the parent, if I am going to be that far removed from the decision making, then . . . you know, quite frankly, they should just go ahead and, you know, lock him up for a couple of months. . . . If my decision making isn't involved, then, um, I don't understand why they don't just go ahead and take over the whole situation." These comments show that the parents' hesitation is the product of multiple interactions with staff over time in which they have consistently felt ignored, unheard, and overruled by the staff. The parents' lack of involvement with the staff is not a result of perpetual disinterest, but rather a gradual consequence of staff-parent interactions that leaves the parents unfulfilled.

Part of the parents' sense that staff disregards their input comes from the limited communication between them. One barrier to that communication is translation issues for the Spanish-speaking parents. Horatio's mother, a thirty-two-year-old Latina, describes how translation issues prevent her from telling the staff more about her sixteen-year-old son, who is in the north court, the only one of the three courts without bilingual probation officers or drug counselors.

LESLIE: So how do you communicate with her [probation officer]?
MOTHER: I partially understand. She asks me how Horatio is doing at home. I tell her that he is doing fine. They only ask me that, and that is the only thing I am able to answer her. . . .
LESLIE: If there was an officer that spoke Spanish . . . how would you feel?
MOTHER: Well, that would make a big difference. I would feel much better.
LESLIE: In what way?
MOTHER: In that if she wanted to ask me more questions, I could understand more. Or if I want to ask her something, I could do it. Right now I can only answer the question that she asks me. Like, I cannot have an actual conversation.

This logistical problem could serve to potentially alienate Horatio's mother even more from the process, as she is literally unable to share information with them. The fact that Horatio's mother can only answer a few questions (and that the staff does not press her for more answers) also curtails the court's ability to know how he is doing. While there may be many other reasons why parents do not tell the staff more information, having no bilingual staff in the north court is a clear factor in Horatio's case. And while staff does have many other ways to find out about the youth's performance in school and drug treatment, its insistence that parents contribute to staff assessments is compromised if it can only communicate with some of the parents. Finally, this translation issue can also reflect upon how the staff views the parents—as recalcitrant, passive, or disinterested in their child's progress—when, in effect, it could be a structural barrier built into the court's daily operations.[9]

While it may seem easy to reduce the lack of communication to language barriers, many of the English-speaking parents also described frustration with the lack of meaningful interactions with the staff. Henry's father suggests the staff could talk more in depth with the parents to come up with an effective treatment plan, saying, "I don't think they have a clue. . . . I've never sat down with Derek [probation officer], and said, 'Okay, this is our family situation.' . . . I do think that, uh, some of that probably should be taken into consideration, uh, as far as trying to determine programs, and stuff that they should be in." When asked if he would be open to that kind of conversation, he said yes, adding,

> I've given you more information here in thirty minutes than probation has ever asked me for. . . . All they wanna know is, "Do you have a dog in the house [presumably for the safety of probation officers when they make a home visit]? Is there anyone else in the house?" So when they come by they know what to expect . . . Nobody's sat down to say, "What do you do for a living? How does that . . ." I work in the music business. I mean, I, I do concerts, so he's obviously exposed, although I don't hang out with cokeheads and drug addicts and drunks and such. But, um, he does have exposure to the music industry.

These comments suggest that the staff has missed an opportunity to engage the parents by not initiating a conversation with them about their youths' cases. Henry's father seems more than willing to strategize with the staff in crafting its sense of his son's workability; however, the staff has not yet discussed with him how to deal with his son.

Ben's mother also feels she had very limited contact with the staff: "[They] never come here [to the house]. I know he was drug tested here a couple of times. . . . They haven't really spoken with his father." Similar to Henry's father, Ben's mother implies the staff members do not appear to want to get the parents' input on their children, since they only come to the house to administer drug tests for weekly compliance reports to the court versus talking to her or Ben's father about him. This is the same father the staff described earlier as "laissez-faire" and disinterested in the drug court. From the mother's perspective, the staff has never really tried to talk to the father.

The question is not whether the staff should know the parents more intimately to be effective; it is how do parents perceive staff's engagement with them and how does that shape their willingness to work with the staff to address their children's noncompliance. Most of the parents I interviewed did not see the staff getting to know the families in any great detail. A logical follow-up question for understanding parental involvement would be this: If the staff is not trying to break down these barriers, why should parents trust it to make the right decisions for their children?

COLLATERAL CONSEQUENCES
OF PARENTAL INVOLVEMENT

The families recognized some advantages and disadvantages to the drug court taking over parental control. These collateral consequences are often ignored or not considered in great depth by the staff in its decision-making process. Yet all the parents took them very seriously, further affecting how they may or may not share information with the staff. This subsequently facilitated or limited the staff's work in assessing the youth's noncompliance. Parents did note two advantages to the drug court staff being the primary agents of social control over their children. The first is the relief resulting from not having to be the bad guy. Orlando's mother says that "one of the main things that has been helpful to me is that I don't have to be the bad guy, or there's gonna be a consequence not necessarily from me but it's gonna be from them." Greg's father agrees, "It's an easier life. Before that, you were responsible for, you know, making sure he went here and went there and then, you know, and the arguments and the conflicts and stuff that came in, and that's the frustration. It's not healthy." In addition, the staff was able to offer help in mediating family tensions, especially between divorced parents who shared custody but lived separately. Greg's father describes such a situation: "The rules at his mother's house are a lot different than the rules over here, but the—it was, it was kinda, really, it was a breath of fresh air in many respects, because we didn't know how to deal with him, and we didn't know how to control him in the right way to where it was a positive kind of, you know, situation. It always felt you were fighting. You never wanted to leave him alone, and you know, you couldn't have a life. You just couldn't. You know, so in so many ways it's—it's been nice." The parents who recognized these advantages were more likely to cooperate or cede control to the staff. They viewed the youths' problems as more than they could handle and welcomed the court's intervention to reestablish some kind of order in their youths' lives.

Parents also outlined many negative collateral consequences to the court intervention, regardless of where they fell on the involvement continuum. These consequences related mainly to the logistical, financial, and psychological strains created by the youth's drug court involvement on the entire family. Just as drug treatment counselors discuss addiction as impacting the drug user's family, the drug court intervention also could affect the family. For example, Gemma's family moved to a new neighborhood, thirty miles north, to get her away from negative influences. While Gemma's mother accepted this change because "it was way better to save her," she also noted the difficulty in leaving their extended family: "We used to have a house down there, and we used to live with all my sisters, and my mother, and [it] was really hard to do that [move]."

Other families made new living arrangements. For example, two mothers moved back in with their ex-husbands/separated spouses to make it easier for their sons to adhere to all the court obligations. Ben's mother, who moved back in with her ex-husband, explains, "He [Ben] was my first priority and top job. And I was willing to do that. I don't like living here." That choice ironically impacted the staff's view of her, as she occasionally would leave the house to spend time with her boyfriend, placing the father in charge. That led the staff to view her as a hypocrite with Ben, who she wants to obey her rules when she is not always there to enforce them.

Many parents admitted that the court obligations affected their jobs, either in terms of cutting back hours, missing work, or quitting altogether. Ben's mother mentioned having to reduce her workload as a masseuse by half to focus on her son. Similarly, George's father, a plumber, talked about having to cut back on hours to drive his son to and from his drug court appointments. This affected his pay as an hourly worker. Kevin's mother uses her lunch hour to drive her son from school to treatment to make sure he was not marked noncompliant for being late to treatment. She also reduced her hours in a dental office to be at court on Wednesdays. She outlined the consequences of that decision, saying, "I'm very lucky at my job, that, um, I can't work on Wednesdays. But, that's the most important thing for me, is to get him there on Wednesdays, see what he's doing. I wanna sit there in court. So, I'm sacrificing. Like I could go full-time work. I could get health benefits. I'm giving it up to make sure that my son is there in court . . . so I can see what's going on . . . because the system will not—if he can't get there—I mean, he's had a problem before once where we had a miscommunication." Kevin's mother does not get a sense that the staff adequately considers the families' sacrifices in its decision-making process. She has reduced her hours to part time, sacrificing health insurance, to make sure her son gets to court on time. She did this because Kevin was once late to court due to a bus. The staff did not excuse his tardiness, even though, to her, Kevin was not at fault. While she did not explicitly state her objections to the court policy, this statement indicates how the court's insistence on individual accountability obscures the fact that the families have to get involved to make sure the youth is accountable. If the youth tries to get to court on time but cannot because of public transportation issues, then it is up to the parents to get the youths to court on time. This then affects the parents' work options, as Kevin's mother outlines well, which can then lead to another type of strain on the family (e.g., less income, no benefits). It is unclear whether the staff knew of the court's influence on the mother's work schedule and if it would have affected their decision. At the same time, given the staff's limited communication with most parents, including Kevin's, it would seem highly possible they did not know, further conveying the notion to the mother that the staff does not really care about their family as much as maintaining the system.

Forrest's mother, a thirty-eight-year-old African American, discussed similar sacrifices that she took to make sure her seventeen-year-old son remained in compliance with the court. She says, "Since Forrest's been having a lot of issues, and, when I was working, it was hard for me to get him around, to get him focused, to, I took six weeks off of work [in real estate and retail] to get him focused." Other parents simply quit work altogether. Charles's grandmother, a sixty-two-year-old African American, retired early from her job at Walmart to make sure her sixteen-year-old grandson stayed on track. Benito's mother also stopped working, which she stated was the most difficult part of drug court for her:

MOTHER: I had to give up my job to be there for my son.
LESLIE: Okay. Not just to go to court but to drive him around to the different—
MOTHER: Exactly.

Both Charles's grandmother and Benito's mother, a thirty-eight-year old Latina, were able to stop working only because of their alternative streams of income (Charles's grandmother could collect Social Security/pension, and Benito's mother could rely on the incomes of her husband and daughter, who lived with them). These practical constraints on the families and youths to stay in compliance with the court demonstrate the complexity of youth accountability in the juvenile drug court. That is, it is not simply based on the youth's motivation. On a sheer practical level, youth accountability depends on the entire family's efforts, including moving and taking a loss of income.

Parents also face more financial burdens when the staff issues normal remedies for the youths. Austin's mother, a thirty-four-year-old Latina, describes how she is now completely responsible for the financial costs because her ex-husband stopped working when he found out about the court bill. She says,

Once he knew [about the bill], he stopped working. He is working on his own now, so there is nothing I can do. I would have to pay for a lawyer, and honestly I do not have the money for that. . . . I wish they could send him the bill, but it is all on me because I am responsible. . . . I only made the first payments, then I said that I would do it later, because I could not meet payments, so that's why they gave me this date [in revenue and recovery office], which is tomorrow. . . . I have to go and make payment arrangements.

While the court does not charge interest, the parents are expected to go to the probation department's revenue and recovery unit to set up a payment plan. The court expects them to pay a minimum amount every month until the total amount is paid off, for however long is necessary. If they can only pay five dollars a month, that arrangement is fine. However, if parents miss a payment and are working, the court has the option to start garnishing their wages. Ignacio's mother, a 48-year-old Latina, explains how this happened to her:

> I had made a plan because what they are charging for Ignacio is over $6,000. Then I made payments of $30 a month. . . . Sometimes I was giving more, $40 or more. But for two months I supposedly gave $25. Because of those two months, I received a letter that they sent the bill to my company. They are now taking away 25 percent [from my paycheck]. Then I told them, "no," because I am the only one who pays the rent here. . . . I then called again so they could bring it down. They brought it down to 10 percent instead of 25 percent. It is about $100 for each check.

So while the youths are the ones generating the fees based on the normal remedies issued for their noncompliance, parents end up being primarily responsible for paying them. Many parents felt this was unfair and wanted their children to pay the fees. James's mother says, "I would like the court to force these youngsters to pay for their debts, because there [at the court] you can see parents of all economic classes. . . . Parents have a hard time paying for these debts. I think if the court forced them [the youths] to pay their debt once a week by requiring them to work, it would help them a lot. This way they would think about it before involving themselves in problems." Curtis's sister, a twenty-eight-year-old Latina, concurs that if youths had to pay the fines, they might think more about what they are doing. She says, "There's kids out there [who] are sixteen or fifteen, they're working part-time or something. Maybe deduct it from their check so they could feel that, 'Oh, God, I don't wanna be on home [supervision].' So that way they, they'll think about it before [they] even do something."

Some parents also talked about the anxiety and stress created by the drug court. Anna's mother, a forty-three-year-old Latina, has anxiety in anticipating the drug court sanctions since "any time she can slip." Austin's mother talks about the stress from trying to meet the drug court's expectations, saying "the most difficult part is that one has to be informing them all the time. I have the stress of calling them all the time. I have to be aware of where he is at and this is hard on me." Charles's grandmother also describes the added strain of having to worry about informing on her grandson:

GRANDMOTHER: The only complaint I have about it is, I have to be very involved in him obeying the court rules. And, there again, they tell him it's his responsibility, and they tell him he's the one that should be calling in and out [for home supervision], and I'm only supposed to be here to support. They'll tell him in front of me, "I didn't tell your grandmother to call in and out. I told you—" And they'll say, "Uh, ma'am, he knows. Don't let him say he doesn't. We've told him." But that's the most that kinda bothered me the first, that I had to—

LESLIE: Okay, the, all the constant tracking and calling and, yeah—

GRANDMOTHER: Yes. And showing up. . . . they might drive up anytime, you know, it's like, "Okay, how do you explain this?" You know.

Charles's grandmother understands the staff's view that her role in her grandson's court case is only a supportive one. However, she states that her role is much larger than that in practice. She also questions how he is supposed to be responsible if she has to keep on top of his whereabouts in case the home supervision officers stop by the house.

This type of strain extends past the parent–drug court youth's relationship. Orlando's mother talks about the constant battle she faces with the other family members about Orlando:

My husband, he, um, he doesn't want to give him as many chances as I do. He wants immediately, he wants him locked up. . . . I have a couple of daughters that don't agree with him being here. Not only am I struggling with him, but I'm struggling with my own immediate family members . . . fighting me on this, you know. And, um, I mean, it all works out at the end. . . .That's when I get really tired of it.

Orlando's entire family is affected by his involvement in the drug court. His parents fight over when to inform the staff, and his sisters want him out of the house completely. While she does see that it "works out at the end," the impact on her mental health is clear in her statements.

Other family members describe the strain of the drug court sanctions on their everyday lives. Curtis's sister describes the most basic tasks like grocery shopping as anxiety laden if he wants to go. She says, "It gets me more stressed out 'cause I'll be the one calling him in every time we have to go, groceries. Sometimes I will tell him, 'You know what? Just stay here. I don't wanna deal with the phone call [to home supervision]. We're leaving to the store. I'm coming back in an hour.' "[10] Other parents mentioned how the court affects their relationships with their sons. George's father says, "Sometimes it [drug court] creates more stress from just the fact that, uh, you know, he gets in a bad mood, he doesn't wanna have to do this."

Lastly, parents talked about how the court feels like a punishment to them. Henry's father sees his life being "in limbo," tied to his son being in drug court. He says,

Um, that's probably the toughest part. Knowing that he's going to be eighteen in two months, and wondering what's gonna happen, are they gonna keep him? Am I still gonna be responsible for, for his actions, um, after he turns eighteen? 'Cause it's all, every parent's dream to get their children to eighteen so that they don't have the responsibility. Um, not that I don't love my son, and, and, you know, I'm not gonna put him out on the street or anything, but it is nice to know that at some point, you know, it's, you've done your job, and, and, you can retire. Or, at least go into semiretirement . . . that's all up in the air now. I have no idea. I would love to be able to . . . when he's eighteen, quit working and, you know, go be a guitar player again. I don't know that I can do that.

Kevin's mother explicitly talks about the drug court feeling like a punishment for the parents. When asked what she likes the least about drug court, she brings up her frustration with the excessive waiting, comparing it to other service interactions: "You know, I—I go to a doctor's—I mean—I don't want to sit there for two hours. . . . You know, my time is my time, too. I'm not the one that's punished." Youths and parents often complained about the court's hearing noncompliant cases first; they felt the compliant youths should be rewarded for their good behavior by going before the noncompliant ones. The court, which started hearing cases around 3 P.M., structured the cases in this way to send the noncompliant youths to juvenile hall before its shift change started at 4 P.M. However, this waiting time for compliant youths conveys the notion to the parents that the staff does not seem to respect their time. Kevin's mother says that lack of consideration leads her to disengage even further from the process. She states, "I feel like they—because of him, they're in their own routine, so they don't have any respect for anybody around them. I'm a professional. I work in an office. We—we try very much to make sure the people don't wait and have to go through that, because all it does is make people angry. And then when you make people angry enough, they're not really going to pay attention to the system or respect it."

CONCLUSION

The ebbs and flows of parental involvement are multifaceted, interactive, and complex. This issue is important to understand to see the limitations of the individual accountability message in the juvenile drug court. Consider the ways that parental involvement affects the youth's accountability in the court. If parents do not support the court's expectations, it makes it hard for youths to adhere to the court's rules and to be accountable for their actions (e.g., parents refusing to attend mandated drug treatment sessions with their children). The staff also might not be able to hold youth accountable if the parents do not report their children's noncompliant actions or they resist the court's ideas for normal remedies.

Parents actively negotiate the extent and impact of the court intervention in their families' lives, even though the court does has the primary authority over their children. While staff suggests the reasons for the lack of parental involvement are due to parents working two jobs, inadequate parenting skills, or frustration with their youths, the parents offer a different perspective that centers on the staff's interactions with the youths and parents. Parents—even those who applaud the court's requirements and influence—do not always mention their child's noncompliance because of financial reasons or because they disagree with the court's response. Some felt they simply became snitches on their children without having any say over their future in the court. Others also noted the limits of the court supervision in teaching their children responsibility, since the staff relied on parents to keep them in compliance.

While I did not emphasize the role of gender, race, and class in explaining the variations of parental involvement, the staff did acknowledge how those factors could affect the way in which parents shared information. For example, the staff often noted that parents of female youths, like Gemma's parents, tended to be overly involved, asking for the court's help to keep their daughters under control, especially regarding inappropriate sexual relationships. Some staff also cited racial and class differences in levels of parent involvement, indicating that youths of color and limited financial means have a more difficult time completing the program. In her 2003 book, *Unequal Childhoods: Class, Race, and Family Life*, Annette Lareau explores these issues to understand educational inequality, suggesting that differing class-based parenting styles can translate into children's performance in school. She argued that the middle-class parenting style of "concerted cultivation" prepared children to have better outcomes in schools that valued such qualities (e.g., cultural knowledge, self-advocacy, and focus on language acquisition and reasoning) compared to the poor parents' "accomplishment of natural growth" style, which had a more removed approach to their children, letting them develop on their own terms.[11] Judge Hooper explains in an interview how racial differences in parenting styles compound a problem faced by all drug court youths: poor impulse control. He says, "Most of them are . . . Hispanic and black. . . . They're the ones that seem to have the most problem getting through the program, because they have less support at home. I'm sorry to say that, but that seems to be true. . . . Most of these parents work, they're overwhelmed. So many of them are single-parent homes, and so it's much more easy for a kid like that to be impulsive." Eva, a Latina drug counselor, concurs with Hooper's assessment of the Latino parents, saying the machismo culture leads Latino parents to view their sons as more independent at an earlier age than other youths and also to see their sons' alcohol consumption as not that big of a deal. She says, "Hispanic culture is very different. It's okay for you know, a son to have a beer with his dad. It starts at an early age, at fifteen, sixteen, most of them work with their parents. So they go home and they have a beer, which, here, of course, it's against the law." Similarly, staff often cited the family's socioeconomic status as a huge factor in its involvement, since the poorer parents had less time or resources to support their youths in the drug court (e.g., Joe's description of the uncooperative parent covering up the youth's noncompliance to avoid paying for custodial sanctions).

However, variations of parental involvement cannot be reduced to gender, race, or class, nor can one assume variations translate into worse outcomes for the poor minority youth in the drug court. Staff members did not agree on the influence of those factors. For example, Joe notes that the white middle-class parents are as uninvolved as the poor parents of color. Moreover, while Hooper perceived minority parents to be the least supportive because of their "overwhelmed" lives, my courtroom observations and interviews revealed that Latino parents tended to inform on their youths more than other parents, especially in instances where they were trying to use the court to reestablish their hierarchy of authority in the household.

The more appropriate question to ask is: Why do parents comply with the court's expectations and in what situations? All the parents—even the most supportive of the court—negotiate when and what information to tell the staff. Part of that could stem from the parents' perceptions of the drug court as simply being one of many court initiatives and programs their children have had to complete. For example, Kevin's mother was frustrated with the drug court staff because of her experiences with a previous probation officer. James's mother confused the juvenile drug court with a regular delinquency court who handled her son's case before. The frequent and prolonged supervision structure of the court also fosters fluidity in parental involvement. The parents have many opportunities to decide whether or not to report on minute details of the youths' behaviors in school, treatment, and home.

Goffman's notion of the internal and external family economies appears to be a better framework in which to understand parental involvement in the court than looking at parental styles or parent demographics. His theory shows how parental involvement is interactive and situational. For example, how do parents view the staff's definition of the youth's dysfunction? How do they come to see their families as benefiting from the reversal of the family information rule? What happens when staff focuses on a disturbance or dysfunction that the parent views as unimportant or not under the purview of the court? On the other hand, parents might tell staff when there are disturbances to the internal economy, but what happens when the staff does not agree with the parents about those disturbances?

Ultimately, the lack of parental involvement boils down to the same issue: the parents do not feel the staff is actively soliciting or considering their input into their youth's progress. And while the staff wants parents to help their children learn accountability, it does not necessarily communicate with the parents how to be effective players in the accountability process. Many parents felt that their efforts never seemed to be enough to appease the staff. If the parents gave up too much control to the court, they were viewed by staff as not being parents. If they tried to maintain control, the staff viewed them as uncooperative. Some parents, such as Kevin's and Ben's mothers, began to distrust or disengage the court. Family involvement, as shaped by the staff's interactions with the youths and parents over time, affects the staff's sense of the youth's workability. That is, the staff's perception of the family as a barrier or partner to its efforts influences its ideas of how to continue motivating the youth to adhere to the court's expectations.

CHAPTER 7

Youth Trajectories in the Court

STAFF WORKS WITH YOUTHS FOR A LONG TIME, rarely giving up on them. For example, Claire, a seventeen-year-old white female in the east court, recently turned herself in after being on the run for six of the seven months that she has been in the court. In discussing her case during a staff meeting, Jerry, a drug counselor, suspects Claire, who is now in juvenile hall, is coming down from methamphetamine use. Weber, the judge, responds that while Claire has "pretty much been AWOL," she hopes Claire will "jump on board soon." On the one hand, the fact that the staff does not terminate Claire seems a hopeful decision. On the other hand, the staff's persistence could simply drag out the inevitable, leading to a worse fate for the youth. For example, one youth asked to be let out of drug court from the beginning, but the staff insisted on working with him for almost a year, using every normal remedy (court sanction) multiple times before finally terminating him from drug court. The staff's prolonged effort stems from the notion that staff does not know in advance what normal remedy will work for a particular youth at different points. The questions become "How does staff figure out what works for which youth? In what instances and when should staff give up on a youth?" Both of these questions need to be asked to understand how final case outcomes are determined in the court.

The answers to these questions can be found by considering the cumulative impact of staff's weekly decisions about youth noncompliance on the youth's workability. Workability refers to the staff's ideas of how to motivate the youth to be able to meet the drug court's expectations and to learn individual accountability. This is an ever evolving process. That is, if the youth does not respond in the expected fashion to a normal remedy, the staff might revise its sense of the youth's workability and try another normal remedy for the next instance of noncompliance. If the youth responds in the expected fashion, the staff might continue along the sequence of normal remedies associated the initial workability type. So, how the staff decides to work with the youth, when the staff decides to change gears in its approach, or when the staff starts giving up on working with the youth all influence how a youth makes progress in the court.

Common Workabilities	Compromised Workabilities
1. Drug oriented	1. Mental illness
2. Corrective oriented (delinquency and nondelinquency)	2. Extreme situations
3. Helping oriented	3. Lost causes
4. Noninterventional	

7.1. Workability types

There are two workability types that shape youths' final outcomes in the court—common and compromised. The common workability types all share one key feature: they are based on the staff's continued belief that youths can be held accountable for their actions. This belief is sustained by seeing if the normal remedies have some effect on the youth. Most youths fall into the first two types of the common workability category: drug and corrective oriented. Compromised workabilities start off much in the same way as the common types but veer off in another direction. This occurs because none of the normal remedies to youths' noncompliance works in the expected fashion. Staff begins to see youths in these types as unable to take responsibility for their actions.

Focusing on workability types recognizes the practical reality that the staff uses many ways to work with youths. Staff members have differing views about the most effective way to work with the youths. Sarah, a probation officer, remarked generally that "the one grand pattern is that they don't go through without relapse." In contrast, Bill, a drug counselor, describes three types of youths in the court:

There is the kind of kid that is going to breeze through drug court, is not going to have a relapse. Quite often those kids are the ones that we help the least because they have not struggled at all . . . they just never had a problem with drugs to begin with, and they just were like situational. They got in situations that caused them to become involved in drug court. . . . The other kind is the kid that is, got a good, good disease. . . . This is the typical kid. And this is the kid that we probably have the most success with is the kid that struggles in the beginning multiple times. You know, it may take eight, half a year of incarceration, or whatever, but multiple times he relapses. We come back, we put him in jail. . . . He is the kid that may or may not stay clean for a long time, but he is going to have to work somewhere recovery principles in order to survive the drug court without being locked up. . . . We have other kids that are so far gone, mostly intravenous drug users, and kids that live on the street and have no social support. . . . They won't even attempt to try, because they don't have nothing invested in trying.

Jack, the district attorney, has yet another take on the youths in the court. He says,

There are those that don't take it seriously. They come in with some trace [of drugs] in their system, and they go through a couple of getting positive tests for three to five days a couple of times before they start to get the point. Then there are those that come in, and they're like ninety-day people. Like about every ninety [days] we have relapse . . . who seemed to have the best intentions. Then there are those whose family interaction is so bad, they're runaways who tend to end up with other people whose habitat is under a bridge, and they tend to do drugs too.

All three staff members describe the youths as using drugs but with different views of the underlying causes and patterns. Bill and Jack note some might not have a drug problem at all and that other youths' main problems are related more to their lack of social support or family stability. As Bill suggests, there are different trajectories for the nonaddicted youths, who will "breeze through" drug court with relative ease, compared to the "good disease" youth, who will probably end up with "half a year of incarceration" before succeeding. Jack sees the patterns as determined by the youths' drug test results, separating out 90-day relapsers from less serious users and those whose real problems are family related.

Individual case histories are presented here to capture each of these workability types. Not all of these cases have final outcomes but indicate the expected progression of normal remedies used in each one. In considering each workability type, gender differences are discussed, as girls and boys faced very different staff responses to similar behavior. Race and class differences are also highlighted whenever possible. These differences are more subtle in tone and influence than gender, since they do not drive staff responses as explicitly. Therefore, racial and class differences are discussed more in terms of how they manifest in some staff descriptions of the youths' character, which serve to shape the staff's overall sense of which youths are still workable.[1] As discussed earlier, the staff is more likely to believe a youth is a gang member if that youth is male and Latino. Here is where the racial differences can influence a youth's case: as the staff repeatedly describes a Latino youth as a "gang" member in its frequent negotiations, the cumulative effect of that descriptive term begins to craft the staff's sense of the youth as being unworkable in the drug court, instead of focusing on the youth's drug problems.

Finally, the case histories illustrate another aspect to workability: the element of uncertainty. The staff might begin thinking the youth's main problem is drug oriented but then realize the youth's home situation is an equally important issue to address. The youth's workability can shift to a more help-oriented line to rectify the home problems or continue in the drug-oriented direction. That shift is not certain. It depends on the court's fluctuating resources, the youth's responses to the staff's decisions, and the various staff's views about which issue is more important to address. The workability types therefore are highly flexible and fluid. More important, workability highlights the tension in the accountability-based model in the drug court: the staff itself recognizes that there are limits to holding youths accountable in practical terms, given that its sense of the youth's workability is contingent upon many outside factors (e.g., parental involvement, available treatment resources) besides the youths' actions.[2]

COMMON WORKABILITIES: EXPECTED YOUTH TRAJECTORIES IN THE COURT

In all four of the common workability types, the staff works with youths to instill a sense of accountability in the youths, using the same normal remedies in various combinations to achieve the desired impact.

Drug Oriented

Given Bill's description of the "good disease" youths, one might expect most youths to fall into this workability type, for which the staff employs normal remedies to stem a youth's drug use. With each new report of drug use, the staff begins to view the youth as someone with a serious drug addiction and thus responds with progressively more severe sanctions. If a youth continues to use drugs, the eventual court outcome is usually a yearlong community-based residential drug treatment program. Consider the following vignette for Eddie, a sixteen-year-old Latino in the south court who has used marijuana and methamphetamine throughout his drug court participation. As the vignette outlines, Eddie's workability involves drug-treatment-related normal remedies in three general phases: continual drug use leading to the 28-day in-custody program, more drug use leading to a 120-day in-custody program, and suspected drug use leading to recommendation for yearlong residential treatment.

Eddie starts the drug court in December after accumulating several positive drug tests for methamphetamine while on traditional probation supervision. He has a tall, chubby frame, shaved egg-shaped head, and acne. While at first glance his physical presence may be intimidating, Eddie is very boyish and charming, especially when he smiles and talks in a soft-spoken respectful voice. At the beginning of Eddie's case, another youth client in the drug court told Julie, the probation officer, that Eddie is a drug addict, as is his whole family (he has an identical twin brother who is also on probation but not in drug court). Eddie starts off the court with a series of positive drug tests in January, for which the staff places him in juvenile hall for five and four days respectively. In early February, he gets another positive test result, and the staff wants to send him away for a month to the probation-run treatment program. Eddie's mother challenges this decision, asking if she can pay for additional confirmation of the drug tests. The staff members themselves get a bit confused as to which tests were new use, but the judge decides to keep the twenty-eight-day sanction in place because Eddie had several tests within a month span.

Eddie comes back from the monthlong program in March but tests positive again for methamphetamine. Staff restarts the normal remedy cycle and sends him to juvenile hall for four days. He does well for about a month; meanwhile, his brother is arrested on a new charge. In mid-April, Eddie gets another positive test for methamphetamine, fails to show up for court, and is on the run. He is arrested on the bench warrant in early May, and the staff decides he needs a "break" from his drug use, sending him to the 120-day treatment program at the probation camp.

When Eddie returns to the court in August, the staff notices he seems more motivated to do well in the program. It commends him for enrolling immediately back in school and also applauding his desire to play intramural football at a nearby school. However, a couple weeks later, Eddie gets a diluted test result, for which he loses ninety-eight sober days. The judge makes a deal with him that he can get those sober days back if he is clean for another ninety straight days. The staff starts to notice some strange but trivial incidents of noncompliance, such as when Eddie reported being stopped by a police officer after curfew when he was in possession of alcohol. One week, Eddie missed a couple days of school, but the staff decides to let it go because that week in court he is "one of the best ones," compared to the other youths on the docket. His brother, meanwhile, is sent to Camp Braddock [a probation camp that is considered one step before California Youth Authority] for the new arrest. Since he got back in August, Eddie still has not enrolled in a drug treatment program and has continually missed his intake appointments. The staff is not sure who to blame for that situation: Eddie says the reason was because he had to watch his younger siblings, but the staff has yet to verify that excuse with his mother.

In late September, Julie, his probation officer, notes that Eddie gets an "interesting test result" after his birthday that shows evidence of methamphetamine, but it is below the court's official cutoff for a positive test. When he gets arrested on a bench warrant in early October, Julie states that test result as positive for methamphetamine and says Eddie told her, "I planned on getting high Friday, but I couldn't stop." She then says, "Duh, that's what we tell you" (that they can't stop). She says, "He's not in recovery." After spending thirteen months in the court, Eddie currently has zero sober days, never making it past the first phase of the program.

For each positive drug test that Eddie gets at the court, staff responds with progressively more treatment-intensive normal remedies, to the point where Julie asserts that Eddie "can't stop" using drugs and is not "in recovery." The staff sees all of Eddie's noncompliance stemming from drug use, even if it is not a positive drug test result. For example, staff interprets Eddie's not showing up to court as a way for him to avoid a normal remedy for a positive drug test result. Over time, staff begins to recognize signs of Eddie's drug use and tests him more frequently than usual.

The normal remedies used here show that staff does not expect youths to stop using drugs right away or completely. Rather, the staff works with the youths to respond immediately to each drug use. It appears Eddie responds favorably to the normal remedies, doing well in the in-custody treatment programs and continuing that progress for at least a short period after being released. The staff discusses sending Eddie to a residential treatment facility but ultimately decides to keep him in the drug court to continue working with him.

While the staff does not explicitly address any racial or class differences in this workability type, the youth's gender does appear to influence the staff's interpretation and understandings of youths' drug-use patterns. The district attorney says in an interview that "the women go in varying directions depending on their, depending on the males that they associate with, who are either providing the drugs or just trying to get them drunk for the usual reasons, or whatever." In a team meeting, Charlie, the public defender, mentions to the other staff that he has noticed that all the girls in the court are using methamphetamine and the guys are hitting on them. He adds that "a lot of our girls are attractive adolescents who don't get a lot of attention at home." Other staff reiterated Charlie's gender-based view of youth drug use, mentioning to me that girls typically use methamphetamine more than marijuana because it helps them control their weight. Consider this vignette for Rita, a white fifteen-year-old in the north court. She is tall with long brown hair and looks much older than her age. In discussing Rita's case during the initial screening meeting, the public defender and drug counselor suggest they need to "fine tune her," as she has already gone to several outpatient and residential drug treatment programs.[3] In fact, she was only one month away from finishing a yearlong residential program when she ran away and used drugs. The difficulty in working with Rita is that she has significant treatment knowledge but does not appear ready to apply it to her life.

Rita starts in the court in late October after being on probation for four years. Bill (drug counselor) mentions to the other staff that she told him she wants to stop using, but he adds that what "keeps her from staying clean are the guys rolling up to her house." The staff also suspects the mother, who is a recovering drug addict, may be still using and has an "endless parade of parolee boyfriends" hanging around the house. Two weeks after starting in the court, Rita tests positive for drugs and takes responsibility by admitting to the staff that she used drugs; she gets four days in juvenile hall. Another two weeks pass by when she admits again to using drugs after her drug test result is positive for cocaine; the staff sends her to the twenty-eight-day program right before the Thanksgiving holiday. She comes back to the court in December but gets another positive test in January. She goes AWOL, and when she gets caught in mid-January, the staff sends her to a group home for girls in the south court's jurisdiction to get her away from the temptations in her home environment. Because of her new home placement, Rita temporarily moves over to the south court and has some adjustment problems at the group home. When I go to visit her there, she tells me she does not feel like she can relate to the other girls, who primarily are there as foster care placements. Rita gets kicked out of her drug treatment program near this group home for having a bad attitude and claiming gang membership during the group sessions. Despite these troubles, Rita manages to stay sober during her time in the group home, accumulating almost ninety days clean before going back to her mother's house in late March. After returning to her neighborhood, Rita starts testing positive for drugs again. She goes AWOL after the fourth positive test, and when she is picked up, they send her to the 120-day program in mid-May. The staff recognizes that the last normal remedy used up most of her custody time. She returns to the court in midsummer and does well for a few weeks. However, when she gets another positive test in August, the staff cannot do anything because of her lack of custody time:

BILL: She recognizes she does have a [drug] problem; however, she's got other issues. For example, when we left, there was a home boy across the street waiting . . .

ALLEN (PROBATION OFFICER): She's got fifteen custody days. Quite honestly, we've exhausted everything we can do with her.

They decide to keep working with her, but a few weeks later Allen says she is now staying full time at her boyfriend's house and is technically AWOL from her home placement. Rita comes to turn herself into the court for an outstanding bench warrant. They end up administratively discharging her from the court.[4] Here is an excerpt from that last discussion:

BILL: Our hope for her—we cut her loose and she reoffends.

ALLEN [REPEATING HIS SENTIMENTS FROM THE PREVIOUS WEEK]: She is on probation already for four years on a six-month misdemeanor. She's done with this, and we're done with her.

[*Later, with Rita and her mother in the courtroom.*]

SAMUELS (JUDGE): I do know it will come to a point where the same courage you had today to surrender [to the court] will come into play with stopping drugs.

Staff sees female drug use as being more complicated than that of males, given its view that the females' drug use is more intertwined with their relationships. While Rita's pattern of drug use is similar to Eddie's, the staff discusses it within the framework of her bad home environment, with her mother's endless parade of parolee boyfriends and Rita's relationships with the neighborhood boys. Rita initially seems to understand and accept the accountability framework, telling staff that she used drugs and cooperating with the staff's normal remedies, such as the group home. Yet despite her seeming workability as a drug-oriented youth, organizational factors shape Rita's case. Her lack of custody time essentially dictates the staff's responses to her drug use toward the end of her time in the court. To reiterate, custody time is based on the maximum sentence that the youth could have gotten as a disposition for her original offense. Since drug court is a postdispositional program, it draws from that bank of custodial time to issue its incarceral-based normal remedies. However, if that time runs out, the drug court staff can no longer use its custodial normal remedies (e.g., 4–5 days in juvenile hall or the 28-day or 120-day probation programs). While it is unclear how long staff would have kept working with Rita if this custody time was not an issue, it is clear that the custody time is the main reason the staff ultimately stops working with her. In the penultimate staff discussion, Allen states that her fifteen custody days prevent the staff from using any meaningful normal remedy for Rita's drug problem.[5] Yet the staff never questions the effectiveness of the model for Rita: in the last staff discussion, Bill suggests that the best hope is for Rita to reoffend and get caught, so the staff can restart the process with a new bank of custody time. Part of that reasoning could be due to her young age. The staff did mention in previous discussions that an older youth might be more able to resist such home pressures. Whatever the reason, Samuels reiterates in his last comment to Rita that it is up to her to stop using drugs, further underscoring the individual accountability notion of drug treatment.

Some youths do manage to turn from their addict ways. Consider this vignette about Rebecca, a white seventeen-year-old in the north court:

> At the time I started fieldwork, Rebecca had accumulated 131 sober days, after having spent most of the summer in the 120-day program. Both her parents are recovering drug users, and the father is often at court with her. She is very engaged in her treatment program (NA meetings), often going to more meetings than the court requires. At one point, Bill, the drug counselor, says "she is talking a lot of good recovery language, so I'm impressed." When she has some drug-testing troubles (e.g., her sweat patch fell off while she was playing sports, she took prescription medication after surgery), the staff believes her explanations. She finishes school and works two jobs. The month before she graduates, the staff discusses her progress. Bill and Allen, her probation officer, commend Rebecca for coming down to their office once a week to get tested, to which Jack, the district attorney, jokes, "She shows up on her clean day." She graduates from the court the next month, with 264 sober days.

Rebecca illustrates the ideal type of drug-oriented workability. Her main problem was drug use, and after several attempts to keep using, she finally realized she needed to stop. In an interview, Rebecca states after finishing the 120-day program that she decided to stop using because of the threat of being sent to the one-year residential program with her next dirty test result. She also adds, "I told myself over again, 'You're done, you're done playing this game, and you're going to be done living this lie, and you're going to be done.' . . . I knew what to do already, it just was a matter of fact of when I was ready or not, like I was finally ready." By saying she was "ready," Rebecca means more than simply staying clean. She also recognizes the long-term consequences of her actions in "playing this game." She says, "If I got high again and got another dirty test, I would go for another year [in the court], and then it would be on my record that I was in drug court. . . . I would miss out in school and wouldn't get my diploma. . . . I just felt like here's your last chance right now to like make it, and it's up to you whether or not you do it or not, and I'm like, I'm doing it." Rebecca made sure to stay in compliance in the court, not just for the sake of being sober but also to clean up her court record and finish school. In stating "it is up to you," Rebecca also highlights the individualistic notion of accountability so heralded by the drug court in which a youth's success or failure is based solely on her own actions and choices.[6]

Corrective-Oriented Delinquency

Staff sees another common type of youth workability that revolves around a youth's delinquent behaviors, of which drug use is just one example. This workability involves either an escalation of remedies or a recycling of different ones in an attempt to get the person away from delinquent peers, behaviors, and patterns. While a youth in this workability type might be doing the same noncompliant actions as a youth with a drug-oriented workability, staff sees his actions as more delinquent versus drug motivated. One simple way that staff makes this distinction is if the youth participant gets caught committing other delinquent acts beyond drug use. Consider this vignette on Ruben, a seventeen-year-old Latino who started in the south court in May 2002. He is medium height and skinny with shaved black hair and large brown eyes. He lives with his aunt and grandmother. Staff's evolving sense of Ruben's workability could be broken down into three parts: general yet trivial noncompliance, growing evidence of gang membership, and a new arrest. Up until the new arrest, the staff still saw Ruben as workable because, overall, he seemed capable of learning to be accountable to the drug court's expectations:

> Ruben has a charismatic personality and appears to be a natural leader among the drug court youth. The staff likes him as well. At the start of the fieldwork period, Ruben is in phase one and in juvenile hall for a home supervision violation; the staff releases Ruben from custody on home supervision again until he gets back into school. He expressed interest to staff in working for his uncle's carpet installation business. Ruben does okay but always has one minor noncompliant issue every week (e.g., an unexcused absence from his treatment program one week, a diluted test another week, tardiness at school and treatment). The staff gives him home supervision, admonishments, or no normal remedy. After a few months, he gets arrested because Julie, the probation officer, puts him on the "hot sheet" after his grandmother and aunt call to say Ruben came home late drunk and was belligerent. The staff releases him without any punishment because his outside treatment counselor comes to court to advocate on his behalf.
>
> Two weeks later (late January), he gets a positive alcohol test when a police officer administers a breathalyzer test after seeing him hanging out with a well-known Latino gang. The staff sends him to the 120-day probation program, given its suspicions that he was drinking before. Ruben does exceptionally well in the program. After coming back to the court in April, Ruben continues to be late for school or skips it altogether; staff discusses the possibility of finding another home placement for him because the grandmother cannot supervise him adequately. After only

three weeks out of custody, he gets kicked out of school and does not show up for court. What follows is part of the staff conversation discussing their options during what it perceives to be a critical moment in Ruben's case:

JULIE (PROBATION OFFICER): Ruben is at his turning point. He is a really neat kid.

JACK (DISTRICT ATTORNEY): Yup.

JULIE: They love him at treatment and he did a 100% program at camp [120-day], but as soon as he gets out he starts to mess up. . . . Home is real tense, with the aunt yelling. He was raised by his grandparents, but the grandfather died and the grandmother is dying. That is why he is with the gangs—he gets more support from the homies. . . . He had a tearful catharsis at [his drug treatment program] about how his homies were pressing him to work more, so he went with his cousin to escape . . .

LOPEZ (SUBSTITUTE JUDGE): How long will it take to get a new home placement?

JULIE: At least a month.

He gets arrested a few weeks later, and the staff sends him back out to the 120-day program. Three weeks later, the staff brings him back to court because of a new charge of attempted murder. He was allegedly involved in a gang-related beating of a rival gang member who was beaten in the head with a steel pipe. At this point, he's been in the court for two years. What follows is part of the staff conversation discussing their options:

JULIE: He told me . . . the gang was pressing him to do work—he ran to east [county] to avoid trouble . . .

JACK (DISTRICT ATTORNEY): His identity is as a gangster, not a doper.

JULIE: And this time he used cocaine, probably to try to numb his pain . . .

CHARLIE (PUBLIC DEFENDER): If he is telling us he wants to change . . . drug court does not take gang entrenched kids for the safety of our kids. . . . He's never brought any of that into drug court. He's been here a long time. We like him . . . I'd like to work with him . . .

O'REILLY (JUDGE): The fact is he is in a gang, and he wanted to try to avoid the gang unit by coming to drug court.

The staff decides to send him to the gang suppression unit to see if it will accept him, but before that can happen the district attorney's office decides to prosecute him on the attempted murder charge. Ruben gets sent to the California Youth Authority.

Ruben's workability differs from the drug-treatment-oriented one in that his noncompliance stems more from other behaviors, such as staying out all night, skipping school, being late for treatment, and getting arrested. The family influence is central to Ruben's workability, as his grandmother often informs the drug court staff that he stays out all night and drinks alcohol. So even though his drug test results are negative, staff still suspects he's not truly clean because of the grandmother's information about his behavior.

A running theme throughout staff's discussion is identifying Ruben's character as either a drug addict or a gangster. For Ruben, the staff clashes along three perspectives of his character, and the staff members use a different description to convey each perspective. Those descriptions serve a practical purpose, as they shape how the staff will respond to Ruben's noncompliance. The district attorney, Jack, repeatedly insists that Ruben is just a "gangster" who has no place in the drug court program. Julie, the probation officer, appears to see Ruben both as a gang-involved youth and a drug addicted youth, as shown by his catharsis in drug treatment. While Charlie, the public defender, does not openly disagree with Jack's view, he suggests that Ruben still has potential to succeed in this program. In the last excerpt, Charlie mentions Ruben's likeability to preserve his workability as a drug-using youth and keep him in drug court. The judge ultimately agrees with Jack in saying only that Ruben is in a gang and does not have a significant drug problem that the drug court could help him address. During this last conversation, the staff members do not really discuss specific actions of noncompliance; rather, they focus on their competing understandings of Ruben's character as completely bad (i.e., full-blown gangster), bad/sick (i.e., gang-involved and drug addicted), or bad/good (likeable gang-involved youth) in assessing his continued workability as a drug court participant.

The corrective delinquency-oriented workability takes a slightly different shape for the girls in the drug court. That is, staff sees girls as delinquent or engaging in high-risk behaviors for actions that are not as severe or frequent as compared to the boys. For example, consider the next vignette with Alicia, a sixteen-year-old Latina in the south court. Staff initially situates her within a drug workability trajectory, only to move more into a corrective delinquency-oriented workability, as a result of the staff's increasing sense that Alicia's main issues are related more to her high-risk behavior as opposed to her drug use:

Alicia is short, extremely skinny, and has shoulder-length curly hair. She lives with her younger brother (who is also on probation) and grandmother. She is smart, astutely observing how the drug court staff worked and pointing out its inconsistencies to me during our interviews. Alicia is also straightforward with the staff, usually admitting to her noncompliance. At the beginning of the fieldwork period, Alicia is attending an all-girls drug treatment program. She wants to switch treatment programs to a co-ed one closer to her house, but the staff wants her to stay where she is. She gets her thirty-day token and does well in both school and treatment. She has a diluted test result that staff interprets as her attempt to get transferred to the co-ed program. After getting four diluted tests in a row, they put her in custody for four days. Shortly afterward, the treatment program informs the court that Alicia tests positive for methamphetamine and that it is terminating her for thirty days. The staff sends her to the twenty-eight-day program in juvenile hall in early November. When she returns to the court in early December, she asks to go back to the all-girls treatment program. She gets a second thirty-day token, while her mother, who now is in a residential drug treatment program, relapses after bringing in a bottle of alcohol into the facility. Alicia does well for a few months, but right before she accumulates ninety sober days to then advance to the second program phase, she tests positive for marijuana. As a result, she loses all her sober time and gets five days in juvenile hall. She starts the co-ed treatment program and a new school. Meanwhile, her mother gets arrested, this time for smuggling immigrants over the border.

Alicia gets another sixty-day token and advances to phase two in late April; this means she only has to come to court every other week. Around this time, staff finds out that she is pregnant and her boyfriend lives in Mexico to avoid an outstanding bench warrant in the United States. She has an abortion and stays in drug court. Soon afterward, the probation officer says the grandma informed her Alicia has been taking "rochas," a drug that does not show up on the normal presumptive test and laboratory reports unless the staff specifically requests it. She admits to relapsing in mid-May and gets home supervision with a stayed weekend in custody to be imposed the next time she is noncompliant. Around the same time, the mother gets sentenced to prison for a year. Alicia does well for a couple weeks but admits to using marijuana in early June. She requests to go to Project Fortitude, a detox program. During that time, the probation officer hears a rumor that Alicia gave Calexi, another drug court client, rochas while at the treatment program.

When she returns from Project Fortitude, she goes AWOL for the weekend. The staff suspects she went to Mexico to see her boyfriend. After getting caught, she gets four days of juvenile hall. The next week, the probation officer and police officer conduct a room search and find a binder with a variety of tagging and a picture with her boyfriend flashing signs of a local gang. They ask the judge to place a no-contact order on the boyfriend. Two weeks later, Alicia leaves home for one night. She gets electronic supervision and then when she begins to miss treatment and school, she receives another three days in custody. In mid-September, she is doing better, but the grandmother is now the noncompliant one by not participating in the drug treatment's mandatory family program. Alicia goes AWOL in late September, and when she is caught a week later, she has a positive test and admits to using drugs. The staff sends her to the 120-day program. After over a year in the program, Alicia now has zero sober days.

Similar to Eddie's drug-treatment-oriented workability that sees his main problem as related to his drug use, staff initially addresses Alicia's drug use with increasingly serious normal remedies. Her noncompliance stems mainly from her positive drug tests. She does well in school and seems responsible enough in that she admits to the staff every time she gets a positive test. As such, it appears to be a drug-treatment-oriented career, with the normal remedies escalating from 4 to 28 to 120 days in custody, as well as changes to her drug treatment program.

However, as her drug use appears to become less frequent, the staff begins to talk more about her general delinquent behavior versus Eddie's case, where the staff talk remains focused on drug test results. For example, after she gets promoted to phase two, staff finds out that Alicia is pregnant and that her boyfriend is living in Mexico, running from the law. The probation officer also mentions that Alicia was using rohypnol (rochas) and allegedly gave it to other girls in the court. This latter action seems particularly egregious given that she did it in front of the treatment facility, and the drug is commonly known as the "date rape" drug, endangering the girls even more. The staff issues normal remedies to Alicia for her positive drug tests, but those remedies are situated within a more general discourse of delinquency instead of her drug use.

As a result, the staff begins to talk more about her dangerous behavior and the need to take her out of her environment. A major contingency here is the family dynamic. Over time, the grandmother begins to reveal more noncompliance to the probation officer, such as Alicia staying out all night and taking the rochas. What's interesting in Alicia's situation is that she is honest about her drug use with the staff, admitting to using and even volunteering to go to a short-term community-based detox program on her own. It appears that she is willing to take accountability for her noncompliant actions by telling staff and to be accountable for those actions such as offering to go to a detox program. Yet instead of recognizing her efforts and working with her on her drug use, the staff focuses more on Alicia's delinquent behaviors, highlighting her recklessness, manipulation of her grandmother, and going out all night.

The staff's discussions about Alicia are highly gendered. For example, the staff sees Alicia's pregnancy as a potential obstacle, whereas it often talks about fatherhood as a wonderful motivator for males to stop using drugs. The staff also does not see the girlfriends of male clients in the same way as the boyfriends of female clients. The former are not seen as a significant bad influence on the youth in the same way as the latter. Note the difference with staff's responses to Ruben's reckless behavior: Julie, the probation officer, sees Alicia staying out one night as high risk, while Ruben stays out for several nights. It also takes a police officer seeing Ruben with a local Latino gang for staff to start talking about his gang issues, whereas one mention of Alicia's boyfriend in Mexico triggers a room search by the probation officer and police officer, who find some gang material (e.g., binder and picture).

While the delinquency focus seems outside of drug court's purview, it actually fits in quite well with the drug court's model of accountability. The court's normal remedies are designed not only to teach youths to stop using drugs but also to teach them how to make better decisions in general. In this regard, some youths with a delinquency-oriented workability could be considered by staff as successful graduates of the drug court. Consider this next case of Jimmy, a seventeen-year-old Latino, in the north court.

Jimmy is tall, with a medium frame and dark hair. The staff appears to like him but also thinks he is an extremely strong-willed guy who has some problems with authority figures. He gets released early from the 120-day program at the beginning of November with seventy-seven sober days. He does well but has some minor problems at school when he uses inappropriate language and then gives a false name to the school disciplinary staff. Bill describes Jimmy as having "a victim complex that the principal is out to get him," but he also sees how Jimmy gives the school officials "all the ammo in the world" for that. The staff makes him write a 500-word essay about honesty and proper use of language in school. He continues to get into trouble at school and treatment, typically for fights with other guys about girls, as well as driving around without a license. The staff gives him community service for those incidents but then sends him back to the 120-day program in early January after he lies about a positive drug test result for methamphetamine. The staff considers long-term residential treatment at that point, but the probation department (who pays for it) objects because of financial costs. He comes back to drug court in early April. He gets suspended from school twice for defiant behavior over the next month and continues to drive without a license. Bill notes that he is doing well at treatment, despite the school troubles. He goes into juvenile hall for four days for the first school suspension but manages to avoid going into custody for the second suspension because staff allows him to stay with his mother, who is having surgery. The staff switches him to a stricter probation-run school called Visions. The next week, the staff talks again about his driving without a license and not going to school which it attributes to the father making him go on a house-painting job instead. A month later, the staff shifts gears and discuss Jimmy's remarkable progress:

BILL: This kid has made the most remarkable turnaround in attitude—everything. I don't know if Visions got him to change, but he decided to get through this—partially because he is eighteen soon, so he sees the light at the end of the tunnel. I sat with him a long time and talked today, and his attitude is real good. He still has these moments where he acts out, but all around . . . if he continues on this path, I'm for giving him the full benefits of graduation when he turns eighteen the following month.

SAMUELS: He will have been with us fifty-one weeks when he gets his six-month token. He had a real rough start . . .

BILL: He was on his way to Project Arise.

He graduates from drug court in mid-August with 228 sober days; at the time, he is still in adult school but has already completed his drug treatment program.

The staff interprets and responds to Jimmy's noncompliant behavior after his release from the 120-day program within a similar workability frame as Ruben's. His problems were not really drug related as much as they were about his bad attitude and behaviors that got him into fights at treatment and in school. It's important to note that in contrast to Ruben, Jimmy's delinquent actions are not as severe. Jimmy's fights are seemingly innocuous ones over girls, and there is also never any indication of a gang affiliation with Jimmy. So the staff is more likely to see him as capable of finishing the program. Yet, in contrast to Alicia, whose delinquency is more minor in scope, Jimmy gets a far more lenient staff response for his noncompliance, such as community service for driving without a license or fighting at drug treatment.

In addition to illustrating gender differences in youth workability, the comparisons between Jimmy, Ruben, and Alicia highlight the unpredictable nature of a youth's workability. Had probation recommended the long-term residential treatment, Project Arise, instead of the 120-day program when Jimmy lied about the positive drug test result, perhaps the staff would have seen him as more of a drug-oriented type of youth. His tenure in the court would have ended prematurely at that point without success, as they would have vacated his case. Instead, the staff sees him as having a most remarkable turnaround, giving him the full benefits of graduating early from the drug court around his eighteenth birthday.

Corrective-Oriented Nondelinquency

Staff also encounters noncompliant youths with no identifiable drug problem or serious delinquent lifestyle. Staff employs normal remedies to motivate
them to stop their noncompliant behavior, typically related to either school
or home. The next vignette is about Christopher, a white sixteen-year-old in
the south court. He rarely gets a positive drug test, and, like Ruben, he is
well liked by most of the staff. The problem with Christopher is that he does
not go to school or treatment, so the normal remedies focus on encouraging
him to do something productive with his time. The vignette shows his workability starting off like Ruben, as a period of general noncompliance where
staff suspects drug use but eventually focuses more on school issues.

Christopher is medium height, with an average frame and black hair. He
lives with his parents and younger sister in a ranch-style home in a
middle-class neighborhood near the court. He starts the program in early
October; in the screening meeting, staff discusses that he already has had
extensive drug treatment, including a residential program over a year
ago. The staff debates the extent of his drug use, noting he has a drinking
problem, but his last positive drug test is from over three months ago.
The public defender then suggests they give him a shot, and if there is a
problem they'll move him out to another program.[7] He is continually in
trouble for not going to school or treatment, receiving either no normal
remedies or short-term ones for nonattendance. During this entire time,
he tests negative. Staff advances him to phase two by mid-April. He gets
a job and asks to do Narcotics Anonymous [NA] meetings instead of his
current more intensive treatment program, which conflicts in hours with
his new job schedule.

He eventually gets a few days in custody for not coming to court,
being absent from school, and not providing the staff with a pay stub as
proof of employment. At that point, the drug counselor tells the staff that
Christopher has been skipping school on and off for months. Christopher
gets demoted back to a phase one weekly schedule in mid-May. He continues not to go to school or to provide proof of employment or proof
of attending NA meetings. At the same time, he consistently tests negative and accumulates 180 sober days by mid-June. He finally enrolls in
an independent study school program at the end of June. The staff
advances him to phase three in early July. He now only has to come to
court once a month. In early August, he has two failures to test (losing
his 221 sober days) and gets five days in juvenile hall for not providing
any documentation of his NA meetings and employment. The judge then
decides to make a deal with Christopher. If he signs up for the GED program (which was the school option he wanted in the beginning) and stays

clean, he will be terminated administratively from drug court and successfully from probation. Three weeks after the deal, he gets a positive
test for alcohol and goes in the Hall for a few days. He then signs up for
the GED and provides proof of NA meetings. In early October, when
he has accumulated thirty-three sober days, the judge administratively
discharges him from the drug court but successfully terminates him from
probation.

In contrast to the youths in the other workability types, Christopher is not
getting into too much trouble, either in terms of drug use or delinquency.
For example, he is not testing positive, like Eddie, nor is he staying out all
night, getting arrested, or hanging out with gang members, like Ruben. As
such, the staff has less opportunity or need to punish him, and he advances
more quickly through the program. The critical contingency here is that he
is not getting caught for any noncompliant behavior. For example, I observed
the mother telling the drug court police officer during a home visit that
Christopher was drinking alcohol. Christopher wasn't home at the time to
be tested, so he could not be punished for that reported incident. Christopher had chosen a drug that is very hard to detect, since it leaves the body in
such a short period of time.

Staff members told me they knew that Christopher was manipulating
them, describing him as someone who would make a great car salesman or
politician later in life. He can talk his way out of many normal remedies,
saying he has proof of compliance but never showing it to staff. In these
instances, it appears he is betting on the chance that the staff will forget to
verify or ask for the proof the following week. According to his drug
counselor in the court, "he's a good guy, but he is just lazy . . . he is very
unmotivated." During a ride-along, the same drug counselor says he sees
Christopher as one of those youths who keeps doing what they are doing
until they want to stop on their own.

It may seem premature for the judge to do an administrative discharge
for Christopher. He is not yet eighteen years old, nor has he accumulated
any significant amount of sober days. His mother has played a main factor in
the judge making this deal. She comes to court to advocate for her son, who
has been in the juvenile justice system for an extended period of time:

CHRISTOPHER'S MOTHER: We'd like to see him get off probation.
O'REILLY (JUDGE): We would too.
MOTHER: He's been on so long. It's dragging on forever. There's no end in
    sight.
O'REILLY: It's kind of his fault.
MOTHER: I know, but from before he's doing good. He's a good guy.
O'REILLY: We always liked him. . . . He always got something to tell us.

MOTHER: He paints a good picture. He's a good kid at the heart of it. . . . I'd
   like to see him be done with that part of it so he can move on . . .
O'REILLY: We're going to make a plan.
MOTHER: Okay. A plan with an end?
O'REILLY: Yes.

At this point in his workability, Christopher has been in drug court for ten
months and was in a yearlong residential treatment program in Fresno before
that. Because he manages to show some kind of partial accountability by signing up for the GED, attending NA meetings, and holding down a job,
Christopher is administratively discharged from drug court. With this decision, the staff seems to acknowledge tacitly that it cannot work effectively
with him anymore.

Home troubles are another major reason leading to nondelinquent
corrective workability. Again, the gender difference becomes apparent as
parents of girls, especially fathers, typically bring up more instances of noncompliance to the staff. For example, the stepfather of Audrey, a sixteen-
year-old Asian American female in the south court, calls Julie, the probation
officer, every time Audrey comes home after curfew. Regardless of how well
she is doing in other areas of the drug court (e.g., treatment, school, negative
drug tests), the stepfather constantly requests that the staff put her on home
supervision, to the point where the probation officers start calling him the
"sup nazi."

> Audrey started the program in July. She is a tall Asian-American girl with
> long hair and an athletic build. When screening the case, the probation
> officer says she is a "tough little thing" who "smacked her mother's
> boyfriend" and her mother. Sarah, the probation officer, describes
> Audrey as a "real druggie" who used cocaine every day in eighth grade.
> The staff determines quickly that she is smart, quick, and witty. Charlie,
> the public defender, reads from her file that when "the probation officer
> asks [her] what can I do to assist you," she said, "get me a carne asada
> and my boyfriend's address." She lives with her mother and stepfather. A
> couple weeks later, she gets put on electronic home supervision because
> the grandmother reported that she stayed out until 1:30 A.M. and was
> "under the influence." The staff was not able to drug test Audrey in time
> to see if the grandmother's claim was true.
>
> Audrey does well for a few weeks and gets a thirty-day token of sobri-
> ety. At the parents' request, the staff puts her back on electronic home
> supervision because she came home at 11 P.M. and was drinking over the
> weekend. In court, the judge gives her this warning:
>
> O'REILLY (JUDGE): One of the biggest of rules of drug court is to follow
>   the family's rules. . . .

AUDREY: Sir, it's not that I want to violate home sup[ervision], it's just that teenager thing.

O'REILLY [JOKING]: Get out of here.

CHARLIE [TO AUDREY]: Don't talk anymore.

A couple weeks later, she is arrested for another home supervision violation in which she left home without permission. She gets released from custody. A couple weeks later, the stepfather calls the probation officer demanding that she be put back on home supervision. The staff describes the stepfather as being too harsh:

JULIE (PROBATION OFFICER): Audrey's stepdad was really upset with her. Everyone else is pleased.

CHARLIE (PUBLIC DEFENDER): He's always upset . . .

JULIE: I told the dad she'd admitted she violated curfew for a few days, and there was an argument, and she said sarcastically, "Yeah, I'm high." I told the stepdad to focus on the positive and that she has been testing clean.

O'REILLY (JUDGE): Yeah.

JULIE: She's doing okay at school and fine at treatment.

O'REILLY: Yeah

JULIE: At most, community service for the curfew violation. I don't even think Audrey needs that.

O'REILLY: Yeah. How do we tell the stepfather to stay out of it?

JULIE: When I asked the father to be more positive, he said, "I am. When she washes my car, I give her five dollars."

The judge just gives her a stern warning about obeying her parents in front of the stepfather and mother. She does well for another couple weeks until the stepfather complains during the drug court hearing in front of the other youths, leading the judge to hold a private family conference after court.

As with Christopher, the corrective remedies for Audrey pertain not to the youth's drug use or delinquency but to other issues of noncompliance, which in this case are family conflicts. While this chronic noncompliance seems serious, the curfew for Audrey (as with all sixteen-year-old probationers) is technically only 6 P.M. In another discussion, Julie tells the judge that Audrey probably does not get out of treatment by that time. Yet with the stepfather constantly reporting Audrey's noncompliance, the staff has to address such troubles in a way that placates the parents. After three months in the program, she is only in the first phase with fifty-five sober days.

This kind of workability contains the unintentional possibility of turning what would amount to a status offense into a more serious delinquent act.

Staff could interpret and respond to a missed day of school or curfew problem as a probation violation. While Christopher does not necessarily go into
custody for missing school, Audrey's home troubles do lead her to get placed
on home supervision three times and sent to juvenile hall for a few days—all
within the span of a couple months. While the staff recognizes the overzeal-
ous nature of her stepfather's reactions, it does have to respond to his reports
of her misconduct, building up an official case record of "probation violations" that later could start to depict a pattern of delinquency.

Helping Oriented

This type of workability centers on getting youth participants some kind
of specific help that is not related to their drug addiction or general delinquent behavior. The staff sees these youths' drug use and other acts of
noncompliance as part of a more general problem with their environment,
such as difficult parents, an overcrowded household, or extreme poverty. The
staff's responses focus on addressing those problems. So, the intention of staff's
responses in this workability is to help the youths, instead of just treating
their drug use or correcting some kind of bad behavior. What is interesting
to see is that the staff does try to help the youths as much as it can. Yet the
ultimate goal of that extra work is to stabilize the youths' setting so that they
can do the drug court program and learn accountability.

In the next vignette, the staff views Grace's drug use and noncompliance
as the result of a bad home situation. Grace is a white fifteen-year-old in the
south court. She is fairly skinny, has shoulder-length wavy brown hair, and is
about five feet five inches. She has a loud voice and talks very fast. In general,
her workability centers around the staff's efforts to get her out of a very bad
home situation, in which her alcoholic mother is in the last stages of cirrhosis
and is schizophrenic. Once the staff finds a bed for her in an all-girl group
home, it works on keeping her engaged in it:

> At the start of the fieldwork period, Grace is in phase one, with thirty-
> eight sober days. She attends Visions, a probation school. After about
> a month, she tests positive for methamphetamine but does not show up
> for court; the judge issues a bench warrant. She is arrested a week later,
> at which point the staff sends her to the 120-day program for multiple
> reasons:
>
> O'Reilly (judge): How about Grace?
> Charlie (public defender): Twenty-eight.
> O'Reilly: Okay . . .
> Mark (clinical therapist): She already did the twenty-eight-day pro-
>   gram. We need to give her the 120-day program to give time to work
>   out a new home placement for her.

CHARLIE: 120-day program.

O'REILLY: This is for what, not showing up and a positive test?

Two weeks later in early December, a bed opens up in a group home for girls, so the staff sends her there instead of the 120-day program. A couple weeks later, she tests positive for cocaine, for which she goes into custody for five days. After that, Grace does extremely well in the group home and the drug court, accumulating various incentives. The only issues of noncompliance relate to her behavior in the group home; the drug court supports the group home's rules and encourages Grace with positive feedback.

The staff does not issue any normal remedies for her noncompliance until late March, when she tests positive for methamphetamine. Staff puts her into custody for three days, and Grace loses over ninety sober days. The staff frames that test as a reaction to Grace being upset over her mother's alcoholism and a sense that she will be in the group home forever. After getting released, Grace does well for a few weeks until she tests positive again for methamphetamine in mid-April. The staff puts her into juvenile hall for four days but does not put her on home supervision afterward:

JULIE (PROBATION OFFICER): Grace said some guy at school gave her some methamphetamine. . . . I think she should do five days in custody.

JACK (DISTRICT ATTORNEY): Five.

JULIE: She said she really wants to get clean. I told her, "I believe you."

O'REILLY (JUDGE): Four days . . .

JULIE: Should she go on home supervision?

CHARLIE (PUBLIC DEFENDER): No, she is already on it at the group home—it's a living home sup.

After this stint in juvenile hall, Grace has no significant noncompliant incidents, advancing to phase two in early July. She excels in the probation school, transferring to a continuation school in August. She also finishes her treatment program in July and moves into an aftercare program. During this entire time, she is living in the group home, whose staff arranges for her to see a psychologist and also helps her find a job. At the end of the fieldwork period, she has 182 sober days, getting her six-month token of sobriety, and is promoted to the third phase in the court.

The gender differences factor into Grace's workability, as it was much easier to find a bed in a group home for a female versus males. Once in the group home, Grace gets a series of intermittent positive drug tests. Instead of following the escalating normal remedies as found in a drug-treatment-oriented workability, the staff interprets those tests as Grace's adjustment and reaction to being in a group home and tries to find remedies to help her stay engaged in the group home. The staff decides to issue more lateral normal remedies of short-term custodies (five days, three days, four days). One time, the staff also decides to not to release her on home supervision, recognizing that her group home is, in essence, home supervision. With this intention of helping Grace with her home situation, the staff focuses on keeping her motivated and encouraged. The judge often gave her extra incentives and also praised her more extensively than the other youths. This is all to stabilize her to be able to stay in compliance with the court, which she does by finishing school and treatment. The helping workability depends on the problem not exceeding the court's resources. When youths have an extremely difficult home situation, the staff usually does not see them fitting into this workability.

Noninterventional

While perhaps the rarest of workability types, there are situations in which youths sail through the program with no significant instances of noncompliance. The staff does not have to do anything to shape the youths' behavior. It assumes the youths either do not have a drug problem in the first place or that they were scared straight early on. An instance of this type is Manu, a sixteen-year-old Latino who started in the north court in June. He is fairly tall, with shaved dark brown hair and a round face. Manu lives in a remote part of North County, over twenty miles from the courthouse, where the public bus runs infrequently.[8] The closest treatment program is on a Native American reservation.

> Manu has not had any positive drug tests, except for one diluted test result that staff excused because he had been working outside in the sun doing construction during the summer and was drinking a lot of fluids to avoid dehydration. While he does not always make it to court, he does call to say he cannot find a ride to get there. When he is in phase three of the program (224 sober days), he gets suspended from school once for a "tagging" incident, but staff dismisses it as a miscommunication between school officials and him. They give him community service for that incident. The judge reviews his case and says "he's been pretty steady in reformness." He graduates early in March because he completed his drug treatment program, had no positive drug tests, and had 280 sober days.

What's interesting to note is that staff uses these youths like Manu as further evidence to how the program works, versus recognizing that perhaps the youths should never have been in the program at all. In some ways, these youth do serve to boost staff morale in that they are succeeding in the program. Consider this excerpt from the staff discussion on Manu on the day of his graduation:

BILL (DRUG COUNSELOR): Manu must have been one that the screening committee had a hard time with.

SAMUELS (JUDGE): Absolutely right—he's also GSU [gang supervision unit].

BILL: Yes he was.

SAMUELS: There were war stories about him before he came, but he's been more pleasant than others.

BILL: He is headstrong, so when he puts his mind to something, he'll do it.

On paper, Manu is seen as a really bad candidate for the program, yet he manages to do well in the court. One implication to having these youths in the court is that they take up resources (e.g., treatment and school slots, staff supervision time) that could be applied to other youths who need more attention. Ultimately, though, staff can claim victory over youths for whom they did relatively little work.

In all the common workability types, the staff tries various normal remedies to convey a message about accountability where youths learn to make better decisions and take responsibility for their actions. For the drug-oriented workability, the staff sees the youth's main problem as drug-related and predominantly uses normal remedies such as drug testing, drug treatment, and custodial stays in juvenile hall to curb the youths' drug use. For both the delinquent and nondelinquent corrective workabilities, the staff focuses on curbing other types of noncompliant behaviors through normal remedies that are not as therapeutically oriented, like community service, house arrest, and juvenile hall. The helping workability involves finding alternative solutions to the youths' non–drug-related problems, after which the staff can focus on the youths' drug use issues. The nonintervention workability features little staff guidance in the youth's trajectory through the court, as the youth appears able to be accountable on his own initiative.

At the same time, the juvenile drug court staff recognizes that some youths will present problems that it will be unable to address. Identifying who those youths are is not so clear in the beginning stages of their time in the court. Depending on the youths' actions and contingencies present at that time, the variations on common workability types could eventually turn into compromised workabilities.

COMPROMISED WORKABILITIES: UNUSUAL YOUTH TRAJECTORIES IN THE COURT

This section looks at how staff starts to see certain youths as having compromised workabilities. These youths have an extreme situation of the issues and challenges discussed in common types. The main difference that leads some youths to fall into the compromised workability is that they cannot be held accountable in the same way as the youths in the common workability types. If the youths are mentally ill, they cannot be held responsible for their actions. If the youths' problems are so severe that the court cannot respond, the staff considers the youths' situations as too unstable for them to take accountability for their actions. And if the court's normal remedies repeatedly have no visible impact on the youth, the staff considers the youth unable to learn accountability in the drug court.

Even though staff recognizes youths might fit into these compromised workabilities, it still continues to work with them to try to have some positive effect. The youths may fluctuate between workability types as the staff tries different normal remedies to influence their behavior.

Mental Illness

Unlike the other explanations used to explain youth noncompliance (e.g., unwillingness to accept responsibility for actions, disadvantaged socioeconomic or family situation), mental illness provides an amnesty function for youths because staff does not necessarily expect them to be responsible for their actions.[9] In this light, staff considerations of mental disorders create potential tensions in the court's accountability-based model. In contrast to traditional juvenile court settings (Arrigo 2002; Emerson 1969; Jacobs 1990) that have to decipher if a defendant is sick mentally or delinquent/criminal to determine the extent and nature of the defendant's accountability, the juvenile drug court has the additional task to decipher whether the youth is mentally ill and/or drug addicted, as well as if he or she is delinquent.

This added layer of decision making poses several logistical challenges for the staff that is limited in its organizational responses to youth with mental disorders. While the court's clinical therapist could do mental health counseling, he only does so if the drug court team mandates counseling. In addition, while the staff can order psychological and psychiatric evaluations for the youths, it does so typically while they are in custody. Youths taking certain psychotropic medications were not allowed in the probation camp, which was too far from psychiatric hospitals to get the necessary care if the youths had problems. Perhaps the biggest limitation lies in getting psychotropic medication for the youths. The only way the court can provide uninsured youths with medications is if they are in juvenile hall for at least thirty days, so the court-appointed psychiatrists can monitor them. However, given that the juvenile drug court cannot legally impose that length of stay just for this purpose, the staff comes up with other official reasons to put a youth in juvenile hall. All of these contingencies affect how the staff works with youths in this workability type.

The staff's decision making is constrained, as it cannot hold youths accountable for behaviors caused by their mental illness. The longer the youth goes through the court with an undiagnosed mental illness or a diagnosed illness for which he does not have the appropriate medication, the increased possibility that the staff might suspect the youth is just faking it to get away with bad behavior.[10] The staff could potentially hold one undiagnosed youth accountable for the same action committed by a diagnosed youth who would be absolved from any responsibility.

Diana, a seventeen-year-old Latina in the east court, best exemplifies how mental illness can affect a youth's workability. Like many of the poor and Latino youths in the court who the staff suspects of having a mental illness, Diana did not have a documented mental illness, nor did she have health insurance to get a diagnosis and treatment.

> Diana starts the court in mid-October. She is a little plump, with a baby face and long wavy black hair. She appears really shy and quiet during the court days, not interacting with the other youths or staff. She lives with her mother, who the staff sees as an incompetent parent. The screening committee notes Diana has regularly tested positive for marijuana and has used PCP in the past. Her record also shows she assaulted her mother and got into a fight with a girl at school. In December, she gets arrested for a DUI, ending up in a psychiatric hospital on a seventy-two-hour hold. The staff puts her on home supervision because the official petition for the DUI has not yet been filed in the court. The next month, she tests positive at treatment for marijuana when the staff brings up her psychiatric hold again. No normal remedy was issued. Two weeks later, they formally handle the DUI in the court and do not give her a punishment, stating her psychiatric hospital stay was a sufficient response.
>
> In February, the staff discusses how Diana is missing school a lot, needs psychotropic medication, and lacks support from her mother. Diana gets suspended from school in March. She also has a tampered sweat patch, for which she was supposed to spend two days in custody. Because she has an abortion scheduled for later that week, the staff decides to rescind that custodial normal remedy. She keeps missing school and court over the next few months. The staff avoids giving any normal remedies, citing her abortion. An excerpt from one staff discussion during that period is as follows:
>
> JILL (DRUG COUNSELOR): She is saying she is depressed.
> CHARLIE (PUBLIC DEFENDER): Saying? She had an abortion. . . .
> SARAH (PROBATION OFFICER): Diana canceled her first appointment [with the court psychologist] because of menstrual cramps. . . . The mother was referred to parenting classes and there was also the tutoring . . .

JILL: She is not going to school . . .

JACK (DISTRICT ATTORNEY): I think we've lost our credibility with her because we've given her too many breaks.

JILL: Yeah, she said yesterday, "I don't think locking me up will help," and I said, "It's your responsibility to go to school, it's your responsibility to go to treatment, and it's your responsibility to go to drug court." . . . When I went over there [her house], she was bundled up on the couch watching TV.

CHARLIE: That's what you do when you are depressed.

Diana does eventually see the court psychologist, who recommends she get another evaluation by a psychiatrist for medications. In mid-May, she changes schools because of the excessive absences but ends up failing the semester for lack of credits. She tests positive for cocaine and does not come to court. She comes three weeks later and tells the court she had appendicitis. The staff decides she does not have to go into custody. In early July, she gets a positive drug test result, for which she goes to the twenty-eight-day program. After getting released, she starts to miss school again. At that point, Hooper says, "I don't know what to do with her."

She turns herself into the court in late August. The staff puts her in juvenile hall for seven days on suicide watch because it notices some marks on her wrists. She stays in juvenile hall for a few weeks until she can get assessed for psychiatric medication. The psychiatric staff thinks she might need medications at night and that her problems could be related to sleeping issues. When she gets out, she starts doing better, accumulating ninety sober days and advancing to phase two in September. She also is going to school and getting more support from the mother. Yet she is also waiting to see a psychiatrist for a full medication evaluation and continues to have sleeping problems. She gets kicked out from school and treatment in November and has a presumptive positive test for marijuana.

Diana's case shows how mental illness issues come up in staff discussions when it sees the normal remedies as ineffective. While some staff members have different ideas about her workability, with Jill saying she needs to take more responsibility and Jack and Charlie saying she is depressed, the staff's perceptions of Diana's mental health issues prevail over most of its decisions about her noncompliance. Initially, the staff is very lenient in responding to her noncompliance of the DUI arrest compared to other youths, mainly because of her psychiatric hospitalization after that arrest. The staff's mental-health-influenced responses also can redirect or prolong the youth's trajectory in the court as the staff waits for mental health treatment instead of using normal remedies to respond to a youth's continued noncompliance. For example, the judge authorized her evaluation for psychiatric medication in April, but Diana was still waiting for that screening in October, due to institutional delays in getting psychiatric care for uninsured youth. In the meantime, she continued to not attend school regularly, ran away from home for a few weeks, and tested positive for drug use, for which she received little or modified normal remedies because the staff kept waiting for the evaluation. Even though it is not using normal remedies to do so, the staff continues to try to teach her responsibility by keeping her in the drug court. But because no mental health responses are available, she is effectively in limbo, where she is not held accountable or treated for her illness. At the end of the fieldwork period, she had accumulated only 110 sober days of the 365 required to graduate, despite having been in the court already for a year.

Staff often is less divisive in discussions about a white youth's mental health issues, paying more attention to responding to the youth's psychological problem than determining an appropriate punishment for noncompliance. This is mainly related to the fact that the white youths, who were predominantly middle class, had the private resources such as health insurance to verify the court's diagnosis or expedite the process. In the next vignette, Luke is a white sixteen-year-old in the east court. The staff interprets his noncompliant behavior as related to his mental illness, which was documented in his file before starting the drug court. He lives with his grandmother, who is retired and with whom he has occasional fights. His father and mother, who are divorced, live in Los Angeles, and neither is able or willing to take care of him right now. His time in the court could be seen in two phases: the first involves the staff focusing on Luke's mental illness as the main source for his noncompliant behavior. The second phase of Luke's tenure in the court veers more toward addressing home issues as the grandmother starts having health problems and becomes physically unable to take care of him:

Luke started in the court in December after having been on regular probation for only a few months. He is medium height, with cropped brown hair, big round brown eyes, and a stocky wrestler's build. His court file states he is bipolar and has AD/HD. He goes to a special school for dually diagnosed youth and is currently on five different kinds of psychiatric medication. The first week he is in the drug court, he gets into trouble on the school bus for yelling obscenities at the bus driver. The staff views this behavior as a result of his mental illness.[11] In addition, a positive drug test result for amphetamine is also understood to be a result of one of his medications, Adderal. His grandmother calls staff when she feels Luke is disrespectful with his abusive language and yelling at her. In these instances, the staff discussions center on whether or not he is taking his medication, and staff usually just admonishes him and extends home supervision. In court, he always expresses remorse for his actions; in one instance, he asked staff to put him on home supervision because it helps him stay out of trouble. As he told me afterward: "I can't get structure by . . . doing the bad thing I keep on doing over and over again . . . so I might as well put on the table and say, "Put me on house arrest, please."

After advancing to phase two easily in March, he admits to drinking alcohol and goes into custody for the weekend. When he gets out, he starts to have a negative attitude in drug treatment. He also has a couple sweat patches that fall off. Because the school calls to verify that the patches fell off while he was playing football at school, the staff does not consider them to be tampered tests. The grandmother then starts having some health problems and tells the court that she can no longer take care of him. The father starts looking into military schools for him. In late April, Luke tests positive for methamphetamine and marijuana. Instead of punishing him, the staff decides to administratively discharge him, because the father comes to court with information on a twenty-four-hour school for troubled youth in Utah that is ready to accept him the following week. The father says his work hours are too long for him to supervise Luke adequately. The district attorney says to the other staff that, "in the range of what we get here, he's not that bad," and that Luke was just "self-medicating." Luke was in the court for five months.

The first phase of Luke's tenure in the court addresses his drug use, which appears to follow the typical path described by staff: getting to ninety sober days without any problems but then messing up, as evidenced by him admitting to using alcohol. Yet Luke's workability is shaped by an additional lens of his mental illness that is already documented in his court file. Unlike Diana, Luke's noncompliance in the court is explained entirely by his mental illness. Staff interprets Luke's conflicts with grandmother as a result of him not taking medication and focuses its responses on getting him to take it. After staff considers the medication issue stabilized, it begins working with Luke within the traditional accountability-based approach.

Luke's workability is ultimately hampered by the court's inability to resolve the home placement issue so that he can continue to stay in drug court. When discussing the father's plan to send Luke to a boarding school for troubled teens in Utah, the judge resists, saying he does not have to allow this transfer because Luke is a ward of the court. However, the court realistically has no alternative placement option. The limits to court's *parens patrie* become clear here, since the father has the ability to exert greater influence over his son because of his financial resources. That does not stop Judge Hooper from making these remarks to the father and grandmother:

LUKE'S DAD: I want to help him.
HOOPER: I think he is a pretty good kid.
FATHER: So do I.
HOOPER: I think partly the way he acts is because of rejection, and the fact he has been bounced around—and bounced around again . . .

After court, I see Luke's grandmother talking to another youth's mother, saying, "We're doing the best we can."

The staff blames the family in this case for Luke's compromised workability in the drug court. It does not try to figure out how to fix the home situation with the grandmother, offering her support to help supervise her grandson. Instead, it blames the family for rejecting him. So his potential to be held accountable is ultimately curtailed by his family situation, not his mental illness. The court's shortcomings in its approach are hidden in this interpretation. Who knows what would have happened if the staff had focused more on improving his relationship with his grandmother instead of his adherence to taking his medication, especially considering his mental health issues were largely under control without significant court intervention. The youth's mental health issues can lead sometimes to other compromised workability types that lead to failure in the court. That is, the mental health issues effectively skew the staff's perceptions about other possible and perhaps more effective workability types for that youth.

Extreme Situations

This type of workability occurs when the staff does not have the available remedies to address the youths' trouble in any meaningful way. More often than not, the youths who fall into this category have exaggerated situations of one or some of the typical barriers—a bad home situation, drug addiction, delinquent behavior, gang membership, or transportation problems—that most youths face in the court. This affects the staff's ability to work with them, as there becomes a clear mismatch between the youths' problems and the staff's normal remedies. In general, these youths are predominantly poor and Latino. When the court does not have the resources to treat, correct, or help the youth to hold them accountable, it moves them out of the program.

In this next vignette, Paulino is a fifteen-year-old Latino in the south court. During the screening meeting, the staff notes that he is coming from another intensive supervision probation program, Changes, and while he appears to be in a local Latino gang, he does not have enough custody time to be an eligible candidate for probation's gang suppression program. His family situation is so unstable that the staff skips several steps in the sequence of normal remedies to send him to a residential program after only a few months.

> Right after starting in the court, Paulino admits to staff that he drank alcohol and stayed out all night. His older brother also drinks alcohol, and they go out all night together quite often. The family is receiving multisystemic therapy, an intensive form of family counseling, through the school district. His family situation is difficult, in that there are reports that his father is an alcoholic and abusive toward his mother, and Paulino often has had to prevent the father from hitting his mother. The mother eventually gets a restraining order against the father. Meanwhile, Paulino gets jumped by rival gang members who stab him on public transportation on his way to drug treatment. Later, when he is drunk, he falls out of his window and breaks both his arms, requiring surgery. The staff does not issue any normal remedies because Paulino is in the hospital for his injuries. Soon afterward, the mother allows the father to come back into the home because she cannot handle the children without him. Paulino then drinks vinegar to try to avoid testing positive and continues to violate curfew by staying out all night. At this point, the father shows up to court with the school family counselor. The father requests long-term residential drug treatment (RTF) for Paulino. The staff detains Paulino in juvenile hall until he gets a psychological evaluation, a prerequisite for the court to start that process. Charlie, the public defender, summarizes the evaluation, stating the dilemma as follows: "He probably will abscond from a residential setting, but then it said because his father is abusive and drinking, to send him home is a mistake. So, because of that, he recommends RTF." Julie, the probation officer, adds the psychologist also recommends sending him "as far away from [here] as we can find." She says the psychologist "believes the minor is depressed, but he doesn't realize he's depressed. It comes out as anger." Staff decides to keep him in juvenile hall until he can be placed in a residential treatment program.

Paulino's case demonstrates an extreme workability type in which staff quickly recognizes the mismatch of remedies to the problem. It is rare to have the public school system fund such an expensive form of family therapy. This adds to the staff's sense of the severity of the family troubles. Paulino's drug use also has more serious consequences than other youths. He does not just drink alcohol; he ends up in the hospital for surgery after falling out of a window while drunk. Even if he wanted to go to drug treatment, the threat of gang retaliation while he is out in public impedes his ability to travel safely to the treatment program. Given there is no other family in the area to watch after Paulino, the staff sends him to residential treatment after only two months in the program.

Other kinds of extreme workability take longer to develop. Staff may think that it can handle these youths' problems but then eventually realize that its normal remedies are not sufficient to address the magnitude of the issues. Consider the case of Felix, a fifteen-year-old Latino in the south court who has a history of marijuana and methamphetamine use. His mother, a recovering drug addict, is very supportive of her son, and her fiancé takes him to NA meetings. His aunt and grandmother also are very involved in his life. In fact, the aunt advocated once for a residential treatment program in Mexico instead of drug court. Felix's tenure in the court features three distinct phases of extreme delinquency and drug use. The first centers on an immediate suspension due to a new arrest; the second involves an extreme version of him resisting arrest; and the third results in termination after injuring a police officer while trying to avoid arrest:

> Felix started in the south court in the beginning of November. He appears very innocent, with a baby face, wavy brown hair, and a slightly chubby frame. Within a week, he gets arrested on a new charge of car burglary. He is suspended from drug court and gets sent to probation camp until end of January, when he is accepted back into the drug court program. He starts off well, but the probation officer tells the other staff that the mother is worried about taking him off of home supervision. Against her advice, they take him off home supervision because he is already in treatment and school.
>
> A couple weeks later, he is back in juvenile hall for an incident at school in which he resisted arrest. It also took three probation officers to control him as he was getting booked into juvenile hall. He stays there for ten days, partly due to the school trouble and partly, as the drug counselor noted, to "detox in the hall." After he gets out, he gets into some minor trouble at school and court, for which he receives no punishment. He then gets a thirty-day token for clean time and appears to be doing well.
>
> He goes on the run for a few weeks. While he is being arrested, he tries to run away from five police officers. In the process, he breaks one of the officer's arms. The officer has to retire early because of his injury. The drug court suspends him a second time until he can get arraigned on that charge a couple weeks later in mainstream juvenile court. He gets sent back to drug court but goes on the run shortly thereafter. At that point, the staff has the following conversation:
>
> RAUL (DRUG COUNSELOR): He can't stay clean.
> JACK (DISTRICT ATTORNEY): It is not just staying clean. He can't stop living a crooked life. . . .

O'REILLY (JUDGE): I agree with Raul. He really has a problem with marijuana.

Felix turns himself in two weeks later, and the following week a substitute judge (Lopez) is on the bench. Here is the final discussion about Felix at the end of June:

JULIE (PROBATION OFFICER): I recommend sending him to Changes, which has a lot more power than drug court . . .

CHARLIE (PUBLIC DEFENDER): He did turn himself in.

LOPEZ (SUBSTITUTE JUDGE): You have to explain that to me, why they talk about a kid who turns himself in as if it is a good thing. The reason they turn themselves in is because they have nowhere else to go.

JACK (DISTRICT ATTORNEY): The cops chase them in.

CHARLIE: He came in with his mother. He wasn't on the streets.

JULIE: Felix told me he'd like to come back to drug court. My fear is he is so noncompliant. He said he wants drug court because he gets more supervision. I said that's not true—we couldn't find him ever to test him.

CHARLIE: How old is he?

JULIE: Fifteen.

JACK: When you cost a [police officer] guy's career, there has to be some consequences.

CHARLIE: We already dealt with that. . . .

JACK: We told Felix next time we're going to send you to Changes.

JULIE: We need to do what we say; otherwise, the kids know they can do whatever they want.

LOPEZ: There needs to be some consistency . . .

[*The following is a side conversation among Joe (probation officer), Raul (drug counselor), and Sharon (court analyst), who were sitting behind me in the audience*]:

JOE: There is a safety issue. We aren't armed.

SHARON: I'm losing officers in the field cause of stuff like this.

[*Back to the staff's discussion.*]

JULIE: We could send him to Project Fortitude [twenty-one-day detox program], but I'm afraid they would send him home, and then he would relapse immediately. He doesn't have the tools yet.

LOPEZ: What's the rec? Changes?

JULIE: Changes at a minimum 240 [days].

Felix's trajectory in the court features extreme versions of staff's remedies and youth's noncompliance. Felix gets suspended twice from the drug court after getting charged for a car burglary and resisting arrest. He gets sent back to the drug court both times due to a fortuitous contingency that O'Reilly heard those cases and kept referring him back to drug court. While O'Reilly and others probably expected Felix to then fall into a common workability type, Felix's noncompliance escalates quickly. The staff stops trying to figure out how to help him address drug issues, to the point that Julie hesitates sending him to a community-based detox program, because Felix "doesn't have the tools yet." The staff starts talking about Felix as a delinquent who requires the more intensive supervision of Changes, the probation program which Paulino was in before drug court. There are other larger issues outside of Felix himself that inform his workability: staff sees the need to have more consistency for the rest of the youths and to maintain the safety of unarmed staff in the field. The court also needs to show the police officers that it is serious about dealing with delinquent youth to maintain its working relationship with this external agency, upon whom the staff depends to arrest youths.

The next vignette about Vanessa, a seventeen-year-old Latina, shows the extreme version of the helping workability. Vanessa is not able to be held accountable under the typical drug court model because of her extreme home situation, which staff depicts as one of the worst child protection services cases it has seen. Her biological parents abandoned her, and her foster father molested her. Judge Samuels says he previously dismissed her case in dependency court two years earlier because he thought the foster father had already died. However, he is still alive and recently returned home after becoming terminally ill and wheelchair-bound.

> Vanessa starts in the north court in early January. She has a medium build with wavy dark brown hair. Allen describes her initially to the other staff as having a history of running away from Images, home, and RFG, a 120-day probation program for girls. One week after she starts drug court, the staff has the following discussion:
>
> ALLEN (PROBATION OFFICER): Vanessa didn't go home last night.
> JACK (DISTRICT ATTORNEY): The molester is in the house.
> CHARLIE (PUBLIC DEFENDER): He died over the weekend . . .
> JUDGE SAMUELS: She is a foster kid who was molested by the dad, and the guardian aligned with her husband. . . . What we don't know is the emotional stuff she is going through . . .
> ALLEN: We need to improve the eligibility process to screen out these kinds of cases.
> CHARLIE: No one else would take her. We had to try.
>
> Vanessa goes on the run the following week. She gets arrested on a bench warrant two months after the drug court police officer heard she was

hanging out with gang members. She tests clean, but the staff has to figure out a new placement for her since her foster mother does not want her back. They send her to the twenty-eight-day program. She goes back to live with her foster mother and goes on the run a week later. She is arrested on a bench warrant less than two weeks later, when the staff sends her to RFG, which is connected to the juvenile hall. The foster mother again states she does not want her back.

While Vanessa is in the RFG program, the staff tries to get her into a group home. Vanessa does not want to go, and the staff fears she will run away from that program. Two months later, the staff shifts gears to see if her friend's mother would be willing to take her in. That does not work out, so a month later, the staff arranges for her to interview at Job Corps, a yearlong residential vocational program. She has now been in RFG for four months, during which time she has started to make a lot of progress in school. Her teacher writes a letter to Job Corps stating, "Vanessa has developed into being an academic student. She's truly desiring a higher level of learning. She works diligently. . . . Teaching her is a joy . . . [she is] setting goals and is determined to make her life special." Ten months after starting the court, the last five of which she was detained in juvenile hall, she appears in court one last time before going to Job Corps. She tells the staff, "I learned a lot. I did . . . I learned how to respect other people and their opinions." . . . Judge O'Reilly says, "I really hope you do well at Job Corps." He then says that she could get a great job afterwards and that he looks forward to hearing good things from her. Vanessa says, "Me too."

Vanessa's case is interesting in that it shows how far the staff will go to work with a youth. Even though it knew of her horrific home situation from the onset, it still accepted her because, as Charlie says, "we had to try." This indicates the staff would work with almost any youth, even if drug use is not the main problem. However the staff does not acknowledge that it does not have the necessary resources at its disposal to work with Vanessa. The staff instead uses normal remedies for a completely different purpose here. The staff sends her to the 28-day and 120-day program each time she gets rearrested. Typically, the staff would reserve those normal remedies to respond to youths' increasing drug use and to teach them accountability. The staff made an exception with Vanessa because she had a long history of running away, and the staff needed time to figure out new home placements for her. In the end, the staff was able to send her to another program, Job Corps, in which she would get free housing while receiving vocational training. Ironically, Vanessa was able to end on a positive note and even learned what the drug court hopes every youth will learn—such as setting goals and how to respect people—without having to go through the court's accountability-based framework of normal remedies. So while she does not graduate from drug court, the staff was able to work with her to get her on a positive path through Job Corps. At the same time, the staff has some success with her only because it kept her locked up in RFG for months as it transitioned her to Job Corps.

Lost Causes—Nothing's Working

Staff may take a long time to recognize that normal remedies will not impact the youth in any meaningful way. In these trajectories, the youths are not doing anything extremely bad. These cases differ from the extreme ones in that the staff cannot easily identify the youth's problem. Even if the staff knows the problem, the staff believes the available remedies should be sufficient to have some positive effect on the youth. This belief stems from the sense that the remedies would help other youths with the same issues. Consider this example with Jude, a fifteen-year-old Caucasian who has been in the south court for over a year. Jude refuses to comply with any of the court conditions, despite being punished several times for his noncompliance. The staff essentially runs out of ideas on how to influence him in any long-lasting way. Jude's trajectory in the court could be summed up in the following phases: (1) open resistance to the court, telling staff he does not want to do drug court; (2) unstated resistance yet continued noncompliance; (3) a positive potential shift in momentum; and (4) total noncompliance, leading to placement in a residential treatment facility.

Jude is short and skinny. Some of the staff says he has the "little man" complex and a "jockey stature." He lives with his parents and brother. He had just gotten out of the 120-day probation program when I started fieldwork. He is consistently late for court and regularly does not go to treatment or school for the next month. When Jude does not show up for court one day, a bench warrant is issued. He gets picked up a couple weeks later, and at that point the district attorney suggests "cutting him loose" from the court. They decide instead to detain him, pending a screening for a yearlong residential drug treatment program (Project Arise). It turns out that he was in that program before but ran away from it. He and his mother told the public defender at that point that he did not want to do drug court. The staff sends him back to the 120-day program in November. Jude tells the judge again that he does not want to do drug court. Julie (probation officer) says that Jude told her, "I love the life."

When he gets out of the 120-day program, Jude expresses interest in Job Corps but is too young to be eligible. As before, he does not go to school or treatment, and the staff has a hard time finding him to administer drug tests. He gets five days in juvenile hall for these absences. Staff finds out that he has been deleting its messages on the home machine and that he leaves school thirty minutes after his father drops him off. He does not come to court either. He goes on the run in late March, and when he is arrested almost a month later he admits to using marijuana. At this point, he has been in the drug court for fourteen months. The staff decides to detain him in juvenile hall until he can get into Project Fortitude, the twenty-one-day detox program. The staff chooses this option because the twenty-eight-day Probation program has been closed due to budget cuts. It takes over a month to get him into detox, during which time staff discusses him as "dragging the whole program down" (public defender), a "waste of time" (drug counselor), and a "classic drug addict" (judge). At the same time, the staff also says that he is a likeable youth who just does not want to listen to anybody.

Jude finally is accepted into Fortitude but gets kicked out for fighting. When he goes home, his brother, who is a heavy methamphetamine user, attacks him because he thinks Jude has drugs. Judge O'Reilly says, "this kid is messed up. He's done every program short of CYA [California Youth Authority]." They decide to give him eight hours of community service for getting kicked out of detox, because he appeared to bond with a counselor there. Jude seems to do better the following week, going to school once and testing negative.

However, the next week in early July, he stops going to school and does not come to court; the judge issues another bench warrant. A couple weeks later, he gets arrested and they detain him for several weeks to screen him for long-term residential treatment. Judge O'Reilly says, "Of all the kids I wish would age out of the juvenile justice system," it would be Jude." The judge discusses the possibility of sending Jude to Camp Braddock, one step before CYA. He says that Camp Braddock is "not a treatment place, but I'm not convinced any treatment will help him." Julie, the probation officer, convinces the other staff to delay that decision while they pursue other residential treatment program options. She says, "One of my concerns of Camp Braddock, he's the youngest of the lot, and the smallest, and he'll come out with worse tricks." The staff does find a residential program that interests both Jude and his family. The judge vacates his case from drug court pending his completion of the residential program.

Jude ends up with the same outcome as Paulino (long-term residential treatment), but it took the staff over eighteen months to get to that point, as opposed to only two months with Paulino. The time difference is because the staff feels it can work with Jude. He has a family who is involved and seemingly stable. Jude is also not committing any egregious delinquent acts like Felix did. However, staff tries various approaches to work with Jude, none of which appear to have any effect on him. The parents are also largely ineffective in controlling Jude. The staff eventually runs out of ideas on how to work with him. At one point, the judge says, "I've never seen a more unmotivated kid." Raul, the drug counselor, adds, "All the kids, I get a pretty good sense; this kid, I can't." Staff finally sends Jude to residential treatment after exhausting all their other options on how to work with him. While Jude tells the staff many times that he does not want to be in the drug court, and the staff suggests at several points that he is a "waste of time," the staff never seriously considers terminating him. Raul says, "He still has the idea in his head that if he doesn't do anything, he'll get kicked out of drug court." This apparent contradiction brings up an interesting tension in the staff's use of remedies. One could see staff's persistence in working with Jude as simply an attempt not to grant a youth's unreasonable request, but staff comments are more suggestive of their desire that something positive may eventually click in the youth participant.

Another variation of this ineffectual workability could pertain to youths whose problems are not drug related. Consider the following vignette on Sinh, a sixteen-year-old Asian American in the east court. He was initially accepted into the program in early October. During that conversation staff does not discuss his drug issues, but rather the fact that his older brother went through the drug court and graduated. They also talk about his difficult family situation. The probation officer, Joe, says they have the "nastiest home" he has ever seen, describing how when he went to the home the mother was just playing in the dirt. Moreover, the mother does not speak English, the father is never home, and Sinh lives in a cramped tiny apartment with nine other siblings. However, staff does not consider those barriers initially to be significant, given Sinh's older brother faced the same barriers and managed to graduate from drug court. Sinh also has plenty of custody time (1,200 days) for the staff to use its normal remedies to instill in him a sense of individual accountability. Sinh's time in the court incorporates three phases: general noncompliance in school and treatment, suspension from drug court, and the staff's acceptance of his noncompliance and a revised approach.

> Sinh is short and skinny, with straight black hair that falls just below his ears. He never tests positive for drugs the entire time he is in drug court. His noncompliance is related to his nonattendance in school and treatment. He goes AWOL from late December until early February, when he is arrested. He gets a new charge at that time for resisting arrest and gets sent to the 120-day program.

He returns to the court in late April and has the same issues of not going to school or treatment. He avoids getting any normal remedies by telling the court that he is in the process of signing up for school; however, the probation officers are convinced he is not doing anything. They discuss terminating him, but he shows up with a business card from a school official as proof that he is registering for school. Judge Hooper admonishes him at that point, saying that if he is to stay in drug court he also needs to go to school; otherwise, they will send him back to mainstream court, and the likely disposition will be gang supervision unit. The staff believes a job will help motivate him, since that was what turned around his brother. In late May, he gets arrested again for breaking into a car. This time, he gets suspended from drug court pending the new charge.

In mid-June, the mainstream court sends him back to drug court for rescreening; when the substitute judge asks him why he wants to stay in drug court, he tells her that it "helps me stay off drugs—they pee test me once a week and the PO [probation officer] comes to check on me to see how I'm doing." The staff conditionally accepts him back into the court for four weeks, because they believe he will benefit from the intensive supervision. However, he continues to avoid registering for school, and the staff has difficulty finding him. They reconsider kicking him out of drug court in July because he still has yet to enroll in school or treatment. Judge Hooper says, "I ask him if he does anything," adding that he acts like he has Alzheimer's. Later, he says, "he just kind of comes in here with a bewildered look and that's it." The issue with school and treatment continues for another month when the probation officer says he is at his limit with Sinh. They plan to terminate him at the end of August, but Sinh comes into court that day with proof of a job. The only thing he does somewhat consistently is come to court. He does test negative for drug use (although the probation officer says he gets tested only once a week at court, since he is never at home, school, or treatment, where the probation officer goes to test the youths). In late September, the staff discussion returns to what they are doing for him:

HOOPER (JUDGE): Drugs are not his problem.
CHARLIE (PUBLIC DEFENDER): Life is his problem.
HOOPER: Why keep him then?
CHARLIE: He wants to.
SARAH (PROBATION OFFICER): Right. Perhaps drugs are not his problem anymore because we are his support system. . . . This kid has little attention in his life except for us.
HOOPER: He has absolutely no structure at all.

SARAH: I know. It's sad.

HOOPER: That's the way it is. All right, we keep him. We've got to be flexible.

The staff recognizes that Sinh does not have a drug problem. He seems to have more of a delinquency-oriented workability, as he gets arrested and suspended once from drug court for breaking into a car. Staff keeps him in drug court even though it is unclear what he gets out of it. During the five months after being conditionally accepted back into drug court, he says he is trying to enroll in at least five different schools but never seems to be at any of them. Over the entire fieldwork period, the only time he attended school or treatment consistently was when he was in the 120-day program. Each time the staff is about to terminate him, though, something happens—either he states that he wants to stay or he brings in enough proof of some kind of compliance—and the staff postpones the decision.

In many ways, Sinh's workability parallels that of Christopher's corrective nondelinquent workability. They started the program around the same time and have trouble mainly with registering and attending school. They both are always on the verge of getting kicked out of the court but manage to show some kind of proof of compliance to avoid that outcome. What is different between the two cases is that Christopher and his parents communicate well with staff. Sinh does not talk much with any of the staff, nor do his parents (his father is always out working, and the mother does not speak English). In addition, the staff typically can find Christopher at home, whereas Sinh is never at home. As a result, Christopher eventually gets off probation successfully, while Sinh remains in the drug court, always on the verge of getting terminated.

These compromised workability types all appear to be leading to negative case outcomes. But the distinction between common and compromised workability types does not map directly to a youth's chances of succeeding or failing in the drug court. Several youths with common workabilities could end up failing the program, and some youths with compromised workabilities could do well in the drug court. Diana could still finish the drug court and graduate. Sinh also could graduate, especially given that the staff has modified its expectations of his compliance. The distinction between common and compromised workabilities is more about how staff continues to view the youth as tenable or not in the court and what it uses to measure the youth's progress.

CONCLUSION

Messing up is a normal and anticipated occurrence in the drug court. Staff expects youths to be noncompliant at some point and uses a variety of normal remedies to correct that behavior, reemphasizing the accountability framework to the youths. Staff also expects youths to have a halfhearted or inconsistent response to those remedies and still continues to work with them. In these common workability types, the staff tries various normal remedies to instill a message of accountability, whereby youths learn to make better decisions and take responsibility for their actions. If the normal remedies associated with that workability do not work, the momentum shifts to compromised workabilities in which the staff modifies its expectations from accountability to other goals.

It is important to emphasize that the staff starts working with all youths within the common workability trajectories. Once a youth participant starts the program, it takes a few months to get him settled into the drug court routine. In this initial phase, a youth may test the limits of staff, either by not attending school or by testing positive. In those instances, staff decides on normal remedies to get the youth back on track. These remedies usually include continued home supervision and short-term custody. Depending on the youths' responses, their workability type takes shape. The staff's sense of youths' workability diverges depending on the evolution of this cycle between youth noncompliance and staff's imposition of normal remedies. Therefore, workability highlights both the youth's and the staff's involvement in the youth's ability to be accountable. That is, the frequent interactions between the youths and staff shape and direct the staff's sense of the "true problem" and what normal remedies to use. If the youth is messing up, the staff might impose a particular remedy and increase supervision. Once the youth begins to perform better, the staff eases up on its supervision. If the youth falters again, the staff can choose to repeat or escalate the remedies.

What is interesting to note is that the same normal remedies (e.g., home supervision, short-term custody) could be used in all the workability types, but the staff's intention differs depending on the specific workability. For example, the staff might decide to place a youth in the 120-day probation program either to have time to dry the youth out (the drug addict), to get him away from his peers (the delinquent), or to give staff more time to place the youth in a job training program (the youth with an abusive home situation). The distinction among the common and compromised workability types then comes from the various progressions of those remedies in each one. For example, the drug and extreme (e.g., abusive home) workability types may both call for custodial normal remedies initially to address youths' noncompliant behavior; however, with the youths' continued noncompliance, the drug workability could call for more treatment-oriented remedies (e.g., changing outpatient treatment program, short-term community detox program), whereas the extreme workability would call for expedited removal from the drug court into a more appropriate program (e.g., long-term residential program or job training program).

As a conceptual tool, workability allows for researchers to understand youths' progression through programs in a more naturalistic perspective than simply the youths' official program status. As stated earlier, one could conceive of the juvenile drug court as comprising four formal phases based on the juvenile's sober days and time in program, leading to one of two outcomes: graduates or failures. Yet in practice, the breakdown of phases and outcomes is not as straightforward. Staff-accepted positive drug test results (and sometimes diluted test results) could reset sober days back to zero and instances of noncompliance could lead to a phase demotion or delay in phase advancement. Youths' progression, then, is not simply tied to the official phases, because they could cycle back and forth between the phases.

Workability also provides a better framework to understand the various ways that youth could exit the program, other than the assumed categories of graduate and failure. The staff has three other options of final outcomes: administrative discharge, vacated case, or suspended case. Staff might administratively discharge youths like Christopher and Rita if it no longer has the legal jurisdiction over them. Vacated outcomes refer to youths like Paulino who were sent to long-term residential drug treatment programs. Finally, if someone like Ruben gets arrested on a new offense, the court suspends the youth until that case is resolved in mainstream juvenile court. While not officially considered final outcomes, vacated and suspended cases could be considered as such since most of these youths do not get re-referred back to the court. Consider table 7.1, which shows the differences in outcomes of the 103 youths I observed who achieved a final status in the program by the end of my observations.

Almost two-thirds of the youths fell into one of these three categories: 64 percent of the final outcomes are not graduates or failures. The workability

TABLE 7.1
Percentage of final youth outcomes (N = 103)

Outcome	Total
Suspended	15.5
Vacated	10.7
Administrative discharge	37.9
Failure	11.7
Graduate	24.3

NOTE: The percentages add up to 101 due to rounding error.

framework illuminates the steps that lead the staff to these different outcomes. For example, it uses a particular sequence of normal remedies for a drug-workability youth whose case might be ultimately vacated when the staff sends him to long-term drug treatment. The staff might use another progression of normal remedies for a delinquent youth it views as a gangster more than a drug addict and ends up suspending. Despite failed or doomed prospects for the compromised workability youths, the staff keeps working to try to have some kind of impact on them. While none of the compromised types shown here leads to an official successful outcome as a drug court graduate, they are not automatically considered failures either, as the staff often vacated or administratively discharged their cases.

Another way to look at these outcomes is to consider how the youths' gender and race might influence the staff's interactions with the youth over time, as illustrated in Table 7.2. Some race and gender differences do appear in these outcomes. The main gender differences appeared in the administrative discharge and graduation outcomes. This can be explained in two ways. Female youths were administratively discharged for getting pregnant, and they were punished for more behaviors (e.g., curfew violations) than male youths, leading to lower graduation rates (11 percent of females versus 27 percent of males).[12] Comparing final outcomes within racial categories, a higher proportion of whites were administratively discharged (44 percent versus 35 percent Latinos). Looking at the reasons for this difference, it appears that staff administratively discharged whites more for moving to another state, while it discharged Latinos mainly for being pregnant. Moreover, a higher proportion of whites were sent to residential treatment (16 percent compared to 8 percent Latinos), suggesting that staff sees them as more amenable to treatment, while a higher proportion of Latinos were suspended (22 percent compared to 12 percent whites). Again, while I do not

TABLE 7.2

Percentage of final youth outcomes by race and gender (N = 103)

	Race			Gender	
Outcome	Latino (*n* = 51)	White (*n* = 43)	Other (*n* = 9)	Male (*n* = 85)	Female (*n* = 18)
Suspended—New charge	22	12	0	16	11
Vacate—Residential treatment	8	16	0	11	11
Administrative discharge	35	44	22	35	50
Fail	8	9	44	11	17
Graduate	27	19	33	27	11

have the families' socioeconomic status information, race and class appeared highly correlated in this study. In my observations, the white families were more likely to be middle class than the Latino families. Such a disparity influences final outcomes, in that white families can afford to move their children out of state (e.g., administrative discharge) or, in some cases, pay for long-term residential treatment (e.g., vacate—residential treatment). While this is a retrospective analysis, it does lead me to question why staff did not see Latino youths as being equally amenable to treatment as white youths, especially if they all started with the same common workabilities. How might the staff have worked differently with "untreatable" Latino youths before they were arrested on a new charge?

At the same time, I hesitate to reduce the youths' outcomes solely to their gender, race, and class as it affected the staff's sense of their workability. Looking at the staff use of descriptions as a proxy for race, the effect is not so clear-cut. Going back to the gang member description, the staff was open to having gang members in the drug court if they were not posing a serious risk to the community. Victor, the sixteen-year-old Latino discussed earlier, epitomizes this concept. The staff opted to keep him in the court even after the district attorney described him as a gang member, because he was an accomplice rather than a sophisticated and violent member. At the end of the fieldwork period, Victor was well on his way to graduating from drug court.

The concept of unpredictability described earlier helps to reconcile the idea that race, gender, and class may play a role on the youth's outcomes. As the staff mentioned, it never knew which youths would respond to a particular normal remedy at what point in their workability. Sometimes it seems that the staff should have let go of youths like Jude much earlier than it did. Yet the staff's open-minded try-and-see approach works with other youths, such as Vanessa, for whom staff goes an extra mile to help. As shown with Vanessa's case, the staff comes up with creative responses to do what it believes is necessary to have the intended effect on youths. The question is how and when to decide who benefits from this approach, another court program, or, as Schur (1973) suggests, "radical nonintervention." Perhaps it would be better for the staff to recognize earlier in youths' workability that certain problems are beyond the scope of the drug court's realm, and to cut youths loose from the drug court before they go through months of short-term custodial normal remedies only to end up with being administratively discharged or terminated. These decisions are not just based on the youth's race, class, or gender, but a variety of organizational factors that affect how the staff manages youths.

The (In)justice of Discretion: Drug Courts as Therapeutic Punishment and Therapeutic Justice

THE FUTURE FOR DRUG courts in the United States appears bright. They have achieved widespread support among liberal and conservative policy makers alike, as well as many academics who study drug policy. Advocates applaud the courts' potential to reduce the prison population and to provide drug treatment to a previously underserved population of drug users. Drug courts are being incorporated into state drug policies across the country, including New York, where the Rockefeller Drug Law reforms passed in 2009, earmarking $50 million to expand the existing 175 drug courts in the state. On the federal level, the Office of National Drug Control Policy sees drug courts as a critical component in its plans to meet the nation's treatment priority of reducing drug abuse and addiction. Its 2009 National Drug Control Strategy states that "for individuals whose drug use has brought them into contact with the criminal justice system, drug courts combine the power of the courts with the renewing potential of treatment to foster a community of support and to change drug-using behavior" (U.S. Office of National Drug Control Policy 2009, 2).

The policy research on drug courts suggests that they offer a structured and effective way to keep drug offenders from relapsing and from recidivating. This study does not mean to contradict or nullify those findings outright; rather, it poses additional questions about how drug courts assess client noncompliance, which other studies have largely taken for granted. For example, even if drug courts do appear better than previous strategies to deal with drug offenders, what is the cost to the offenders? Is the drug court's form of treatment helping drug offenders? This study problematizes the treatment-legal fusion in therapeutic jurisprudence as well as explores how drug courts represent a broader trend toward individual accountability to tackle social problems like poverty and racial inequality. The central question is this: Are drug courts truly therapeutic or are they simply a new form of punishment under the guise of help?

Blurring Lines between Law and Therapy: Theoretical Implications of Drug Courts

Drug courts have two interesting features for sociologists of law and punishment: their reintroduction of discretion into legal decision making and a treatment-centered approach toward drug offenders. Compared to the draconian mandatory minimum sentencing policies in which judges' discretion was essentially absent, drug court judges have much more flexibility to craft responses to offenders. As seen in the previous chapters, the judge and staff could handle a youth's noncompliant behavior in a variety of ways, depending on how they interpret the seriousness of that behavior. If the youth came home late one night, the staff could dismiss the incidence altogether if the youth had been doing well, or they could formally consider it a probation violation if the youth had been struggling in other areas and needed a reminder to behave better. For the same kind of noncompliant behavior, a youth could get community service, house arrest, or a three-month stay in a probation camp. Drug courts then appear to offer a way to improve upon the traditional juvenile court model of *parens patrie*—that is, taking on a parental role to teach youths how to adopt more appropriate lifestyles.

At the same time, there has been no significant discussion about the limits to that discretion. This study has shown how staff decisions about normal remedies are often highly contested and negotiated. Those decisions—which are largely made in the backstage team meetings—are not on the official court record. As a result, they cannot be used in any kind of appeal process. This leads me to question, as other scholars (Baar 2002) have, if drug courts are simply repeating the mistakes of the pre-Gault juvenile court era, when judges sometimes gave harsh sentences to curb troublesome behavior without any significant regard to the youth's due process. In short, is the drug court's discretionary decision-making process, in its current informal form, helping offenders or leading to an overreaching of the law?

Wexler and Winick (1991, 2003) write extensively about the idea that the law can be used as a therapeutic agent. In practice, that means drug court judges are not just referring offenders to treatment programs; they are becoming familiar with drug treatment approaches and incorporating that newfound knowledge into their decision-making process. While this may seem like a good approach to improve the collaboration between the legal staff (e.g., judge and attorneys) and therapeutic staff (drug counselors), one could also view this confluence of legal and therapeutic realms as a way to dilute both areas of expertise. For example, the public defender often agreed with the other staff to incarcerate a youth if it seemed appropriate as a treatment intervention, even though he could have argued for a more lenient response on legal grounds. Similarly, when considering drug test results, judges tend to focus on evidence of the youth's progress in getting clean rather than legal issues; yet they do need to maintain the legal integrity of the interpretations and responses to drug test results. A prominent critic of drug courts, the Honorable Judge Morris Hoffman (2002) has criticized the role of the judges as quasi social workers, stating they have no business in going beyond their legal expertise. I am not necessarily in agreement with that extreme position, but I do maintain that the judges and lawyers need to remain firmly grounded in the legal orientation of the cases.

For the most part, Judges O'Reilly, Hooper, and Samuels did not let their therapeutic knowledge overshadow legal considerations, reminding the team of the legal limits to their approach. Yet even when staff members keep those lines drawn, their decisions made under the guise of treatment often become muddled in the details of negotiating youths' noncompliant status. In addition, the workgroup culture of the drug court staff can lead to groupthink moments. The staff is so used to working together to come up with a therapeutic response that it might not be able to say no to one another's suggestions (Quinn 2000/2001). At the very least, it is a complicated balancing act to combine therapy and law, especially if the court's focus on offender noncompliance obscures or overshadows its ability to consider issues of guilt and innocence. In my study, it was only under extreme circumstances that the attorneys or judges raised the legal standards of evidence in their decision-making process, akin to what Berman and Feinblatt (2005) suggest in their study on problem-solving courts. While that makes sense to some degree, since the majority of the decisions were based on trivial behaviors, the question remains as to how many of those trivial decisions should have been considered more carefully under the legal framework.

The drug treatment programs working with the court face the same issues of balancing law and treatment. Their staff is increasingly focused on providing updates to the court about the offender's compliance rather than just treating the offender. Two treatment agency directors regularly attended the juvenile drug court hearings and often stressed the lack of youth accountability to encourage the staff to issue a normal remedy. They never came to report good news, only bad news for which they wanted the court to serve as their backup. This shift from treatment to discipline is found in other social settings like schools and social welfare agencies that are turning more attention to managing unruly behavior through punitive measures.[1]

The increased link between law and treatment affects drug treatment programs in other concrete ways as more of their treatment slots are dedicated to the mandated court clientele. Nancy Wolff (2002), who studies mental health courts, a parallel movement to drug courts, discusses how treatment becomes compromised in two ways as programs increasingly accept offenders as clients. She describes how the programs may water down their original model as they spread their resources to provide services to additional court clients or they exclude noncriminal clients to free up space for the court-referred clients.[2] These types of changes are also found in drug treatment programs in which voluntary self-help programs (e.g., Alcoholics Anonymous) are filled with court-mandated clients. Residential therapeutic community programs now place time limits on parolees' stays due to funding constraints, modifying their model, which used to allow people to live on site indefinitely to maintain their sobriety.

Beyond the practical conflicts raised by combining mandated and voluntary clients in one program, there is a philosophical one as well. Drug courts are essentially coercing people to adopt the identity of a drug user or drug addict, as expected from self-help treatment and cognitive-behavioral change treatment programs, even if they do not choose the label for themselves.[3] This is especially difficult to do with youths. One of the tenets cited in most drug treatment programs is to avoid the people, places, and situations that tempt drug use. Adolescents' worldview runs counter to that tenet: their most influential agent of socialization is peers (versus family, school, media, or church), and many of them engage in "magical thinking", in which they know of the dangers of drugs but still believe they are immune to their risks. Forcing someone to choose to change is an inherently unrealistic goal. At the very least, it is difficult to assess in practice.

Such a treatment-oriented approach may not be entirely different from its more punitive cousins. Consider all the ways that drug courts can be equally, if not more, punitive than therapeutic in practice. The frequent review of cases allows the staff to find instances of noncompliance that might have otherwise gone unnoticed, and for which the offenders would have been subjected to some kind of normal remedy, such as a short-term stay in jail. In this study, some youths spent so much time in custody that they used up their maximum possible sentence time. Others received extended sentences, as the staff used their new arrests to add more time than would normally have been issued in another court. Therefore, even if offenders graduate from the court, they could spend a significant amount of time in custody for noncompliance along the way. If the offenders fail, all the documented moments of noncompliance as "probation violations" build up cases of "seriously delinquent" youths that follow them outside of the drug court, if they are arrested on a new charge.[4] As Stanley Cohen (1985) points out in *Visions of Social Control*, the "community correction" option is not a true alternative to traditional corrections. In citing Lerman's research on California community projects, Cohen illustrates how those groups spent

time in custody for nonlegal reasons, such as "violating treatment expectations, administrative convenience, missing a group meeting, sassing a teacher,
the threat of 'community explosion' or 'acting out,' or community pressure
or even diagnostic purposes" (71). Through their use of "invisible discretion," drug courts and other "alternative" programs represent the blurry lines
between "crime and delinquency nets . . . [which] get tangled up with other
welfare, treatment and control nets" (61).

I suggest that while drug courts and, by extension, therapeutic jurisprudence, can be seen as therapeutic, they also could be considered a form of
new penology under the guise of help. They are not like other new penology programs because their stated goal is to help rehabilitate drug users. To do
so, they respond to each individual's actions differently within the context of
his or her progress in drug treatment. In this way, the drug courts are managing individual offenders' therapeutic risk rather than their risk of danger
to the public. This therapeutic risk is primarily internally focused toward
themselves.

At the same time, the courts have some characteristics of the new penology, as they adopt actuarial tools (e.g., drug testing) to interpret individual
acts of noncompliance. So while the drug court may seem to be just another
version of traditional legal decision making based on staff workgroups, discretion, bias, and experience, its actuarial tools legitimate the subjective work
as objective fact. For example, even if the staff members debate a test result
amongst themselves in their team meeting, off the record, they can use the
test as grounds for sending a youth to juvenile hall for a few days. If the youth
or parent protests the test result, the staff can state during the formal court
hearing that they cannot dispute the laboratory result, shutting down any
further questions.[5] So, drug courts represent a transformed view of new
penology in which risk is transformed from an overtly punitive focus to a
more therapeutically oriented one. Given the ways that drug courts use
custodial-based normal remedies to respond to offenders' noncompliance,
however, the results of therapeutic penology could be equally or more
punitive if the offender is unable to meet the court's therapeutic goals.
Furthermore, staff can interpret the offender's therapeutic risk as possibly
leading to a larger public safety risk. For example, Jack, a district attorney,
often cited the public safety concern of drunk driving to argue for a harsher
normal remedy for youths suspected of drinking alcohol.

By emphasizing individual accountability and laying the groundwork for
punitive outcomes for those who fail, drug courts' potential is not one of
reducing incarceration but of reproducing existing social inequalities. Michael
O'Hear (2009) addresses this notion in the *Stanford Law Review*. According to
O'Hear, drug courts could further racial disparities in the justice system
through their selection bias in who gets into drug courts and the predictors

of success from the court. Offenders who are ineligible for many drug courts are those charged with selling drugs or those with previous felony convictions. People with these charges are disproportionately minorities, not because they are more involved in drug-related activities but because unequal law enforcement practices target poor minority drug offenders.[6] White offenders get a shot at redemption through treatment, while black offenders go straight to prison. Moreover, among the offenders accepted into drug court, those who are more likely to succeed are married, employed, or have a high school degree, characteristics more likely to be found among the middle-class white drug court clients than minority clients.[7] In these ways, drug courts pose a more dangerous threat to identifying and rectifying racial inequality because of their emphasis on the individual offender as the sole driver of his fate. Offenders who fail are seen as not taking responsibility for their own actions, and their behavior is pathologized more than before.[8]

POLICY RECOMMENDATIONS FOR DRUG COURT PRACTITIONERS

I could easily conclude that we must completely reconsider having drug courts in the first place. However, drug courts do have the potential to help drug addicts stop using, to keep drug offenders in their communities instead of in jails, and to enable successful drug court clients to reintegrate more easily back into society, since their felony charges are reduced or dismissed. The following five policy recommendations are suggested to mitigate the unintended punitive consequences of the drug court intervention and to facilitate its stated therapeutic goals. These recommendations are designed for policy makers contemplating a drug court in their area, as well as for existing drug court practitioners who may want to rethink their existing policies and approaches to the offenders.[9]

Allocate More Upfront Resources

The drug court staff makes its decisions based on its constantly evolving notion of youths' workability—that is, how they can most effectively persuade youth to comply with the court's expectations. Instead of using the current let's-see-what-happens approach, I would recommend devoting more upfront resources to figuring out workability. While I do agree it is wise not to overly label or stigmatize a youth early on, staff could easily do more in its baseline assessments to identify any major problems that could affect the youth's performance in the court. This does not necessarily require extra resources but rather a shift in thinking about how to engage the youths. For instance, the staff can probe more deeply in its initial assessments.

Rather than asking about drug history only, they can ask about current interests and future goals as well. Staff could then use that information in crafting individualized treatment plans to keep youths engaged in the program. That is, the staff could find incentives that catered to the youths' interests or help them work toward future goals to inspire them to stay in compliance with the court. Additionally, the staff can incorporate the principles of motivational interviewing, which involves active listening, empathy, and encouraging the client to want to change, instead of prescribing a treatment route for each client.[10]

One helpful upfront resource that would require additional funding is a mental health evaluation for every youth entering the court. Some staff expressed their desire to have this information, regardless of whether the youths had a documented history of mental illness. Their rationale was that many of these youths suffer from some sort of undiagnosed depression or mental health issue that would inevitably hinder their ability to do the drug court program successfully. So, to know the potential psychological issues in the beginning would help the staff identify which youths would be able to stay in the drug court and which youths should be transferred to another program. Judge O'Reilly once shared with me in an interview that he hesitated to order mental health evaluations because of the potential stigmatizing effect of having them in their file. I would argue that these types of evaluations could yield more benefits than harm, if they are used solely to identify ways to better work with youths. Moreover, the reality was that the staff ended up ordering evaluations for many youths anyway, and, up to that point, had already stigmatized them in another way by incarcerating them for noncompliant behavior, which could have resulted from mental health issues. Besides O'Reilly's hesitations, the main obstacle to implementing such a policy in the court was financial concerns. This often-cited budget limitation is extremely short-sighted, given the potential cost savings if the staff does not have to waste court resources on youths who should be in counseling or who need medication. Consider Diana's case: staff spent countless weeks discussing her possible mental health issues but did not have an evaluation performed until she had been in the court for months. Had they identified her depression earlier, perhaps they could have been more effective in using the court's resources to find the most appropriate treatment program for her needs much earlier. They might have also saved hours of staff time discussing her lack of accountability during court hearings.

Use Different Styles of Communication with Parents

It is telling that Henry's father said he had told me more in thirty minutes during our interview than he had told any of the staff members in the three months his son was in court. Had the staff taken the time to ask him or any of the parents about their ideas, it could have discovered more ways to solicit parental input. In addition, the staff's ongoing communications with the parents should go beyond simply checking in. It should clarify any misconceptions on both the staff's and the parents' part about each other. As noted earlier, the staff's perceptions of the parents do not always match up to the reality of that family's situation. This disconnect hinders its ability to hold youths accountable, which it claims is the main purpose of the court. Joe, the probation officer, mentioned ruefully that parents often wait until the crisis point before telling staff about their noncompliant youth. He suggested that the staff could have responded better if the parents had told them earlier. However, staff should recognize its complicity in not reaching out earlier to the parents or having enough bilingual staff to work with Spanish-speaking parents.

Many could dismiss this idea of more substantial communication as implausible given the lack of parental engagement. However, the drug court is unique from other courts, in that the staff does have regular contact with most of the families because of its weekly reporting format. Therefore, it could serve as a model in how to work with families beyond a weekly phone call asking such routine questions as "How are things? Any problems?" For example, a more honest communication could allow staff to rearticulate the court's goals and to find out ways the parents feel silenced, overburdened, confused, or misguided. Such conversations do not need to happen every week, but they should be frequent enough to allow staff to understand how parents are trying to work with the court or how they want the court to work with their youth. The conversation should also enable staff to give the parents feedback about how their efforts are inadequate and why. More attempts to communicate with parents in a substantive way could help staff keep them engaged.

Let Go of Unworkable Youths Earlier in the Process

While the staff's persistence in working with youths is commendable, I would recommend not hanging on too long to chronically noncompliant youths. I am not suggesting an increased form of the weekly staff reviews, but rather a broader critical reflection of what Judge Hooper often asked: "Can this kid do the program?" A central component to that questioning should be geared to the court itself—namely, whether it has sufficient organizational resources to help youth do the program. If not, the court should stop thinking it can make a youth learn to be accountable when it does not have the ability to support the youth in that process. In those cases, the youth should not be labeled as failures in the court. Instead, they should be given one of the nonpunitive exits (e.g., administrative discharge or vacated case) currently offered in the court.

One might suggest that such a change would eliminate the all-important "stick," or leverage, to hang over clients as the external motivation for them to engage in treatment. Yet there were clear cases where the staff delayed the inevitable—for example, Jude, who resisted the staff every step of the way. Even if the staff keeps an unworkable youth in the court, it often is not giving the full drug court intervention. One youth in this study, Sinh, was kicked out of the court but was taken back, only to be almost kicked out again. By the end of the fieldwork period, the staff only expected him to show up for court each week to be considered compliant. The question remains: if the youth simply does not want to change or have sufficient internal motivation, at what point does the staff just cut the cord?

Rethink the Therapeutic Intervention and
the Court's Reliance on Drug Testing

While I do not pretend to be a drug addiction specialist, I would suggest a critical rethinking of the model of mandated drug treatment for youths. Instead of making youths spend nine hours every week in a group-based drug program learning about the dangers of drugs, perhaps a better therapeutic intervention would be to engage them in other activities that develop their skills and goals in a more positive light. For example, many of the youths who played sports felt the negative physical impacts of drug use on their performance. If the staff arranged sporting activities and encouraged youths to participate, then these activities might serve as a motivator for youths to stop taking drugs in order to perform better athletically. Many family members also suggested jobs as the best treatment for youths—teaching them responsibility and the value of hard work and earning one's own money. The drug court staff did allow youths to work, but only in the advanced phases of the program. Instead of seeing jobs as a reward for doing well in treatment, the staff could use employment as a form of treatment. Both of these forms of treatment would certainly address the boredom that many of the youths said they felt in outpatient treatment. Switching up activities that could count as treatment hours might help them stay more invested in the program and, even more important, introduce them to activities that can help them resist going back to using drugs.[11]

One way to fund these activities is to reduce the frequency of drug testing. While the staff considers rigorous testing a prime way to keep youths accountable, the staff's decisions about drug test results were not always based on scientific findings from the laboratory. The youths also saw how drug test results could be altered and that the staff did not always respond consistently to results. Therefore, drug testing does not necessarily serve as a fail-safe indicator of a youth's progress in drug treatment. However, if the court did not drug test as often, it could reallocate the field-based staff's time to focus more on counseling the youths and connecting them to various programs they might like. As it stands now, the drug counselors and probation officers spent most of their time going around to the youths' schools, drug treatment programs, and homes to do drug tests on the youths. What would happen if they could spend more time just talking with the youths instead of having to watch them while they pee? How would the staff's team meeting discussions change if they focused less on ambiguous drug test results and more on motivating the youths?

Review Sanctions for Their Possible Negative Effects on Youths

Building on the findings from the youths and parents' interviews, I would suggest a more comprehensive review of the drug court sanctions, which I have redefined in this book as normal remedies, to see the ways in which they become countereffective. In making decisions about youths' trivial behaviors every week, the staff might not consider the impact of its normal remedies on the youths. For example, the frequency and repetitive nature of issuing home supervision whenever youths were slipping might lead staff to forget the implications of such a normal remedy on the youth and family. Youths might start to feel imprisoned in their own homes, leading to the possibility of decreasing their motivation to do the program. Moreover, for families the financial impact of these sanctions cannot be ignored. Parents are charged thirty-five dollars a day for home supervision and thirty-seven dollars a day for juvenile hall. This cost certainly affected how the parents viewed the court's effectiveness in working with the youths and impacted the amount of information they shared with the staff about them. Another example is the staff's response to a diluted test result in which the youth's sober days are taken away until the youth accrues ninety more sober days. Recall Peter's words about the direct impact of this court's decision on Christopher's desire to do the program—as Peter said, he just gave up. In reviewing the normal remedies, the staff could take a page from the public health approach to drug treatment in which a guiding principle would be to do no harm.[12] In other words, at what point does the court's response—intended to instill more individual accountability in the youths—have the opposite effect on the youth, who then begins to blame the program and develop more resistance to the accountability message?

All of these recommendations are based on one critical question: Are juvenile drug courts the best way to deal with youth troubles and drug use? If so, for which types of youths and in what ways should we apply these court interventions?[13] This study has intended to show the limitations of the model when it is applied to youths who have no drug problem or to youths who have other types of problems that the court cannot sufficiently address. Again, this question is not to suggest we dismiss the drug court model entirely, but rather to caution policy makers not to automatically adopt it as the next best step in juvenile justice and drug policy reform. In our eagerness to divert offenders from prison, we must carefully consider whether diversions such as drug courts reduce the prison population and effectively treat drug addiction.

Drug courts can serve as a promising vehicle to shift the criminal justice system's approach to drug offenders away from punitive policies, but only if they maintain a strong connection between the individual offender's accountability and the court's accountability to the offender to provide the necessary groundwork for the offender to do the program. Herein lies the danger with drug courts' popularity. They focus only on individual accountability, ignoring what Geoff Ward and Aaron Kupchik (2009) call system-level accountability, or the recognition that the court itself must have enough resources or capabilities to achieve goals for individual accountability. This study attempts to reverse that emphasis, focusing more on the places in which the system itself is unaccountable, or, more accurately, how staff crafts notions of individual accountability that are not based on the youths' choices but organizationally bound interpretations of their actions. Divorcing these two levels of accountability in the analysis of drug courts only increases the sense that offenders do not deserve help if they cannot help themselves. Accountability-based penal policies have the potential to further exclude the socially marginalized populations and exacerbate existing racial inequalities while ignoring how the state has failed in fulfilling its responsibilities to its citizens. It is not just the fact that the unaccountable client is the new undeserving client; he is living in a blameless state. While it might be perfectly legitimate for a government to hold people accountable for abusing drugs and endangering others, it is also imperative to hold that same government accountable for providing viable economic and educational opportunities for people to stay sober. Any policy featuring that kind of dual accountability would be true drug reform.

Appendix A

Methods

This study employed ethnographic methods to provide a naturalistic account of the staff's decision-making process in the juvenile drug court. By "naturalistic" I mean that I attempted to obtain an understanding of the local meanings about youth drug use, youth noncompliance, and staff work practices. I paid particular attention to how staff articulated those meanings to each other in the court, as well as to me in our informal conversations and interviews. My fieldnotes attempted to document the decision-making process as it unfolded, without any editing based on analytical presuppositions or hypotheses. To facilitate this, I strove in my fieldnotes to record "thick descriptions" (Geertz 1973) and used a grounded theory approach (Charmaz 2001; Glaser and Strauss 1967) to analyze my fieldnotes. That is, I began to notice specific areas (e.g., varying uses of drug test results, seemingly inconsistent staff responses to different youths, and staff disagreements about youth actions) that appeared relevant to my study. At that point, I then sought negative cases to enhance my initial understanding of the phenomena. I used that expanded paradigm to inform my interviews with staff, youth, and parents to further supplement my courtroom observations. What follows is a more detailed account of the methods used in the study during the two fieldwork periods in 2003–2004 and 2007.

Start, Stop, Start

I obtained access to the field site through contacts made at a previous field site. The same organization provided treatment services for the juvenile drug court. I initially started fieldwork in the beginning of September 2003. However, on my first day of fieldwork, the treatment provider—through whom I had access—found out it had just lost its contract with the county to provide services to the court. I pulled out of the field for a month while the treatment agency considered its options. After it appealed the county's decision and was given an extension through December 2003, I restarted fieldwork in October. When the county denied the organization's appeal, I got approval from the new treatment provider for my project. The new provider allowed me to continue the project and did not require any changes to the research design. I completed the first fieldwork phase in October 2004.

Once in the field, I had almost complete access to the staff and youth participants during the drug court days. In addition to the precourt team meetings and court hearings, I was allowed to observe the screening meetings, in which staff reviewed prospective youth clients, and policy-related meetings regarding drug testing and general operations. I also received the weekly summary report that outlined the youth's sober day count, program phase, and, in some reports, a brief description of the youth's progress that week. Finally, I had more limited access to the treatment programs, observing a few programs with staff and youth client approval.

I did not have official access to the schools but was able to see many of the clients during my ride-alongs with the field-based staff. I also did not have access to the youths' official court files during the first fieldwork period, nor was I allowed into the juvenile hall facility to see the youths when they were locked up. Toward the end of the first fieldwork period, I did go on a public tour of juvenile hall and the girls' probation 120-day program (both located next to the main juvenile court) during an annual open house for the community. I also visited the probation camp facility, located about an hour from the main juvenile court, which housed the 28-day and 120-day drug treatment programs for boys.

Being Everywhere and Nowhere: Breadth versus Depth

Initially, I envisioned playing a neutral role in the first fieldwork period, focusing equally on the youths, their parents, and staff. However, that did not happen, as the youths and families saw me as staff. This identification largely resulted from my focus on the staff's team meetings. While I tried to sit apart from staff, various probation officers, police officers, or drug counselors sat next to me in the audience to observe the court hearing. I also had difficulty in balancing my time and attention between the staff and youths. For example, every week I had to decide whether to stay in team meetings before the court hearings or hang out in the waiting area with youths and families. While I knew I could collect detailed fieldnotes about all the youths in team meetings, I was not as sure about which youths or families I would see in the waiting area. I decided to stay in the team meetings and to talk to youths during the breaks in between the meetings. Ultimately, I chose breadth versus depth, focusing on the court operations from the perspectives of the staff members instead of getting fewer detailed perspectives of the court from the youths and families.

This choice was strategic but also practical. For example, many of the activities occurred simultaneously. Since I was looking at three courts,

I experienced scheduling conflicts in whether to interview youths at treatment, go with staff on ride-alongs, or attend a team meeting. I sometimes skipped court hearings to meet a youth from another court at his school or treatment program to interview him, only to find out that he did not show up that particular day or that he had to leave before I got there. I also focused on the staff because I felt uncomfortable asking youths to open up their lives to me. They were under such scrutiny already by the drug court staff, the treatment providers, their families, and their schoolteachers. To add another adult asking about their private thoughts seemed overly intrusive and unfair, especially when I had no incentives to offer them. In retrospect, I could have spent much more time with a smaller group of youths in hopes of building enough rapport to get honest and detailed answers about what they thought of the court. To do that, I would have had to be more aggressive in trying to get to know certain youths, making more contact with them outside of the court setting and trying to get access to visit them when they were incarcerated. However, these endeavors would have required much time to get data on just a few youth participants rather than on the entire court and staff work practices. This limited focus definitely informed and motivated the second phase of fieldwork, where I chose to exclusively focus on youths and families to get information I could not obtain during the first phase of data collection.

The issue of where to focus my attention manifested also among the various staff members as well. The field-based staff commented that I was always with the public defender, with whom they had occasional disagreements in the team meetings. If I started spending too much time with field-based staff, the public defender commented about me becoming one of them. In both situations, I began paying more attention to whom I talked to during the court sessions and with whom I scheduled ride-alongs.

FOCUSED ATTENTION: DEPTH VERSUS BREADTH

I went back into the field for two additional months in 2007. The purpose of that second phase was to focus exclusively on the youth clients and their parents' perspectives of the court. Returning to the field allowed me to fill in the gaps in the analysis done after the first fieldwork period. I also had had some time to further reflect upon the main themes raised in the first analysis, such as the financial strains on the parents and the staff's multifaceted use of drug test results. I was able to obtain a small grant to pay the youths twenty-five dollars and families fifty dollars for their interviews. In this two-month phase, I conducted forty-eight interviews with twenty-four youths and twenty-four parents/legal guardians. I focused my court observations on only those youths' cases. Additionally, I was able to get access to their court files, so I was able to see their original offenses, past juvenile court involvement, and history of tenure in the drug court.

During the first fieldwork period, I spent the majority of my time with the public defender, district attorney, clinical therapist, and field-based staff. I was able to connect fairly easily with all of the staff based on some mutual interest. For example, I had a lot in common with the public defender in terms of political beliefs; he often told me the "war stories" of his time as a former grassroots community organizer. I was about the same age as many of the field-based staff, so we conversed easily about various social activities or family issues. I also had some familiarity with the drug treatment and drug court philosophy from my previous research and work experience, so I was able to converse with the probation officers, drug counselors, judges, district attorney, and police officers on those levels.

Staff initially saw me as an outsider, as a young undergraduate student doing a paper on the court. Some staff also saw me as liberal simply because of my academic identity—a police officer and the district attorney, who were self-proclaimed conservatives, half-jokingly asked me to explain my "socialist" views to them. Despite my numerous attempts to tell them my age or work background, most of the staff never seemed to retain the fact that I was a graduate student doing doctoral research (and then an assistant professor during the second phase of research), nor that I had previous work experience setting up a similar juvenile drug court in New York. I initially struggled with that misperception of my educational status and understanding of the program, feeling the need to show them how much I already knew. I quickly accepted that it was beneficial to be seen as a naive girl to get the staff's own views of the court and work. Within a few months of the first fieldwork period, the staff appeared completely comfortable in having me in the team meetings. Many times, the staff referred to "my book," saying that I should make sure to write down a particular quotation in my ever-present notebook. The staff sometimes asked me what I was writing, mainly out of curiosity about why anyone would want to write down its discussions and also out of amazement as to how illegible my writing was.

A related issue to my overidentification with the staff was my struggle in deciding when to intervene in its decision-making process. I often had to hold my tongue when I saw staff being seemingly inconsistent or acting against protocol. In the end, I did point out a few things to staff if the discussion seemed to veer toward a negative outcome for the youth. That is, if staff was about to issue a normal remedy to the youth for something that contradicted a prior staff decision, I discreetly would tell one of the staff members what was discussed previously. I did not intervene if the staff confusion could help the youth avoid the punitive normal remedies. While unbalanced in substance, my intervention did not appear to change the staff's decisions significantly, especially since I was pointing out what the staff had already decided to do. However, I cannot say with absolute certainty that my interventions did not influence the decisions in some way. I only did this during the first fieldwork period, when I had a more intimate familiarity with the cases and the staff.

In general, I was less comfortable with the youths compared to the staff and parents during both fieldwork periods, mainly because I had nothing in common with them. I did not share the same type of adolescent experiences, nor did I come from the same family or class background. I also did not have an intimate knowledge of contemporary youth culture (e.g., music, clothes, jargon). This disconnect became painfully clear when one youth asked me what CD I was listening to in my car. When I told him, he said that was what his mother listened to. Instead of trying to pretend that I knew these things, I simply stated that I was old and completely ignorant. I would then ask them to explain to me what they liked. During the first fieldwork period, I also emphasized that I was simply a student trying to get through school. This seemed to work well, as we were all students of some kind, and the youths were interested in helping me finish school. I also found the youths to be much more open and approachable on a one-on-one basis. My most productive interviews with youths occurred before the court, when other youths had yet to arrive, or after court, when the other youths had already left. It was much easier in the second fieldwork period to relate to the youths since I had a clearer separation from the staff in the court hearings. I also explicitly stated that my purpose was only to interview them and their parents for their perspectives of the court. In the second fieldwork period, I conducted all the interviews in the youths' homes, which further put them at ease and helped me to get them to open up about their feelings about the court.

I was able to establish a good rapport with all of the parents during both second fieldwork periods. While I did not interact much with the parents during the first fieldwork period, I occasionally had informal conversations with some parents during the court hearings. Because I do not speak Spanish, I could only interact with the English-speaking parents unless their children translated for me. In the second fieldwork period, I did have a translator to communicate with the Spanish-speaking parents. Despite having a third person present, these interviews proceeded with the same flow and ease as the English-speaking ones. Overall, the parents seemed to recognize that I sympathized with their situation of having to constantly answer to the court authority and understood that I wanted their honest opinions about how to improve the court. All but one parent seemed open to talking with me, with some talking much longer than the allotted time frame. It seemed they did so not because they were compensated for their time but because they wanted to talk to someone about the court.

Presentation of Data

Writing field notes poses its own challenges in ethnographic data. If you cannot tape record peoples' conversations to catch their precise words, how do you represent the conversations in your notes? What if you capture some of their words but not all? While some might try to summarize the conversation or only focus on the key players in the interaction, I kept close attention to who was speaking. If subjects were talking too fast or too softly for me to understand all of their words, I wrote, "Charlie?," which then came out in the field notes as, "Charlie said something I don't catch." This allowed me to preserve the naturally occurring interaction for the subsequent analysis. As a result, my field notes had a mixture of direct quotations and indirect quotations. This follows what Emerson, Fretz, and Shaw suggests in *Writing Ethnographic Fieldnotes* (1995, 51): "consider the handling of direct quotations in moving from jottings to fieldnotes. Only those words actually taken down at the time are placed in quotes; a portion of the direct speech missed at the time is paraphrased outside the direct quotes. As a general practice, speech not written down word for word at the time should either be presented as indirect quotation or paraphrased." However, when it came to writing up that often jumbled flow of conversation in the final ethnographic text, I faced another challenge in presenting a readable conversation that preserved the staff's dialogue with my less-than-perfect transcription of that dialogue. For readability in the final manuscript, I removed the partial direct quotations from the dialogue. So, while I have opted to remove the quotations for the clarity of the text, that does not mean I was taking field notes or that I selectively wrote down snippets of staff conversations in a haphazard way.

I want to emphasize the importance of maintaining the distinction between direct and indirect quotations during the data collection process. As Emerson, Fretz, and Shaw (1995) state, it helps to keep the ethnographer true to members' meanings and to not fill in the gaps of the conversations herself; it also proves to the reader that the ethnographer was really there in the setting. Duneier (1999) also maintains the importance of not using one's own words to re-create local conversations, especially if the ethnographer is not from the same social position as the members in the setting. For these reasons, I would encourage ethnographers to continue this practice of field note writing if tape recording is not an option to uphold methodological rigor and analytical preciseness.

Validity/Verification

Using a grounded theory approach can be difficult because of the enormous amount of detail captured in the fieldnotes that requires extensive verification. That is, the court setting had so many unique voices to consider that it was hard to know what I was capturing in my analysis. I asked myself the following questions: How do I know why one staff member might view the youth as noncompliant or compliant? What drives the team's decision—the particular youth or the organizational factors or both? Are the youths and parents lying to me about what happened in the court? I used two different verification strategies to ensure my analysis had appropriate validity in its findings.

During the first fieldwork period, I asked staff members about specific cases during the breaks or after court to make sure I had a clear understanding of their perspective about what happened. I also brought my findings back to the field, at least partially. I circulated an early version of a chapter on mental health issues to all the staff and conducted informal interviews about it with all three judges, the public defender, and the district attorney. I also asked the drug counselors and probation officers for feedback, but in general most of them had not read it completely and/or did not have any concrete responses to it. I sent the staff a completed version of the dissertation but did not receive any feedback.

I took a more comprehensive but focused approach in the second fieldwork period by focusing only on twenty-four youths' cases, which allowed me to compare in more detail the youths' and parents' perspectives to the staff's perspectives. I was able to compare the youths' account of their drug court history with their official court files. Moreover, I could observe the staff's discussions about the youths and parents and also compare them to the youths' and parents' perspectives.

This naturalistic approach to understanding the drug court is steeped in the Chicago School tradition of Robert Park and Everett Hughes and the symbolic interaction tradition of Herbert Blumer. These traditions do not presume a preexisting theoretical framework to inform or expand their data. They strive instead to show how people make sense of their everyday lives and then to see how social structural forces constrain or shape those lives, if at all. Given the complexity of the juvenile drug court staff's decision-making process, such an approach seemed to be the best way to depict it as accurately as possible. To assume that staff's views of youth actions are simply reflections of larger theoretical ideas about therapeutic jurisprudence is overly deterministic. Yet to assume its decisions are independent or free from the organizational context in which it makes those decisions is equally naive. This study has attempted to balance such views—to show the multifaceted and multilevel aspects of social control in the drug courts while maintaining a healthy respect for the staff, youths, and families individually negotiating social control in their interactions with one another.

Appendix B

Concepts and Terms

28-day: Short-term in-custody drug treatment program for a maximum of 28 days.

120-day (drug dorm): Long-term in-custody drug treatment program for a maximum of 120 days.

Administrative Discharge: Final outcome used by staff when it does not have the legal jurisdiction to continue working with the youths. These youths are technically not considered failures but also have not done enough to be granted the full privileges of the program graduates.

AWOL (absent without leave): Youths who have run away from home.

Bench warrant: An order issued by a judge for the arrest of an individual, typically when the youth fails to show up for court.

Clean time (see sober days)

Custody days: Maximum amount of time that youths can be incarcerated for the offense for which they have been found guilty. The amount of custody time the youths receive becomes a crucial factor in how staff works with them in the program.

Dilutes: Ambiguous urinalysis drug test results where there is not enough creatinine in the urine to confirm the levels of drug use.

Drug dorm (see 120-day program)

ESP/electronic supervision: Intensive form of house arrest where youths must wear an ankle bracelet that tracks their movement to ensure they stay inside the house.

Home supervision/house arrest: An alternative to juvenile hall where youths are to remain at home unless they are in school, treatment, or out with a parent. They are supposed to stay inside the house and cannot even be outside on the patio or in the yard.

Incentives: Rewards for youths' good behavior, such as phase promotions, sobriety tokens, movie tickets, and gift certificates.

Normal remedies (sanctions): Staff's punishments for youth noncompliance, or what is called "sanctions" in drug court terminology.

Parens patrie: A concept initially used in medieval English courts, it justifies the legal intervention of the U.S. juvenile courts, who assume the parental role over a youth's life if necessary.

Presumpts/presumptive: Drug test in which a treated strip of paper is dipped into urine, providing instantaneous results.

Sanctions: Penalties for violating the court's expectations. (See also "normal remedies.")

Sober days: The court's official record of a youth's sobriety. It is determined by the youth's drug test results, with each new positive test resetting the count back to zero. To graduate from the program, the youth must accumulate 365 consecutive sober days.

Stay: Delayed sanction, meaning the court will enforce the sanction when the youth commits another noncompliant action.

Suspended: This outcome is used after a youth is arrested on a new offense. The suspension lasts until the case is resolved in mainstream juvenile court. If the offense is serious enough, the youth typically does not return to drug court.

Therapeutic jurisprudence: Initially conceptualized for mental health law, a new legal movement in which the courts view the law as a therapeutic tool, considering how the law can both hurt and help an offender.

UAs/Urinalysis: The most common form of drug testing which measures the drug levels in the creatinine of a person's urine.

Vacated cases: Situations in which youths are sent to one-year residential drug treatment programs and are removed from the court docket.

Workability: The staff's sense of how it can best influence a youth to adhere to the court's requirements. There are common workability types (e.g., drug-oriented, corrective-oriented, helping-oriented, and nonintervention) with which the staff uses normal remedies in different combinations to get the youth to learn accountability. Compromised workability types (e.g., mental illness, lost causes) are when the staff is unable to hold the youth accountable, either due to its lack of resources or the ineffective impact of its normal remedies on the youth.

Appendix C

Additional Resources

This list is not comprehensive but is intended to provide additional resources about drug courts, problem-solving courts, and restorative justice.

Drug Courts

Descriptive Information

American University Drug Court Clearinghouse

http://www1.spa.american.edu/justice/project.php?ID=1

The Drug Court Clearinghouse Project, housed at American University since 1994, tracks drug court information and activity across the nation.

Overview of Policy Research

National Development and Research Institute (NDRI)

http://www.ndri.org

A nonprofit research and educational organization, NDRI publishes reviews of drug court evaluation research.

Practitioner-Related Information

National Association for Drug Court Professionals (NADCP)

http://www.nadcp.org

This site contains fact sheets and resource materials for people interested in planning a drug court.

Technical Assistance, Research, and Information

Center for Court Innovation

http://www.courtinnovation.org

This nonprofit think tank helps courts and criminal justice agencies to aid victims, reduce crime, and improve public trust in justice. It has implemented and evaluated several drug courts in New York and provided technical assistance to other drug courts across the country.

Office of Justice Programs, Bureau of Justice Assistance

http://www.ojp.usdoj.gov/BJA/evaluation/program-adjudication/drug-index.htm

This federal agency provides overview information and evaluation about drug courts.

Drug Policy Reform and Drug Testing
Drug Policy Alliance
http://www.drugpolicy.org/
This organization promotes policy alternatives to the drug war. It has state-by-state information about drug policies, as well as information about drug testing, especially in school settings.

PROBLEM-SOLVING COURTS

This movement includes not only drug courts but also mental health courts, domestic violence courts, and community courts. The common theme is to respond to crime in more creative ways than simply adjudicating the individual offense.

Center for Court Innovation
http://www.problemsolvingjustice.org
This Web site provides specific information for practitioners and academics about problem-solving courts, including white papers, fact sheets, and curriculum.

National Center for State Courts
http://www.ncsconline.org/d_research/ProblemSolvingCourts/Problem-SolvingCourts.html
NCSC provides information for state courts based on its collaborative work with the Conference of Chief Justices, the Conference of State Court Administrators, and other associations of judicial leaders. The site provides an overview of problem-solving courts, including a toolkit for people interested in starting one in their jurisdiction.

THERAPEUTIC JURISPRUDENCE

International Network on Therapeutic Jurisprudence
http://www.law.arizona.edu/depts/upr-intj/
Overseen by one of the founders of therapeutic jurisprudence, David Wexler, the International Network on Therapeutic Jurisprudence is a clearinghouse and resource center regarding therapeutic jurisprudence developments across the world.

Therapeutic Justice Center
http://therapeuticjurisprudencecenter.org/
Established by the other founder of therapeutic jurisprudence, Bruce Winick, the center is run by Laurie Silvers and Mitchell Rubenstein. It conducts original research, sponsors conferences, and trains judges and lawyers in the concepts of therapeutic jurisprudence.

RESTORATIVE JUSTICE

A related movement to therapeutic jurisprudence, restorative justice involves restoring the people most affected by a crime, including victims, offenders, and community. Programs include victim-offender mediations, family group conferencing, and sentencing circles.

Center for Restorative Justice and Peacemaking
http://www.cehd.umn.edu/ssw/rjp/Resources/RJ_Dialogue_Resources/default.asp
This center is run out of the University of Minnesota School of Social Work in collaboration with Marquette University Law School's Restorative Justice Initiative (http://law.marquette.edu/cgi-bin/site.pl?2130&pageID=1831). Both sites have overview information, scholarly articles, and training materials about restorative justice.

Notes

Chapter 1 Inside the Black Box of Drug Court Justice

1. All names of youths and staff have been changed for confidentiality purposes.
2. See Clear (2007) on neighborhood disadvantage and families; Pager (2003, 2007) for more on employment chances; Western (2006) for life course; and Manza and Uggen (2006) for the impact of felon disenfranchisement on politics.
3. E-mail communication with Leonora Fleming, research coordinator at the National Drug Court Institute, December 17, 2009.
4. One of Wexler and Winick's earliest books, *Essays in Therapeutic Jurisprudence*, published in 1991 by Carolina Academic Press, provides a good overview of therapeutic jurisprudence. See also Corvette (2000) for a summary.
5. Burns and Peyrot (2003) discuss this notion of tough love therapy further in their study of how judges in adult drug courts try to compel defendants to change.
6. In this regard, drug courts resemble contemporary forms of parole and probation where violations for minor infractions (e.g., missed appointments, positive drug tests) could lead to reincarceration.
7. The social constructionist literature considers how people attribute meaning, based on their own understandings and localized settings. As Spector and Kitsuse (1977) suggest, the analytical task is to focus on the social process of definition of a social problem that in this case would be the notion of youths' noncompliance.
8. In his 1984 book, *Inside Plea Bargaining*, Douglas Maynard, an ethnomethodologist, characterizes how these seemingly innocent "person descriptions" contain the court actors' implicit interpretations of the defendants and their "motives" behind their actions to covertly direct the plea bargaining process. For example, he mentions one case of Frank Bryan who is charged with resisting arrest and disorderly conduct in which the judge's description of the defendant as "the poor chap" shaped how the defense attorney and prosecutor subsequently proceeded to present the "facts" of the case to result in a more lenient plea bargain.
9. Feeley and Simon, as well as Garland, both mention these types of diversion and court-mandated drug treatment programs but do not expand upon their relationship to the new penology or culture of control. Garland mentions a cousin to therapeutic jurisprudence—restorative justice—as somewhat promising, but essentially states that it is too early to tell how it fits within the culture of control. Similarly, Feeley and Simon walk the line between calling for more diversion programs for drug offenders while also situating drug testing within the new penology of managing "risky" offenders on parole or probation.
10. Michel Foucault (1977) discusses this concept of the panopticon to highlight new forms of social control. He describes Jeremy Bentham's proposed organization of a prison in which the cells were organized around a central tower such that the inmates would think there was always someone watching them from that tower.

11. Mirchandani summarizes Habermas's argument in his 1996 book, *Between Facts and Norm*, as follows: in a rational deliberative democratic state, the dispersed state control increases the citizens' ability to monitor the state's functions and to collectively protest when it disagrees with that state function.

12. For comprehensive reviews of drug court evaluations, see Belenko (2001); Berman and Feinblatt (2005); Hepburn and Harvey (2007); Huddleston, Marlowe, and Casebolt (2008); and Butts and Roman (2004) .

13. Hasenfeld makes a distinction between people-processing and people-changing institutions, with the former imposing a new "status" (e.g., delinquent, welfare client) from which to influence a person's behavior to the latter directly trying to alter the "clients' biophysical, psychological, or social attributes in order to improve their well-being and social functioning" (1983, 140). Yet, Hasenfeld also clarifies these categories are ideal types, with many institutions incorporating elements of both. The juvenile drug courts have elements of both types, with its ultimate product being people-changing but its organizational work environment as people-processing. That is, the juvenile drug court is people-changing in that it features extensive staff-client interactions to promote the client's "attribute change," but it is also people-processing in that it has to rely upon several external agencies (e.g., schools, drug treatment programs, family) to achieve its intended goal. Hasenfeld's 1983 study also includes a third category of people-sustaining institutions whose function is to prevent clients' status from worsening, but that is not relevant to the juvenile drug court.

14. Corey Colyer (2007) also analyzes drug courts as a people-processing institution but with a different theoretical and empirical perspective. Colyer (2007, 326) states that the drug court people-processing activities cover four stages: "(a) locating appropriate defendants for participation, (b) discovering an adequate diagnosis, (c) locating compatible treatment, and (d) managing and maintaining the participant once placed." He uses the people-processing framework to analyze the classification work done by the drug court staff primarily in the first three stages of screening, diagnosis, and referral to treatment. As such, the classification work is a series of tasks in the "pre-patient stage" (Goffman 1961) of treatment. Those tasks are also completed primarily by case managers and then presented to the other drug court staff.

    In contrast, my study focuses exclusively on Colyer's last phase of managing participants, or the "in-patient" phase (Goffman 1961) of treatment. I consider the staff's classification work to be the result of ongoing negotiations among all the drug court staff members about the youth's case. As such, this study's empirical focus is the staff weekly assessments of youth compliance. Moreover, in my setting, the concept of compliance applies to more than drug treatment, extending to the youth's actions in school and home as well.

15. For example, some studies of law in action have shown how the organizational structure of court talk (e.g., question-and-answer format of trial witness examinations) shapes the way juries make sense of "what happened" and make decisions (Atkinson and Drew 1979; Drew 1992; Goodwin 1994). Manzo describes the importance of studying such a topic (Manzo and Travers 1998, 11): "for most conventional legal sociologists, the activities that constitute work in legal settings— the talk that makes up plea bargaining, that makes up jury deliberation, that makes up conversations between lawyers and clients—is an annoyance, a stumbling block that exposes the gap that exists between idealized theoretical or philosophical constructs surrounding 'law' and the work of legal actors. This gap . . . has always been a central concern in the jurisprudence and the sociology of law."

16. A similar concept is Harvey Sack's concept of membership categorization devices (1992). Membership categorization devices (MCDs) are descriptive markers that

people use to associate something to a larger reference category to "understand" it. The speaker and hearer both must agree on the use of the MCD for it to make sense; Sacks would refer to this as the consistency rule. Schegloff (2007, 471) explains: "When some category from some collection of categories in a MCD has been used to refer to (or identify or apperceive) some person on some occasion, then other persons in the setting may be referred to or identified or apperceived or grasped by reference to the same or other categories from the same collection. Now this is an optional practice, not a mandatory one, but it does serve to inject into the scene or the activity the relevance of those other categories."

17. See Anspach (1993), Cicourel (1995) and Mann (1985) for more on staff uses of information as occasioned presentations of selected "facts."

18. For example, peoples' welfare benefits are increasingly tied to their efforts to find work. In a *New York Times* article on April 13, 2010, entitled "Plan Would Require Homeless to Work to Qualify for Rent Subsidies," Julie Bosman writes about a new proposal for homeless families that requires at least one adult member to work to receive housing vouchers for free or subsidized rent; they also would have to pay more toward their rent, increasing from fifty dollars a month to 30 percent of their annual salary in the first year. Bosman quotes Linda Gibb, the commissioner of homeless services, who says, "Anybody who can work, is capable of working, and we should help them work." Similarly in educational settings, schools are increasingly evaluated on student test scores and teacher performance measures.

19. As documented in the March 30, 2010, *New York Times* article, "New York Will Stop Paying the Poor for Good Behavior," Julie Bosman reports how the city's efforts to replicate an incentive-based program in Mexico for poor families have not yielded the expected results in the three-year pilot. I would argue this could be attributed to the fact that the program does not make up for the structural inequalities these poor families face every day. That is, paying students to go to school or parents to hold down a job implies their motivation is the only reason driving their performance, instead of under-resourced schools or a volatile labor market.

20. This perspective suggests that drug courts generate what Stanley Cohen (1985) describes as "social and cultural iatrogenesis," in which their intervention produces a new category of undeserving clients: the unaccountable client.

Chapter 2 Setting and Methods

1. That includes both active and inactive (AWOL—absent without leave, in custody, long-term residential treatment) participants. Typically the court has sixty to seventy-five active participants at any given time.

2. Noncompliant events could be a positive drug test result, a missed appointment in treatment, or discharge from treatment. These noncompliant events have to be officially documented as probation violations and heard in the court. Some staff remarked to me in passing that many youths are eligible for drug court but not referred to the program because their probation officers do not have the time to fill out the paperwork to document such violations.

3. If the youths are not accepted into drug court, the judge can choose among a few options. For youths with minor drug issues, the judge would tell them to continue on regular probation and set a ninety-day review hearing. If at that point the youths continue to accumulate probation violations, the drug court might then accept them; if they are doing well, they are kept on regular probation. For a youth with gang affiliations, the judge might refer him to the probation program specifically for gang offenders. Finally, the judge could simply send the case back to the youth's original juvenile court for another dispositional hearing.

4. This observation is based on my visits to youths' homes and communities and staff's comments to me about the youths. I did not have access to official records to verify these views.

5. The percentages of the general population are from the 2000 Census.

6. The program has since switched to a 270-sober-day model and updated the phases to reflect the shortened timeframe. The following description is based on the program design that was in place during my first phase of fieldwork.

7. I should note that in the first three months of my fieldwork, two Caucasian female judges presided over the east court at different times. However, the majority of my observations occurred with Judges Samuels, Hooper, and O'Reilly presiding over the three courts.

8. I should also note that the city contracted with a new treatment agency during the fieldwork period, leading to a massive turnover in drug counselors three months into the fieldwork period. So this total of ten is for the entire fieldwork period; at any given time, only five to six were actually working at the court. The drug counselors listed in the chart are from the new agency that took over in January.

9. These reports were semistructured in that the staff would write a brief paragraph of three to four lines per youth that summarized her progress in school, treatment, and home, as well as latest drug test results. The staff used stock phrases such as "youth doing well in school, parents state he's doing well" or "drug tested clean on March first." The report also listed the youth's drug court phase, sober day count, custody day count, and date of birth. Staff would loosely structure its discussion around these reports, talking first about the noncompliant youths and then going onto the compliant youths. However, the reports were often outdated by the team meeting, as staff would receive last-minute information (e.g., drug test results or school attendance reports) or the youths would have been arrested between the time the report was written and the court day. While these reports are a rich source of information to be analyzed in their own right, the staff's assessments of youth compliance were constructed largely in the staff's verbal discussions in the team meetings. As such, the book does not highlight the use of reports even though it recognizes the value in that kind of content analysis.

10. Most of the substitute judges and lawyers had a working knowledge of the court since they had been doing it for a while. For the few who did not, the regular staff would instruct them about the process. If there were serious decisions that week, the substitute judges and attorneys would often defer the matter until the regular staff returned. As mentioned in footnote eight, the only new staff were the treatment counselors in January. They adjusted fairly quickly to the drug court, as many had previous experience working in the adult drug court or in the drug treatment field in general. The one area of difference was the new drug counselors' sense that the juvenile drug court judges and lawyers did not always accept their treatment expertise about the youths, in comparison to their experience in the adult drug court.

11. This intimacy among staff and youths was further fostered by the fact that many of the staff lived in the same communities as the youths or in neighboring communities. The defense attorney, probation officers, and drug counselors told me they occasionally saw the youths during their off-time in local stores and on the streets. One police officer lived literally on the same street as one of the youths.

12. Some of these agencies, like the drug treatment programs, drug testing laboratories, and private psychologists, did benefit financially from the drug court, as they could bill the city- and state-wide agencies or probation for their services. Yet this did not affect the staff's work in any obvious way since the contracts were with the entire court system, not only the drug court.

13. I will not be focusing on how the staff uses rewards for two reasons. First, while the staff did give out incentives every month and other "rewards," such as phase promotions, sobriety tokens, and movie tickets, the majority of its discussions centered on the "bad" behavior of the noncompliant youths and the corresponding sanction to be imposed. Second, my interviews with youths and parents suggested that the incentives were nice but not necessarily motivating for youths to adhere to the court's expectations. As such, the book focuses exclusively on the sanctioning decision-making process of the staff. While this might seem to skew the view of the court as only negative, the staff did not necessarily consider the sanctions as punishment but rather as part of the "therapeutic" intervention.

14. A more detailed account of the methods and reflexivity is found in appendix A.

CHAPTER 3   WHAT COURT DAY IS HE?

1. Based on my observations of the team meetings, I counted up the number of discussions about noncompliant youths per week in each court and found that the north court had an average of four noncompliant youth per week, compared to the south and east courts which both had an average of seven noncompliant youth per week.

2. To give a sense of the size of this area, I went on a ride-along for seven hours, during which time the drug counselor drove 180 miles to make eleven stops to see nine youth.

3. See also Ulmer and Kramer (1998), who showed how members of different courtroom workgroups used the new sentencing guidelines to advance their own institutional biases. Elsewhere, Harris and Jesilow (2000) looked at the constraining impact of California's three-strikes law on the work group's ability to process cases in their typical manner. Knepper and Barton (1997) also looked at the effect of the workgroup on the court's ability to incorporate the 1980 adoption assistance and child welfare act on child maltreatment proceedings.

4. In addition, they discuss the courtroom actors' sponsoring organizations and task environment (e.g., physical layout of courthouse and external pressures from police, legislative bodies, and media).

5. Indeed, many staff (most prominently, the prosecutor and defense attorney) participated and operated in the same manner in all three courts.

6. As summarized in the 2006 National Institute of Justice report, "Drug Courts: The Second Decade," Goldkamp, White, and Robinson (2002) explored this notion by examining the relationship between judicial staffing patterns and participant outcomes. See also King and Pasquarella (2009) for a summary of research on the impact of judicial styles on drug court client outcomes.

7. This percentage is calculated from the fifty-three youths for whom I knew their neighborhood; there were an additional six youths whose neighborhood I did not know.

8. A couple weeks before, Bill mentioned Olivia to the one of drug court police officers, saying, "I wish my AWOL kids were in [your neighborhood] . . . you are always here." Bill added, "There are two running around my neighborhood. I saw one on Saturday—Olivia." Yates (police officer) said, "Call someone up." Bill said, "I have."

9. This disparity in time that the youth is AWOL does affect the court's assessment of that youth's noncompliance; in this case, it leads to a more severe sanction for Olivia. Officer Grant cites the length of Olivia's AWOL status to justify the longer sanction of the 120-day in-custody program so that she can get back into drug treatment, without adjusting for the fact that she was gone so long because of the north court's lack of police coverage. So the length of the AWOL status—which

drives to some extent the staff's sense of the severity of the noncompliance—should be understood as a function of both the youth's actions and the organizational limitations of the north court.

10. This is different than the specialized cases that the workgroup literature suggests increases the staff's ability to routinize its work. By "specialized," Eisenstein and Jacobs (1977) refer to particular phases of the court process (e.g., arraignments, sentencing). Here the three drug subcourts all handle the same types of cases, with two of them handling additional matters (e.g., new cases, detentions) as they arise.

11. These orientations occurred on Thursdays before the south drug court. In the orientation, Judge O'Reilly talked to the youths and parents about the drug court rules and introduced the staff members. The youths and parents received a paper manual listing all the expectations and policies and also watched a short video about the program. As they watched the video, the staff met in Judge O'Reilly's chambers to conduct its team meeting for the south court.

12. Another complication was that the defense attorney would have to meet with the new youths and families individually to inform them of their rights and to get them to sign the requisite paperwork (e.g., consent forms). At the same time, he also had to meet with the south court's noncompliant youths in detention to hear their side of the story before the team meeting. So the number of new youths affected the amount of time he could spend with the detained youths from the south court and vice versa.

CHAPTER 4   BUILDING ACCOUNTABILITY THROUGH ASSESSMENTS OF NONCOMPLIANCE

1. As mentioned in chapter 2, I refer to drug court sanctions as normal remedies (Emerson 1981), which are a naturalistic interactionist way to talk about how staff decides to use the sanctions.

2. This topic will be explored in greater detail in chapter 6.

3. Because drug testing is a central component to the staff's perceptions of youth noncompliance and has its own unique set of interpretive practices, the next chapter will consider it in greater depth.

4. This cumulative effect will be explored more in chapter 7.

5. I have mentioned elsewhere (2009) that I did find some potential racial differences in the staff's uses of mental health descriptions. Of the total youths ($n = 193$) I observed in the court, white clients were more likely to have some "mental health issue" discussed by staff as opposed to the black and Latino clients. While staff discussed mental health issues for 33 percent of Caucasian youths ($n = 72$), they only did so for 22 percent of black/other clients ($n = 23$) and 16 percent of Latino clients ($n = 98$). At the same time, I cannot attribute this difference solely to race because it is too complicated to separate out in my field notes this factor from the other issues relating to the youths' cases. For more on race and gender differences in terms of the mentally ill in justice settings, see Bridges and Steen (1998); Herz (2001); Lewis (1980); Lewis, Balla, and Shanok (1979); Lewis, Shanok, and Pincus (1982); Rosenfield, Phillips, and White (2006); Thomas, Stubbe, and Pearson (1999); and Westendorp et al. (1986).

6. While Frank's case is an extreme instance, it does bring up the possibility of how institutional racism could translate into discrimination against minority youths in other settings. For example, if a school unfairly identifies a minority student as a troublemaker versus a white student, the drug court staff would only see that difference as one student being more "noncompliant" than the other, unless it saw the overt racism as demonstrated in Frank's school.

7. The staff ultimately decided to postpone this legal maneuvering, opting to wait until the official petition on the resisting arrest charge was filed. But the option to add custody time still remained possible, as Charlie noted in the discussion:

   CHARLIE: Why don't we release him [today] on home sup and when the petition comes down, we'll deal with it. I will tell you, although I shouldn't, [when there is a] new finding, dismiss this petition and true find on the new [one of resisting arrest].

   HOOPER: It is only a year [of custody].

   CHARLIE: I understand, but it is more than what he has now. . . . Don't say I said it.

8. Alicia also describes her conflicted view of drug court in the interview when she says, "I wish I wasn't in drug court because it's not the thing to do or to brag about, but it's helping me. If I wasn't in drug court I think I'd be running wild, smoking, doing all kinds of drugs, and probably overdosed by now. So, in a way, I don't want to be in it, but it's helping me too."

9. Despite that, this interpretive practice of consistency still allows some staff to advocate for a particular normal remedy, serving a strategic purpose in the staff's decision-making process.

10. Similarly, critics of juvenile courts have noted that despite the newfound legal rights guaranteed to youths after the 1967 Supreme Court decision *In Re Gault*, many youths do not fully understand the substance of those rights, such as waiving their Miranda rights and confessing to crimes that they might not have committed.

11. This is similar to what Berman and Feinblatt (2005) characterize as necessary to do when the issue becomes complicated.

CHAPTER 5 SOCIAL CONSTRUCTION OF DRUG TEST RESULTS

1. See Goldkamp, White, and Robinson (2001); Fox (1999, 2001); Paik (2006); Skoll (1992); Weinberg (1996); and Wiley (1990).

2. The sweat patch could pick up methamphetamine use but could not pick up alcohol use, since the staff had to use rubbing alcohol to apply the patch onto the skin. Staff often joked that they did not tell the youths about this discrepancy to keep the youths from drinking.

3. This approach differs from previous research on drug testing that encompasses five general perspectives: legality, morality, technology, deterrence, and implementation. Much of the literature (DuPont 1989; White 2003) and U.S. court decisions on drug testing in the workplace and schools (*Board of Education of Independent School District No. 92 of Pottawatomie County et al. v. Earls, Lindsay et al.* 2002; *Vernonia School District 47J v. Acton* 1995) addresses the legal questions of whether drug testing violates peoples' civil liberties or is legitimate in its attempts to protect the greater public's safety. Sociologists of sport (Denham 2004) highlight the moral aspects, in which drug testing is depicted as a way to keep the "integrity" of the sport where no player has an unfair advantage and to maintain players' status as worthy "role models" for younger and amateur athletes. In addition, some research discusses flaws in drug testing technology (Barnum and Gleason 1994) and security in the testing protocols (Johnston, Michaud and Warner 2009), considering the broader societal implications in terms of the explosion of the drug testing industry (Tunnell 2004) and public opinion about a "growing" drug crisis (Gilliom 1994). The deterrence studies attempt to measure how drug testing influences future drug use and criminal activity, either finding no significant effect (Comer 1994) or showing mixed results of its deterrent effect on a person's drug use and criminal activity (Belenko 2001; Britt, Gottfredson, and Goldkamp 1992; Cullen, Wright, and Applegate 1996; Harrell and Roman 2001; Toborg et al. 1989; Wish and Gropper 1990). Underlying these mixed results are the differences among the types

of settings and people being tested (Borg 2000; Boyes-Watson 1997; Draper 1998; Haapanen et al. 1998; Kleiman et al. 2002; Knudsen et al. 2003; Turner and Petersilia 1992).

4. In interviews, some youths confirmed this assumption, saying they always can test if they are clean; if not, they will try to evade the staff. At the same time, other youths stated getting stressed about having to "piss on demand" (Tunnell 2004); Dominic, who stated earlier that he tried to avoid testing, also says in his interview, "I don't want to be locked up . . . 'cause I can't go pee . . . it's a lot of pressure. . . . And you know you're clean, you're gonna be locked up for no reason. . . . So you're just, you know, pretty much stressing about it."

5. There are several steps to the paperwork to ensure the "chain of custody" for the drug test: the youths and staff must sign various parts of the paperwork at distinct times (e.g., before submitting the urinalysis sample or after removing the sweat patch) and staff must put the paperwork in a certain place with the sample. If these steps are not followed correctly, the staff cannot legally consider the test as positive.

6. See Crowe (1998) for a description of the federal guidelines for recommended cutoff levels for specific drugs, as set by the Department of Health and Human Services. These guidelines are for workplace drug testing but also could be used for laboratories conducting urine testing for any federal agency.

7. There are also examples of opposite situations where staff does not believe the parents and interprets the parents' explanations as "covering" or "enabling" their child's drug use. The next chapter explores this in more detail.

Chapter 6   It's Not Just His Probation, It's Mine

1. In these orientation sessions, the parents mainly listened quietly, asking no questions about the program. Yet, as this chapter will explore, that silence did not mean they understood what was being said. Most of the parents stated in their interviews with me that they did not feel they were adequately informed about the program's expectations of their youths or themselves.

2. There were some extreme cases of abusive parents as well. At least four youths in the first fieldwork period had documented records of sexually or physically abusive parents; those youths were all deemed untenable in the drug court because of their unstable and unsafe home environment. They were quickly sent to residential facilities or to another family member/legal guardian's home to live.

3. The staff did have the ability to refer parents to court-mandated classes to help them improve their parenting. However, it rarely did so.

4. Staff often used these typologies in conjunction with one another to describe parents. For example, staff simultaneously saw parents as being incompetent enablers or unreasonably uncooperative.

5. As mentioned in chapter 4, James tells me about another incident with his parents calling probation when he left the house. However, he explained it as taking his little brother out of the home while his parents were fighting intensely—in other words, to protect his little brother.

6. James went to this boot camp before getting into the drug court program; however, the mom's comments are still relevant, since she is conflating his previous court experiences with drug court under the rubric of "probation."

7. In contrast, there are a few parents who become more involved with the court because of these financial reasons. Greg's dad says he now makes sure the staff uses a different drug test (e.g., sweat patch) on his son so that the test can measure more accurately if the youth uses. He states, "It's a ton of money [to send a kid to juvenile hall], so when I talk to the PO [probation officer] or I talk to the attorney guy

that's there at the drug court thing and I say, "You know what? I just want him on the patch all the time because I wanna know—is he using, yes or no?" Greg's dad brings up another variation to the interactive and situational nature to parental alignment: some parents are not as aware as Greg's dad of the intricacies of the drug court process, especially the drug testing. If they are not monitoring the decision-making process (or asked to participate fully in it), the parents run the risk of increasing their youth's bill with each drug test and incarceration. So one reason James might spend more time in juvenile hall than Greg is not because of his greater noncompliant behavior, but due to Greg's dad, who is trying to prevent more noncompliant behavior from happening.

8. When I asked Kevin's mom to talk more about this incident in greater detail, she did not elaborate further.

9. There is another "unintended" consequence resulting from translation issues: the time delay in finding someone to communicate to the staff effectively creates a "cooling out" period for the parents. Julian's mom, a thirty-seven-year-old Latina, discusses how this affects her motivation to share with the staff: "I have called them, but through my son. I have left them messages. Sometimes they call me back, but when they call I have calmed down already, and I don't tell them what I wanted to tell them." While Julian's mom does bring up another potential problem of using her fifteen-year-old son to communicate her concerns about him to the staff (and running the risk of her son selectively translating), the more pressing issue in her response pertained to the timing. The delay in reaching the staff gives the youth an advantage in that the parent no longer feels the need to tell on him. This cooling out period obviously could manifest among all parents (e.g., if they cannot immediately reach the juvenile court staff), but the linguistic barriers represent a structural opportunity for that to happen. It also then creates an image of the parents to the staff as not being serious—if they constantly call but then retract their threats. When asked how she would react if there was someone who spoke Spanish, Julian's mom responds, "It would be a whole different story."

10. When youths are on home supervision, their parents are supposed to call the probation home supervision office every time they leave and return to the house with the youths.

11. Lareau does make a qualification to state that both styles of parenting have advantages and disadvantages. Despite the fact that it does prepare youths better for school, concerted cultivation places enormous stress on the parents—financially, time-wise—to shuttle their children from one structured activity to another, and on the youths who become more individually focused and less creatively engaged as they do things mainly in preset environments. On the other hand, while accomplishment of natural growth might not prepare youths as well with the language skills to do well in school, it does allow youths more freedom to play in more informal environments and to develop closer ties to their extended families, who often live in the same neighborhoods (unlike the middle-class families whose extended families lived in other areas of the country).

CHAPTER 7 YOUTH TRAJECTORIES IN THE COURT

1. This is similar to attribution theory (see Bridges and Steen 1998) and focal concern (see Steffensmeier, Ulmer, and Kramer 1998) literatures. Bridges and Steen's study (1998) found racial differences in probation officers' accounts of youth offenses and how that affected the ultimate sentencing outcome for those youth. In their study, probation officers are more likely to attribute internal causes (e.g., defendant's criminal personality) to explain a minority youth's offense, compared to the white youth whose offense was attributed to more "external" causes

(e.g., environmental, peer pressure). Bridges and Steen then found that minority youth were subject to harsher sentencing recommendations, partly based on those probation reports. See also Harris (2008, 2009) for a summary of this literature.

2. I should note that the notion of workability does not necessarily address two possible situations in the drug court: (1) when a youth is simply flying under the radar as a result of the staff's attention to other youths on the caseload at the same time, or (2) when youths consistently do badly but somehow avoid detection. More detailed analysis needs to be done to see how those two situations lead to different workability types, if at all.

3. In my first interview with Rita, she does mention her previous experiences in treatment, comparing them to drug court. She says, "I think drug courts are a good program, out of all the programs I've heard of and all the [adolescent treatment programs] I'm with, I think drug court is the best because they don't mess around, and that's what some of us need. We need structure in drug court, and they don't put up with our little games, do you know what I mean? It's a hard program, but it's good. It's worth it."

4. Administrative discharge is a final outcome the staff uses when the youth turns eighteen years old and ages out of probation, the youth moves to another county, or the youth runs out of custody time. In these instances, the staff does not have the legal jurisdiction to continue working with the youths. So, while these youths are technically not considered failures, they also have not done enough to be granted the full privileges of the program graduates.

5. While the staff could technically send Rita to the year-long residential treatment facility, they can only do so if she voluntarily agrees to go. Since she had run away from residential treatment before, the staff did not feel it would be a good option for her now.

6. A few months later, a police officer said he heard Rebecca speak at a school graduation about relapsing after she finished drug court. Bill, the drug counselor, said he knew but was not too worried, since she got right back into "her program" at Narcotics Anonymous. So part of the staff's definition of success is knowing how to stop a relapse from getting too severe.

7. He originally started in another drug court when the program had court five days a week. It ultimately got combined with the south court in March. The summary below refers to what happened from March through October 2004 in the south court.

8. I did a search on the public bus transit Web site: it would take three buses and at least two hours one way to get to the courthouse from Manu's neighborhood.

9. Researchers and practitioners have long acknowledged the challenges associated with the increasing numbers of dually diagnosed offenders in the juvenile and criminal justice system. See Atkins et al. (1999); Grisso and Underwood (2004); Hirschfield et al. (2006); Otto et al. (1992); Teplin (1990, 1994); and Teplin et al. (2006).

10. For example, some of the Thursday staff members disputed a psychologist's diagnosis of Julio, a Latino male, because they thought he wanted to get transferred from probation camp to juvenile hall to get released quicker.

BILL (DRUG COUNSELOR): You can get out of 120 [drug dorm] if [you have a] panic attack?

CHARLIE (PUBLIC DEFENDER): That's what the psychologist said.

SARAH (PROBATION OFFICER): He's not faking it.

SUBSTITUTE JUDGE: Thirty days [in juvenile hall] is not enough if he was committed [legally mandated] to the drug dorm.

Similarly, some of the Wednesday staff wondered if a recent suicide attempt by another Latino male, Martin, was his attempt to "skate" through the program.

Allen, the probation officer, said, "It could be anything. Maybe he used on the weekend and didn't want to go in [so he said it]. It also could be an issue with the parents. The dad has gone to Mexico [they may be separating]."

11. In an interview with me, Luke explained the incident as follows: "Me and my friends, like on the ride home from school, we like to yell outside the windows of the bus and yell at girls that we think are pretty. I don't really say inappropriate stuff, but my friends do, so the bus driver saw my head out the window and my friends were saying like inappropriate stuff, she'd think it was me too. . . . I've never yelled at a bus driver, I've never even said anything."

12. As stated in chapter 2, the staff felt that the pregnant female youths would not be able to handle the many drug court requirements, on top of dealing with their prenatal care. Also, the probation department had a separate program designed exclusively for pregnant girls, to which the drug court referred these girls.

CHAPTER 8   THE (IN)JUSTICE OF DISCRETION

1. For example, schools have increasingly moved to zero-tolerance policies where students are now referred to court for school-related problems: tardiness becomes truancy; student teasing becomes bullying; wearing certain hats and colors become dress-code violations of a "gang-affiliated" nature.

2. Wolff proposes that we rethink how the law can be therapeutically oriented and not separate out mentally ill offenders in their own specialized court where they are potentially stigmatized as having committed crimes because of mental illness. Wolff proposes they should be considered like all other offenders, with their mental health issues entering the legal picture only if those illnesses had a significant influence in the commission of the crime. This is different for drug offenders whose drug use is the reason they end up in drug court. Also, if treated equally, perhaps the mentally ill offenders would face more severe sentencing in cases where their illness goes undetected in the sentencing process, in a similar vein to women facing harsher sentences now that courts have tried to rectify the chivalry thesis.

3. See Cain (1991), De Leon (2000), Rudy (1986), and Skoll (1992) for more about the identity transformation in drug treatment. See also Fox (1999, 2001), Burns and Peyrot (2003), Peyrot (1985), and Paik (2006) for more about the coerced element to some contemporary forms of this type of drug treatment.

4. This punitive nature is found in other problem-solving courts. For example, researchers (Sviridoff et al. 2001) found that the jail times given at Midtown Community Court, the nation's first quality-of-life court, were longer than in traditional case processing: "Although the Midtown Court handed out fewer jail sentences than the downtown court, Midtown jail sentences were typically longer than those downtown, particularly for petit larceny (an average of seventy-nine days, compared to forty-nine days at the downtown court) and prostitution cases (an average of fifteen days, compared to five days at the downtown court)" (8).

5. Simon Cole (2001) has done similar work on fingerprinting to show how legal actors use new technologies as undisputed "facts" of identification when those technologies are prone to subjective interpretations and, by extension, are not completely accurate. Another version of this issue is the "CSI effect" on jury deliberations, as forensic evidence, especially DNA, trumps other evidence as proof of the defendant's guilt or innocence.

6. The following studies detail law enforcement practices in Seattle that focused on certain drugs (crack versus cocaine) and types of drug users/sellers (street open-air markets versus private residences) that appeared disproportionately in minority communities: Beckett, Nyrop, and Pfingst (2006); Beckett et al. (2005); Provine (2007); and O'Hear (2009).

7. Finigan (2009) provides an excellent overview of studies on racial disparities in drug court outcomes. He cites extensively a 2006 study by Dannerbeck, Harris, Sundet, and Lloyd that looked at outcomes for 657 adult drug offenders in ten drug courts in Missouri in which 55 percent of the white participants compared to 28 percent of black participants graduated. They found that compared to the white participants, more black participants were unemployed, unmarried, childless, not living with family, and had lower levels of family support. They also had "significantly lower scores on a composite variable labeled 'community socioeconomic [SES] status' which reflected a combination of their income, the adequacy of their housing, their neighborhood environment, and their employment status" (Finigan 2009, 137).

8. A parallel would be the achievement ideology in education where people believe if you work hard and behave, you will do well in school. This line of thinking obviously ignores disparities in schools, resources, teachers, and facilities.

9. These recommendations speak directly to some of the research areas outlined by Marlowe et al. (2006) in the *National Drug Court Review* for the "second generation" of drug court research, specifically the issues of incentives and sanctions (research questions seven to nine), substance abuse treatment and other services (research questions ten to fourteen), and community supervision and case management (research questions fifteen and sixteen).

10. See http://www.nrepp.samhsa.gov/programfulldetails.asp?PROGRAM_ID= 183#ratings and http://www.motivationalinterviewing.org for more information. One key barrier to implementing motivational interviewing in the drug court is that motivational interviewing calls for no direct confrontation to client resistance.

11. One reviewer questioned what the public health literature suggested about effective drug treatment. Some interventions are now offering early screenings, and in some cases treatment, for substance abuse issues in primary care settings (SBIRT), covering a wider proportion of the population and addressing problematic use before it becomes a more serious addiction. Others advocate for increased use of harm reduction programs, where the emphasis is not on complete abstinence but on mitigating and managing dangerous drug use practices through medical intervention (e.g., buprenorphine for heroin; benzodiazepine, disulfarim, naltrexone, or acamprosate for alcoholism) or reducing collateral public health risks (e.g., HIV/AIDS) through needle exchange programs and condom distribution. However, these interventions are not necessarily conducive for juvenile drug courts for two reasons: (1) the SBIRT prevention-oriented intervention is designed for noncriminal settings to refer people to ostensibly the same kinds of group-based outpatient treatment used by the drug court; (2) the medical-based models are for specific drugs (e.g., heroin) that are not common among the youths in the drug court. While the medicines to counteract alcohol use might be relevant, many are designed to work only after the person stops drinking or has a serious alcohol problem, neither of which resembles the drinking patterns of most drug court youths.

12. See Bezan (2009) for a review of the public health literature and the 2005 report "Public Health Approach to Drug Control in Canada: Health Officers Council of B.C." for more about a public health approach to drug use.

13. Butts and Roman (2004) bring up similar questions in their review of juvenile drug court evaluations but never flesh them out completely.

BIBLIOGRAPHY

Anspach, R. 1993. *Deciding Who Lives: Fateful Choices in the Intensive-Care Nursery*. Berkeley and Los Angeles: University of California Press.

Aos, S., P. Phipps, R. Barnoski, and R. Lieb. 2001. *The Comparative Costs and Benefits of Programs to Reduce Recidivism*. Olympia: Washington State Institute for Public Policy.

Arrigo, B. 2002. *Punishing the Mentally Ill: A Critical Analysis of Law and Psychiatry*. Albany: State University of New York Press.

Atkins, D. L., A. J. Pumariega, K. Rogers, L. Montgomery, C. Nybro, G. Jeffers, and F. Sease. 1999. "Mental Health and Incarcerated Youth. I: Prevalence and Nature of Psychopathology." *Journal of Child and Family Studies* 8:193–204.

Atkinson, J. M., and P. Drew. 1979. *Order in Court: The Organisation of Verbal Interaction in Judicial Settings*. London: Macmillan Press.

Baar, C. 2002. "What the Data Shows." *Fordham Urban Law Journal* 29:1827–1857.

Barnum, D., and J. Gleason. 1994. "The Credibility of Drug Tests: A Multistage Bayesian Analysis." *Industrial and Labor Relations Review* 47:610–621.

Becker, H. 1963. *Outsiders: Studies in the Sociology of Deviance*. New York: Free Press.

Beckett, K., K. Nyrop, and L. Pfingst. 2006. "Race, Drugs and Policing: Understanding Disparities in Drug Delivery Arrests." *Criminology* 44:105–138.

Beckett, K., K. Nyrop, L. Pfingst, and M. Bowen. 2005. "Drug Use, Drug Possession Arrests, and the Question of Race: Lessons from Seattle." *Social Problems* 52:419–441.

Belenko, S. 2001. *Research on Drug Courts: A Critical Review: 2001 Update*. New York: National Center on Addiction and Substance Abuse.

Berman, G., and J. Feinblatt. 2005. *Good Courts*. New York and London: New Press.

Bezan, G. 2009. "Problem Drug Use the Public Health Imperative: What Some of the Literature Says." *Substance Abuse Treatment, Prevention, and Policy* 4:21. http://www.substanceabusepolicy.com/content/4/1/21.

Borg, M. J. 2000. "Drug Testing in Organizations: Applying Horwitz's Theory of the Effectiveness of Social Control." *Deviant Behavior* 21:123–154.

Bortner, M. A. 1982. *Inside a Juvenile Court: The Tarnished Ideal of Individualized Justice*. New York and London: New York University Press.

Bosk, C. 2003. *Forgive and Remember: Managing Medical Failure*. 2nd ed. Chicago: University of Chicago Press.

Bosman, J. 2010. "New York Will Stop Paying the Poor for Good Behavior." *New York Times*, March 30.

———. 2010. "Plan Would Require Homeless to Work to Qualify for Rent Subsidies." *New York Times*, April 13.

Boyes-Watson, C. 1997. "Corporations as Drug Warriors: The Symbolic Significance of Employee Drug Testing." *Studies in Law, Politics, and Society* 17:185–223.

Bridges, G., and S. Steen. 1998. "Racial Disparities in Official Assessments of Juvenile Offenders: Attributional Stereotypes as Mediating Mechanisms." *American Sociological Review* 63:554–570.

Britt, C. L., M. Gottfredson, and J. Goldkamp. 1992. "Drug Testing and Pretrial Misconduct: An Experiment on the Specific Deterrent Effects of Drug Monitoring Defendants on Pretrial Release." *Journal of Research in Crime and Delinquency* 29:62–78.

Burns, S., and M. Peyrot. 2003. "Tough Love: Nurturing and Coercing Responsibility and Recovery in California Drug Courts." *Social Problems* 50:416–438.

Butts, J., and J. Roman, eds. 2004. *Juvenile Drug Courts and Teen Substance Abuse.* Washington, DC: Urban Institute Press.

Cain, C. 1991. "Transformation of Identity." *Ethos* 19:210–253.

Carey, S., and M. W. Finigan. 2004. "A Detailed Cost Analysis in a Mature Drug Court Setting: A Cost-Benefit Evaluation of the Multnomah County Drug Court." *Journal of Contemporary Criminal Justice* 20:315–338.

Center for Families, Children, and the Courts. 2006. *California Drug Court Cost Analysis Study.* San Francisco: Administrative Office of the Court.

Charmaz, K. 1983. "The Grounded Theory Model: An Explication and Interpretation." In *Contemporary Field Research: A Collection of Readings*, ed. R. Emerson, 109–126. Prospect Heights, IL: Waveland Press.

Cicourel, A. 1995. *The Social Organization of Juvenile Justice.* New Brunswick, NJ: Transaction Publishers.

Clear, T. 2007. *Imprisoning Neighborhoods.* New York: Oxford University Press.

Cohen, M., J. March, and J. Olsen. 1972. "A Garbage Can Model of Organizational Choice." *Administrative Science Quarterly* 17:1–25.

Cohen, S. 1985. *Visions of Social Control: Crime, Punishment and Classification.* Cambridge, UK: Polity Press.

Cole, S. 2001. *Suspect Identities: A History of Fingerprinting and Criminal Identification.* Cambridge, MA: Harvard University Press.

Colyer, C. 2007. "Innovation and Discretion: The Drug Court as a People-Processing Institution." *Criminal Justice Policy Review* 18:313–329.

Comer, D. 1994. "A Case against Workplace Drug Testing." *Organization Science* 5:259–267.

Cook, K. 2006. Doing Difference and Accountability in Restorative Justice Conferences. *Theoretical Criminology* 10:107–124.

Corvette, B. B. 2000. "Therapeutic Jurisprudence." *Sociological Practice: A Journal of Clinical and Applied Sociology* 2:127–132.

Crowe, A. 1998. *Drug Identification and Testing in the Juvenile Justice System.* Washington, DC: Office of Juvenile Justice and Delinquency Prevention.

Cullen, F., J. Wright, and B. Applegate. 1996. "Control in the Community: Limits of Reform?" In *Choosing Correctional Options That Work: Defining the Demand and Evaluating the Supply*, ed. A. Harland, 69–116. Thousand Oaks, CA: Sage.

Dannerbeck, A., G. Harris, P. Sundet, and K. Lloyd. 2006. "Understanding and Responding to Racial Differences in Drug Court Outcomes." *Journal of Ethnicity in Substance Abuse* 5:1–22.

De Leon, G. 2000. *Therapeutic Community: Theory, Model and Method.* New York: Springer.

Denham, B. E. 2004. "Hero or Hypocrite? United States and International Media Portrayals of Carl Lewis amid Revelations of a Positive Drug Test." *International Review for the Sociology of Sport* 39:167–185.

Dorf, M., and C. F. Sabel. 2000. "Drug Treatment Courts and Emergent Experimentalist Government." *Vanderbilt Law Review* 53:831.

Draper, E. 1998. "Drug Testing in the Workplace: The Allure of Management Technologies." *International Journal of Sociology and Social Policy* 18:64–106.

Drew, P. 1992. Contested Evidence in Courtroom Cross-Examination: The Case of a Trial for Rape. In *Talk at Work: Interaction in Institutional Settings*, ed. P. Drew and J. Heritage, 470–520. New York: Cambridge University Press.

Drew, P., and J. Heritage. 1992. *Talk at Work: Interaction in Institutional Settings*. New York: Cambridge University Press.

Duneier, M. 1999. *Sidewalk*. New York: Farrar, Straus and Giroux.

DuPont, R. L. 1989. "Never Trust Anyone under 40." *Policy Review* 48:52–57.

Eisenstein, J., and H. Jacob. 1977. *Felony Justice: An Organizational Analysis of Criminal Courts*. Boston: Little Brown.

Emerson, R. M. 1969. *Judging Delinquents: Context and Process in Juvenile Court*. Chicago: Aldine.

———. 1981. "On Last Resorts." *American Journal of Sociology* 87:1–22.

——— 1992. "Disputes in Public Bureaucracies." *Studies in Law, Politics and Society* 12:3–29.

Emerson, R.M., R. Fretz, and L. Shaw. 1995. *Writing Ethnographic Fieldnotes*. Chicago: University of Chicago Press.

Emerson, R. M., and B. Paley. 1992. "Organizational Horizons in Complaint-Filing." In *The Uses of Discretion*, Keith Hawkins, 232–247. New York and Oxford: Oxford University Press.

Feeley, M. 1979. *The Process Is the Punishment: Handling Cases in a Lower Criminal Court*. New York: Russell Sage.

Feeley, M., and J. Simon. 1992. "The New Penology: Notes on the Emerging Strategy of Corrections and Its Implications." *Criminology* 30:449–474.

Finigan, M. 2009. "Understanding Racial Disparities in Drug Courts." *Drug Court Review* 5:135–142.

Foucault, M. 1977. *Discipline and Punish: The Birth of the Prison*. New York: Pantheon.

———. 1991. "Governmentality." In *The Foucault Effect: Studies in Governmentality*, G. Burchell, C. Gordon, and P. Miller, 87–104. Chicago: University of Chicago Press.

Fox, K. 1999. "Changing Violent Minds: Discursive Correction and Resistance in the Cognitive Treatment of Violent Offenders in Prison." *Social Problems* 46:88–103.

———. 2001. "Self-Change and Resistance in Prison." In *Institutional Selves: Troubled Identities in a Postmodern World*, ed. J. Gubrium and J. Holstein, 176–192. New York: Oxford University Press.

Frohmann, L. 1991. "Discrediting Victims' Allegations of Sexual Assault: Prosecutorial Accounts of Case Rejections." *Social Problems* 38:213–226.

———. 1997. "Convictability and Discordant Locales: Reproducing Race, Class, and Gender Ideologies in Prosecutorial Decisionmaking." *Law and Society Review* 31:531–555.

Garland, D. 2001. *The Culture of Control: Crime and Social Order in Contemporary Society*. Chicago: University of Chicago Press.

Garfinkel, H. 1967. *Studies in Ethnomethodology*. Englewood Cliffs, NJ: Prentice Hall.

Geertz, C. 1983. "Thick Description: Toward an Interpretive Theory of Culture." In *Contemporary Field Research: A Collection of Readings,* ed. R. Emerson, 37–59. Prospect Heights, IL: Waveland Press.

Gilliom, J. 1994. *Surveillance, Privacy, and the Law: Employee Drug Testing and the Politics of Social Control.* Ann Arbor: University of Michigan Press.

Glaser, B., and A. Strauss. 1967. *The Discovery of Grounded Theory: Strategies for Qualitative Research.* Chicago: Aldine.

Goffman, E. 1961. *Asylums: Essays on the Social Situation of Mental Patients and Other Inmates.* Garden City, NY: Doubleday.

———. 1969. "The Insanity of Place." *Psychiatry: Journal of Interpersonal Relations* 32:357–387.

Goldkamp, J., M. White, and J. Robinson. 2001. "Do Drug Courts Work? Getting Inside the Drug Court Black Box." *Journal of Drug Issues* 31:27–72.

———. 2002. "From Whether to How Drug Courts Work: Retrospective Evaluation of Two Pioneering Drug Courts in Clark County (Las Vegas) and Multnomah County (Portland), Phase II Report from the National Evaluation of Drug Courts." National Institute of Justice. http://www. ncjrs.org/pdffiles1/nij/grants/194124 .pdf.

Goodwin, C. 1994. "Professional Vision." *American Anthropologist* 96:606–633.

Gray, P. 2009. "The Political Economy of Risk and the New Governance of Youth Crime." *Punishment and Society* 11:443–458.

Grisso, T., and L. A. Underwood. 2004. *"Screening and Assessing Mental Health and Substance Use Disorders among Youth in the Juvenile Justice System."* U.S. Department of Justice, Office of Justice Programs, and Office of Juvenile Justice and Delinquency Prevention. NCJ204956. Washington, DC: GPO.

Gubrium, J., and J. A. Holstein. 2000. *The Self We Live By: Narrative Identity in a Postmodern World.* New York: Oxford University Press.

———, eds. 2001. *Institutional Selves: Troubled Identities in a Postmodern World.* New York: Oxford University Press.

Haapanen, R., G. Boyken, S. Henderson, and L. Britton. 1998. *Drug Testing for Youthful Offenders on Parole: An Experimental Study.* Sacramento: State of California Department of the Youth Authority Research Division.

Habermas, J. 1996. *Between Facts and Norms: Contributions to a Discourse Theory of Law and Democracy.* Trans. William Rheg. Cambridge, MA: MIT Press.

Harrell, A., and M. Roman. 2001. "Reducing Drug Use and Crime among Offenders: The Impact of Graduated Sanctions" *Journal of Drug Issues* 31:207–232.

Harris, A. 2008. "The Social Construction of 'Sophisticated' Adolescents: How Judges Integrate Juvenile and Criminal Justice Decision-making Models." *Journal of Contemporary Ethnography* 37:469–506.

———. 2009. "Attributions and Institutional Processing: How Focal Concerns Guide Decision-Making in the Juvenile Court." *Race and Social Problems* 1:243–256.

Harris, J., and P. Jesilow. 2000. "It's Not the Old Ball Game: Three Strikes and the Courtroom Workgroup." *Justice Quarterly* 17:185–203.

Hasenfeld, Y. 1972. "People Processing Organizations: An Exchange Approach." *American Sociological Review* 37:256–263.

———. 1983. *Human Service Organizations.* Englewood Cliffs, NJ: Prentice-Hall.

———. 1992. *Human Services as Complex Organizations.* Thousand Oaks, CA: Sage.

Hasenfeld, Y., and P. Cheung. 1985. "The Juvenile Court as a People-Processing Organization: A Political Economy Perspective." *American Journal of Sociology* 90:801–824.

Health Officers Council of British Columbia. 2005. *Public Health Approach to Drug Control in Canada.* Victoria, BC: Health Officers Council of BC.

Hepburn, J., and A. N. Harvey. 2007. "The Effect of the Threat of Legal Sanction on Program Retention and Completion: Is That Why They Stay in Drug Court?" *Crime and Delinquency* 53:255–280.

Herz, D. 2001. "Understanding the Use of Mental Health Placements by the Juvenile Justice System." *Journal of Emotional and Behavioral Disorders* 9:172–181.

Hirschfield, P., T. Maschi, H. R. White, L. G. Traub, and R. Loeber. 2006. "Mental Health and Juvenile Arrests: Criminality, Criminalization, or Compassion?" *Criminology* 44:593–630.

Hoffman, M. 2002. "The Denver Drug Court and Its Unintended Consequences." In *Drug Courts in Theory and in Practice*, ed. J. Nolan, 67–88. New York: Aldine de Gruyter.

Huddleston, C. West, D. Marlowe, and R. Casebolt. 2008. *Painting the Current Picture: A National Report Card on Drug Courts and Other Problem Solving Courts in the United States.* Vol. 2, no. 1. Washington, DC: Bureau of Justice Assistance. http://www.ndci.org/sites/default/files/ndci/PCPII1_web%5B1%5D.pdf.

Jacobs, M. D. 1990. *Screwing the System and Making It Work: Juvenile Justice in the No Fault Society.* Chicago: University of Chicago Press.

Johnston, R., E. Michaud, and J. Warner. 2009. "Research Note: The Security of Urine Drug Testing." *Journal of Drug Issues* 39:1015–1028.

King, R., and J. Pasquarella. 2009. "Drug Courts: A Review of the Evidence." *The Sentencing Project.* http://www.sentencingproject.org/doc/dp_drugcourts.pdf.

Kleiman, M., T. Tran, P. Fishbein, M. Magula, W. Allen, and G. Lacy. 2002. *Opportunities and Barriers in Probation Reform: A Case Study of Drug Testing and Sanction.* CPCR Brief. Vol. 14, no. 4 Berkeley: California Policy Research Center.

Knepper, P., and S. Barton. 1997. "The Effect of Courtroom Dynamics on Child Maltreatment Proceedings." *Social Service Review* 71:288–308.

Knudsen, H., P. Roman, and J. Johnson. 2003. "Organizational Compatibility and Workplace Drug Testing: Modeling the Adoption of Innovative Social Control Practices." *Sociological Forum* 18:621–640.

Lareau, Annette. 2003. *Unequal Childhoods: Class, Race, and Family Life.* Berkeley: University of California Press.

Lemert, E. 1967. "Juvenile Court—Quest and Realities." *Trans-Action* 4:30–40.

Lewis, D. 1980. "Race Bias in the Diagnosis and Disposition of Violent Adolescents." *American Journal of Psychiatry* 137:211–216.

Lewis, D., D. Balla, and S. Shanok. 1979. "Some Evidence of Race Bias in the Diagnosis and Treatment of the Juvenile Offender." *American Journal of Orthopsychiatry* 49:53–61.

Lewis, D., S. Shanok, and J. Pincus. 1982. "A Comparison of the Neuropsychiatric Status of Female and Male Incarcerated Delinquents: Some Evidence of Sex and Race Bias." *Journal of the American Academy of Child Psychiatry* 21:190–196.

Lynch, M. 1985. *Art and Artifact in Laboratory Science: A Study of Shop Work and Shop Talk in a Research Laboratory.* London: Routledge and Kegan Paul.

Mackinem, M., and P. Higgins. 2008. *Drug Court: Constructing the Moral Identity of Drug Offenders.* Springfield, IL: Charles C. Thomas Publisher.

Mann, Kenneth. 1985. *Defending White-Collar Crime.* New Haven, CT: Yale University Press.

Manza, J., and C. Uggen. 2006. *Locked Out: Felon Disenfranchisement and American Democracy.* New York: Oxford University Press.

Manzo, J., and M. Travers, eds. 1998. *Law in Action: Ethnomethodological and Conversation Analytic Approaches to Law.* London: Dartmouth Press.

Marlowe, D., C. Heck, C. West Huddleston, and R. Casebolt. 2006. "A National Research Agenda for Drug Courts: Plotting the Course for Second-Generation Scientific Inquiry." *National Drug Court Review* 5:4–31.

Matza, D. 1969. *Becoming Deviant.* Englewood Cliffs, NJ: Prentice-Hall.

Maynard, D. 1982. "Defendant Attributes in Plea Bargaining." *Social Problems* 29:347–360.

———. 1984. *Inside Plea Bargaining: The Language of Negotiation.* New York: Plenum Press.

Mirchandani, R. 2005. "What's So Special about Specialized Courts? The State and Social Change in Salt Lake City's Domestic Violence Court." *Law and Society* 39:379–417.

———. 2008. "Beyond Therapy: Problem-Solving Courts and the Deliberative Democratic State." *Law and Social Inquiry* 33:853–893.

Mohr, L. 1976. "Organizations, Decisions, and Courts." *Law and Society* 10: 621–642.

Moore, D. 2007. *Criminal Artefacts: Governing Drugs and Users.* Vancouver: University of British Columbia Press.

National Conference of State Legislatures. 2009. "Significant State Sentencing and Corrections Legislation 2007 and 2008 and the Budget Impact on Corrections in 2009." *National Conference of State Legislatures.* http://www.ncsl.org/default.aspx?tabid=12682.

National Institute of Justice. 2006. *Drug Courts: The Second Decade.* NCJ 211081. Washington, DC: GPO.

Nolan, J., Jr. 1998. *The Therapeutic State: Justifying Government at Century's End.* New York: New York University Press.

———. 2001. *Reinventing Justice: The American Drug Court Movement.* Princeton: Princeton University Press.

———. 2002. ed. *Drug Courts in Theory and in Practice.* New York: Aldine de Gruyter.

O'Hear, M. 2009. "Rethinking Drug Courts: Restorative Justice As a Response to Racial Injustice." *Stanford Law and Policy Review* 20:101–137.

Otto, R., J. Greenstein, M. K. Johnson, and J. Friedman. 1992. "Prevalence of Mental Disorders among Youth in the Juvenile Justice System." In *Responding to the Mental Health Needs of Youth in the Juvenile Justice System,* ed. J. Cocozza, 7–48. Seattle: National Coalition for the Mentally Ill in the Criminal Justice System.

Pager, D. 2003. "Mark of a Criminal Record." *American Journal of Sociology* 108:937–975.

———. 2007. *Marked: Race, Crime and Finding Work in an Era of Mass Incarceration.* Chicago: University of Chicago Press.

Paik, L. 2006. "Are You Truly a Recovering Dope Fiend? Local Interpretive Practices at a Therapeutic Community Drug Treatment Program." *Symbolic Interaction* 29:213–234.

———. 2009. "Maybe He's Depressed: Mental Illness as a Mitigating Factor for Drug Offender Accountability." *Law and Social Inquiry* 34:569–602.

Peyrot, M. 1985. "Coerced Voluntarism: The Micro-Politics of Drug Treatment." *Urban Life* 13:343–365.

Provine, D. M. 2007. *Unequal Under Law: Race in the War on Drugs.* Chicago: University of Chicago Press.

Quinn, M. 2000/2001. "'Whose Team Am I on Anyway?' Musings of a Public Defender about Drug Treatment Court Practice." *New York University Review of Law and Social Change* 26:37–75.

Robinson, J., and J. Jones. 2000. *Drug Testing in a Drug Court Environment: Common Issues to Address.* Washington, DC: U.S. Department of Justice.

Rosenfield, S., J. Phillips, and H. White. 2006. "Gender, Race, and the Self in Mental Health and Crime." *Social Problems* 53:161–185.

Rudy, D. 1986. *Becoming Alcoholic: Alcoholics Anonymous and the Reality of Alcoholism.* Carbondale: Southern Illinois University Press.

Sacks, H. 1992. *Lectures on Conversation.* Ed. G. Jefferson. Oxford: Blackwell.

Schegloff, E. 2007. "A Tutorial on Membership Categorization." *Journal of Pragmatics* 39:462–482.

Schur, E. 1973. *Radical Non-Intervention: Rethinking the Delinquency Problem.* Englewood Cliffs, NJ: Prentice-Hall.

Skoll, G. 1992. *Walk the Walk and Talk the Talk: An Ethnography of a Drug Abuse Treatment Facility.* Philadelphia: Temple University Press.

Spector, M., and J. Kitsuse. 1977. *Constructing Social Problems.* Menlo Park, CA: Cummings Publishing.

Spohn, C., R. K. Piper, T. Martin, and E. Davis Frenzel. 2001. "Drug Courts and Recidivism: The Results of an Evaluation Using Two Comparison Groups and Multiple Indicators of Recidivism. *Journal of Drug Issues* 3:149–176.

Steffensmeier, D., J. Ulmer, and J. Kramer. 1998. "The Interaction of Race, Gender, and Age in Criminal Sentencing: The Punishment Cost of Being Young, Black, and Male." *Criminology* 36:763–798.

Sudnow, D. 1965. "Normal Crimes: Sociological Features of the Penal Code in a Public Defender's Office." *Social Problems* 12:255–276.

Sviridoff, M., D. Rottman, B. Ostrom, and R. Curtis. 2001. "Dispensing Justice Locally: The Implementation and Effects of the Midtown Community Court." http://www.courtinnovation.org/_uploads/documents/DISPE~6Q.PDF.

Teplin, Linda. 1990. "The Prevalence of Severe Mental Disorder among Male Urban Jail Detainees: Comparison with the Epidemiological Catchment Area Program." *American Journal of Public Health* 80:663–669.

———. 1994. "Psychiatric and Substance Abuse Disorders among Male Urban Jail Detainees." *American Journal of Public Health* 84:290–293.

Teplin, Linda, Karen M. Abram, Gary M. McClelland, Amy A. Mericle, Mina K. Dulcan, and Jason J. Washburn. 2006. *Psychiatric Disorders of Youth in Detention.* NCJ 210331. Washington, DC: Office of Juvenile Justice and Delinquency Prevention.

Thomas, J. W., D. E. Stubbe, and G. Pearson. 1999. "Race, Juvenile Justice and Mental Health: New Dimensions in Measuring Racial Bias." *Journal of Criminal Law and Criminology* 89:615–670.

Toborg, M., J. Bellassal, A. Yezer, and R. Trost. 1989 "Assessment of Pretrial Urine Testing in the District of Columbia." Washington, DC: National Institute of Justice. NCJ 119968.

Tunnell, K. D. 2004. *Pissing on Demand: Workplace Drug Testing and the Rise of the Detox Industry.* New York: New York University Press.

Turner, S., and J. Petersilia. 1992. "Focusing on High Risk Parolees: An Experiment to Reduce Commitments to the Texas Department of Corrections." *Journal of Research in Crime and Delinquency* 29:34–61.

Ulmer, J. 1997. *Social Worlds of Sentencing: Court Communities under Sentencing Guidelines.* Albany: State University of New York Press.

Ulmer, J., and J. Kramer. 1998. "The Use and Transformation of Formal Decision-Making Criteria: Sentencing Guidelines, Organizational Contexts, and Case Processing Strategies." *Social Problems* 45:248–267.

Unze, D. 2007. "Drug Courts Offer Offenders Alternatives." *USA Today*, December 20.

U.S. Department of Justice. 2009. *Summary of Drug Court Activity by State and County*. Bureau of Justice Assistance Drug Court Clearinghouse Project. Washington, DC: GPO. http://www1.spa.american.edu/justice/documents/2150.pdf.

U.S. Department of Justice, Office of Justice Programs. 2004. *State Prison Expenditures, 2001*. Bureau of Justice Statistics Special Report. NCJ 202949. Washington, DC: GPO.

U.S. Office of National Drug Control Policy. 2009. *National Drug Control Strategy*. Washington, DC: GPO. http://www.whitehousedrugpolicy.gov/publications/policy/ndcs09/2009ndcs.pdf.

Ward, G., and A. Kupchik. 2009. "Accountable to What? Professional Orientations towards Accountability-based Juvenile Justice." *Punishment and Society* 11:85–109.

Weinberg, D. 1996. "The Enactment and Appraisal of Authenticity in a Skid Row Therapeutic Community." *Symbolic Interaction* 19:137–162.

Westendorp, E., K. L. Brink, M. K. Roberson, and I. E. Ortiz. 1986. "Variables Which Differentiate Placement of Adolescents into Juvenile Justice or Mental Health Systems." *Adolescence* 21:23–37.

Western, Bruce. 2006. *Punishment and Inequality in America*. New York: Russell Sage Foundation.

Wexler, D., and B. Winick. 1991. *Essays in Therapeutic Jurisprudence*. Durham, NC: Carolina Academic Press.

———, eds. 2003. *Judging in a Therapeutic Key: Therapeutic Jurisprudence and the Courts*. Durham, NC: Carolina Academic Press.

White, T. 2003. "Drug Testing at Work: Issues and Perspectives." *Substance Use and Misuse* 38:1891–1902.

Whiteacre, K. 2008. *Drug Court Justice: Experiences in a Juvenile Drug Court*. New York: Peter Lang Publisher.

Wiley, J. 1990. "The Dramatisation of Emotions in Practice and Theory: Emotion Work and Emotion Roles in a Therapeutic Community." *Sociology of Health and Illness* 12:127–150.

Wish, E., and B. Gropper. 1990. "Drug Testing in the Criminal Justice System: Methods, Research and Applications." In *Crime and Justice*, ed. J. Wilson and M. Tonry. Chicago: University of Chicago Press.

Wolf, E., and C. Colyer. 2001. "Everyday Hassles: Barriers to Recovery in Drug Court." *Journal of Drug Issues* 31:233–258.

Wolff, N. 2002. "Courts as Therapeutic Agents: Thinking Past the Novelty of Mental Health Courts." *Journal of the American Academy of Psychiatry and the Law* 30:431–437.

CASES CITED

In Re Gault, 387 U.S. 1 (1967).

Vernonia School District 47J v. Acton, 515 U.S. 646 (1995).

Board of Education of Independent School District No. 92 of Pottawatomie County et al. v. Earls, Lindsay et al., 536 U.S. 822 (2002).

Index

Page numbers in italics refer to figures and tables.

abortion, 140, 153
absent without leave (AWOL):
  described, 34; disparity in time,
  201–202n9; instances of, 66, 128,
  134–135, 140, 141, 159, 162, 165,
  201n8; unexcused home absence, *44*
accountability: ambiguities in, 8; -based
  penal policies, 182; building blocks of,
  3–6; building through assessments of
  noncompliance, 41–75; conceptual
  map, *13*; described, 9; drug court's
  goal of teaching, 17, 173–174; drug
  test as measuring stick, 76, 86, 98;
  emphasis on individual —, 69–70, 72;
  flaw in, 71; impact of parental
  involvement, 124; -in-action, 9–11;
  individual —, notion of, 136, 182; as
  interpretive practice, 47–48; law in
  action, 9, 11–12; limits to teaching,
  173; mental illness and —, 153;
  message, 3; philosophy of, 12; proxy
  mechanism for differential treatment,
  14; system-level, 182; unaccountable
  client, 16
achieved agreement, 77
administrative discharge, 135, 145, 146,
  169, *169*, 170, *170*, 171, 179, 206n4
admonishments, 137. *See also* warning
adversarial justice, 74
African Americans: final outcomes,
  208n7; lost causes workability, 165;
  racial disparities in justice system, 177;

subcourt, 19; youth demographic,
  17–18. *See also* race
aftercare program, 149
age as issue in sanctions, 60–61, 67–68
alcohol, 176, 208n11: testing issues
  78, 97
Alcoholics Anonymous, 175
anger management classes, 72, 113
arrests, new, 43, *44*, 137, 139, 159, 165
Asian Americans: subcourt, 19; youth
  demographic, 17–18. *See also* race
assessments: decision-making process,
  4, 9, 10, 12, *13*, 29, 41–42;
  parameters of, 42–43; significance
  in crafting workability, 42;
  unpredictability of, 42
Asylums (Goffman), 7
attribution theory, 205n1
AWOL. *See* absent without leave

Bad Kids (Feld), 15–16
Barton, S., 201n3
behavior, monitoring, 42, 84. *See also*
  parents/legal guardians, behavior
  toward
bench warrant, 35, 132, 133, 135, 140,
  148, 161–162, 164
Bentham, Jeremy, 197n10
Berman, G., 174
Between Facts and Norm (Mirchandani),
  198n11
black offenders. *See* African Americans

About the Author

Leslie Paik is an assistant professor of sociology at the City College of New York and the Graduate Center City University of New York. Paik earned her undergraduate degree in literature and society at Brown University and her master's and doctorate degrees in sociology at the University of California at Los Angeles. Her research interests are juvenile justice, law and society, sociology of knowledge, and qualitative methods.

Breinigsville, PA USA
06 April 2011
259310BV00002B/2/P